Foundation Course

UNDERSTAND
MATHEMATICS 1

C. J. Cox & D. Bell

John Murray

© C. J. Cox and D. Bell 1985

First published 1985
by John Murray (Publishers) Ltd
50 Albemarle Street, London W1X 4BD

Printed in Great Britain by
The Alden Press Ltd, Oxford

British Library Cataloguing in Publication Data

Cox, Christopher J.
   Understanding mathematics.
   Foundation course
   Book 1
   1. Mathematics — 1961-
   I. Title   II. Bell, David
   510   QA39.2

ISBN 0–7195 4151–4

Foreword

Children's Understanding of Mathematics 11–16, which was published in 1981, reported the work of the mathematics team of the research project *Concepts in Secondary Mathematics and Science* (CSMS). Christopher Cox was head of department in one of the schools which co-operated with us in the research.

From the beginning he and his colleagues utilised the results we were able to make available. In particular, he noted the lack of success experienced by many children and the errors they committed. This led to the writing of material for use by the mathematics staff in his own and other schools, work which has led to this series of books.

The philosophy behind *Understanding Mathematics* is that, traditionally, the mathematics in secondary school becomes too difficult, too soon, for many children. Thus the exercises here provide a wide range of examples in order to cater for different learning rates, so organised that the learner is encouraged to take some responsibility for the amount of practice needed. The existence and benefits of the calculator and computer are recognised and exercises are provided for their use. Above all, the exercises are full of *interesting* questions and not just lists of sums. Also, the accompanying *Teacher's Manuals* contain a wide range of very useful copyable resource material, which is additional to the detailed guides to all the exercises.

CSMS showed that many children could not cope with the secondary mathematics they were expected to learn. Other research, particularly that reported in the publication of *Children Reading Mathematics* (edited by H. Shuard and A. Rothery) has pin-pointed the special problems faced in conveying meaning through written text. The writers of this series of books have taken the messages to heart and done something about it. Thus the reader is receiving the benefit of tested and well thought-out material written by enthusiastic and dedicated practising teachers.

Kath Hart   July 1984

Preface

Understanding Mathematics is a complete course for secondary pupils in the 11–16 age range. It has proved to be equally as effective with average pupils as with those of the highest ability, its exercise structure providing the flexibility needed to cater for this wide range. All pupils use the same books and follow the same common core, allowing easy transfer between sets and not labelling any pupil as 'lower ability'.

The development of each topic was planned with reference to the findings of CSMS*, resulting in a common core with a less steep incline of difficulty than other texts, although the latter part of each exercise will challenge the highest ability pupil. Each topic is revised at each appearance before being developed further. The Topic Matrix on pages vi and vii of the Teachers' Manual shows the full plan of the course.

The authors thank their publishers for their help, their wives for their tolerance, and all the many teachers and pupils who have helped in the testing and revising of the course.

* Research project reported in K. Hart's: *Children's Understanding of Mathematics*; John Murray

Contents

About this Book

This is the first of our three-book Foundation Course in mathematics. All the work in it has been successfully tried by many different students.

Each chapter is concerned with a **Topic** and is divided into **Exercises**. Almost all exercises have four kinds of question:

Introductory Questions (Common Core) are for everyone.

Starred Questions (Reinforcement) are optional for those who find the introductory questions very easy.

Further Questions (Development) follow. These continue the topic to a higher level.

Boxed Questions (Extension) challenge those who are keen and quick, and give lots of ideas for investigations and practical work.

This structure helps you to learn at your own pace and builds up your confidence.

To help you with homework and revision we have also provided a **Glossary** where you can check on words that you do not understand and a **Summary** of all the first year's work.

Calculators will help you with many of the exercises. Only the four basic functions ($+$, $-$, $\times$, $\div$) are necessary, but $+/-$, % and Memory will be useful.

Computer programs are included and the BASIC used will work on all the popular micros. The few changes needed for some machines are noted in the programs. We will be pleased to hear of any mathematical programs that you write and of any improvements that you make in ours.

1 Flow-charts; Computers; Calculators

A Designing flow-charts

For Discussion

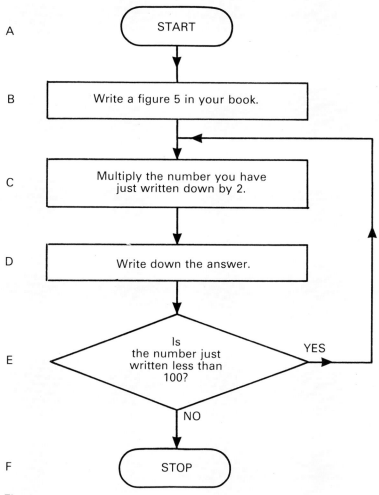

Fig. 1:1

(a) Follow the instructions in the **flow-chart**.

(b) There are three different **frame shapes**: Running track; Rectangle; Diamond. What is each shape used for?

(c) A rectangle must contain one **instruction** only. Rectangle C could not say 'Multiply the number you have just written down by 2 and write down the answer.'

What are the only possible answers to a question in a diamond?

1 (a) Rewrite the following instructions in a sensible order.

To Draw a Circle

Make sure the pencil is sharp.	Draw the circle.
Put point of compasses at marked centre.	Find a pair of compasses and a pencil.
Mark the centre.	Open compasses to correct radius.

Fig. 1:2 radius

(b) Write a question to replace the instruction 'Make sure the pencil is sharp', so that the answer 'NO' means it *is* sharp.

(c) Copy and complete Figure 1:3 for the set of instructions 'To Draw a Circle'. Use your answers to parts (a) and (b).

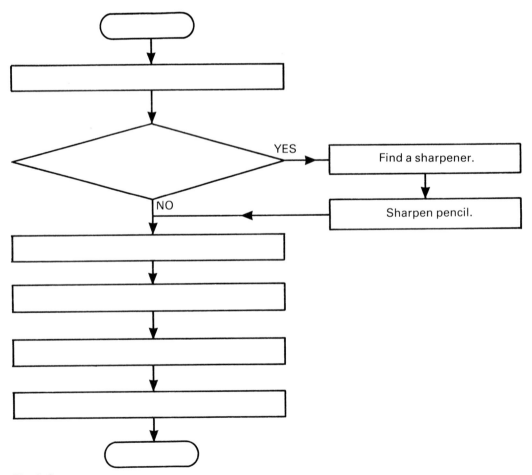

Fig. 1:3

2 A set of instructions telling someone how to perform a task is sometimes called a **program**. Copy and complete the flow-chart in Figure 1:4 for the program 'Pumping-up a Car's Tyres at the Garage'. Use these sentences:

Fix on the pump. Drive to the garage. Stop. Start. Are there any tyres not checked? Replace the dust-cap. Put some air in. Remove the pump from the wheel. Remove the dust-cap.

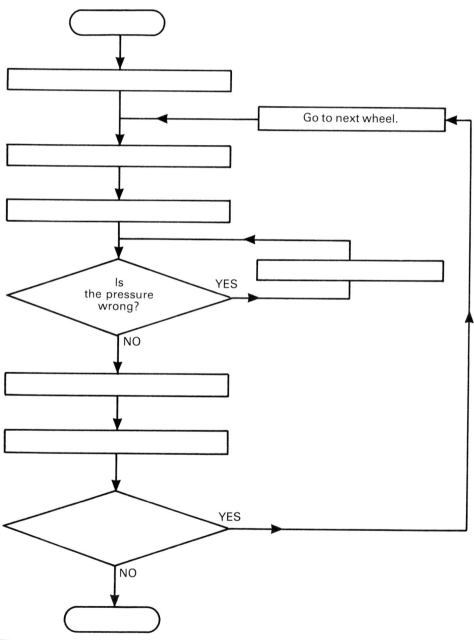

Fig. 1:4

3

3 Copy and complete the flow-chart in Figure 1:5 for the program 'Taking the Dog for a Walk'. Use these sentences:

Stop. Go and get the dog. Did he ignore you? Go back home. Start. Put on the lead. Do you want to walk any further?

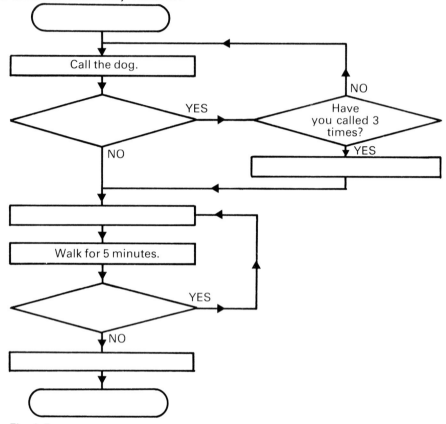

Fig. 1:5

4 Remember that questions must have the answers 'Yes' or 'No'. You should try to make up the question so that the answer 'No' keeps you on the 'main line' down from Start to Stop, whilst 'Yes' takes you sideways to a loop.

Write flow-diagrams for some or all of the following.

(a) To draw an equilateral triangle of side 50 mm.

(b) To make a certain shade of green from blue and yellow paint.

(c) To write down the digits 1, 4, 7, 6, 3, 5, 2, 8, 9 in order of size.

(d) To write the multiples of 4 from 4 to 40.

(e) To use a telephone box.

(f) To buy a shirt or a blouse from a shop.

(g) To start and drive away a car.

(h) To always win at noughts and crosses if *you* start.

(i) Something of your own!

B Computer components and language

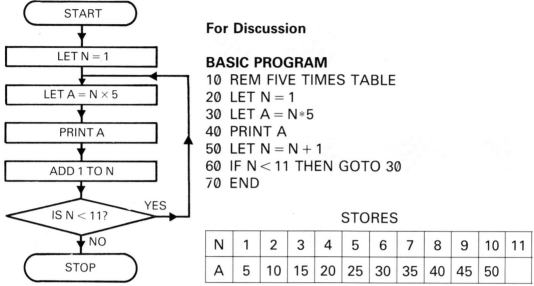

Fig. 1:6

For Discussion

BASIC PROGRAM
```
10 REM FIVE TIMES TABLE
20 LET N = 1
30 LET A = N*5
40 PRINT A
50 LET N = N + 1
60 IF N < 11 THEN GOTO 30
70 END
```

STORES

N	1	2	3	4	5	6	7	8	9	10	11
A	5	10	15	20	25	30	35	40	45	50	

The Basic Program is the set of instructions that you could give a computer so that it prints the five times table on the screen.

REM in line 10 is short for Remark. This is put in to make the program clearer to a human being. The computer ignores any line starting REM.

The sign * is used for multiply, to avoid muddling it with the letter X.

The sign < means 'is less than', so at line 60 the computer will jump back to line 30 if N is less than 11.

The **stores** table shows the changing values of N and A as the computer works through the program.

1 Write a flow-chart and a BASIC program for the Eight Times Table as far as 10 × 8.

2 (a) Copy the stores table and use the program to complete it.

STORES

N						
A						

```
10 REM QUESTION TWO
20 LET N = 1
30 LET A = N + 2
40 PRINT A
50 LET N = N + 2
60 IF N < 10 THEN GOTO 30
70 END
```

(b) List all the numbers that the computer prints.

(c) What does the computer work out in this program?

3
```
10 REM FIVE TIMES TABLE MK II
20 FOR N = 1 TO 10
30 LET A = N*5
40 PRINT A
50 NEXT N
60 END
```
Compare this program with the one in the introduction. Lines 20 and 50 replace lines 20, 50 and 60. We call lines 20 to 50 a FOR ... NEXT loop. The computer increases N by 1 each time it reaches line 50 and repeats lines 30 and 40 until N is 11, when it leaves the loop and goes on to line 60.

Rewrite your program for question 1 using a FOR ... NEXT loop.

4 In question 2, line 50 increases N by 2. We can do this in a FOR ... NEXT loop by adding the instruction STEP 2, like this:
```
20 FOR N = 1 TO 10 STEP 2
50 NEXT N
```
At line 50, N will be increased to 3, 5, 7, 9 and 11, when it will leave the loop. (An 'empty' loop like this can be used to make the computer pause.)

Write a program to write the first ten multiples of 17. One of your lines should read FOR N = 17 TO 170 STEP 17.

5 **The area of a circle is about 3.1 × R × R where R is the radius.**

Look carefully at the flow-chart, then rewrite the program steps in order from 10 to 60 for the area of a circle of radius 3 cm.

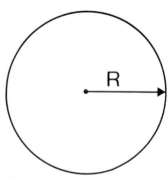

Fig. 1:7

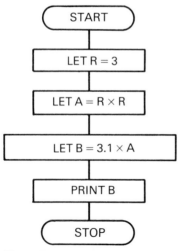

Fig. 1:8

```
REM AREA OF CIRCLE
END
LET B = 3.1*A  (Remember that *
LET A = R*R     means multiply.)
PRINT B
LET R = 3
```

6 The program in question 5 only found the area for the circle with radius 3 cm. For a different circle you could change the value of R in the line LET R = 3, but it is much better to use the following two lines instead:

```
15  PRINT "Please type in the circle's radius."
20  INPUT R
```

At line 20 the computer will wait for you to type in the value of R. Line 15 is not essential, but without it a user would not know why the computer had stopped.

Note that PRINT B prints the value of B on the screen, but PRINT "B" prints a letter B on the screen.

Try these on a computer:

```
10  LET B = 16        10  LET B = 16
20  PRINT B           20  PRINT "B"
```

```
10  PRINT "What is your name?"
20  INPUT N$  (The $ sign tells the computer you are typing in letters not
                  numbers.)
30  PRINT "Hello∧";N$
```

Note: Type a space after the word 'Hello'. The semi-colon (;) splits up two different kinds of printing.

Write out a revised version of the program in question 5 so that any radius can be input.

---

7 The square of a number is the value of the number multiplied by itself, e.g. the square of 4 is 16.

Write a program to print the square of any number. Two of your lines should be:
PRINT "Please type in a number for me to square."
PRINT "The square of your number is∧";R*R

8 The product of two numbers is the answer when they are multiplied together. The product of 3 and 8 is 24.

Write a program to print the product of any two numbers.

9 The perimeter of a shape is the distance round the edge of the shape.

Write a program to calculate the perimeter of a rectangle, given its length and breadth.

10 The area of a triangle is half the product of its base and height.

Write a program to calculate the areas of triangles. You will need these lines:
LET P = B∗H
LET A = P/2
Note that the / sign is used for divide.

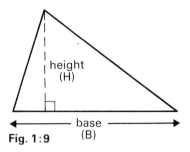

Fig. 1:9

11 Write a program to tell you which of two numbers is the bigger. You will need the following lines:
IF A > B THEN PRINT A;"∧is bigger than∧";B
IF A < B THEN PRINT B;"∧is bigger than∧";A

12 Write a program to make the computer write out ten times any sentence you tell it.

13 Design your own programs.

C Using a calculator

You are probably already quite good at using a calculator. Your teacher will tell you when you may use one to work questions in this book. Most people think it is still important that you can do simple arithmetic without using a calculator. Even with a calculator you will only reach the correct answer if you press the right buttons in the right order. The Using Your Calculator exercises in this course have been written to make you think about this.

In questions 1 to 12 work out the answer 'in your head' first, then use your calculator. Note that the part in brackets is always worked out *first*. If the bracket comes last, as in question 1(e), you should put the answer to it into the memory (or write it down), then start with the first number.

If your calculator has bracket keys, you can enter the questions in the same order as they are printed, e.g. 9 $\boxed{-}$ $\boxed{(}$ 5 $\boxed{-}$ 4 $\boxed{)}$ $\boxed{=}$ ...

1 (a) 3 + 6 + 5   (b) 4 + 3 − 5   (c) 3 × 2 × 7   (d) (3 × 2) × 7
   (e) 3 × (2 × 7)   (f) 4 × 3 + 6   (g) (4 × 3) + 6   (h) 4 × (3 + 6)

2 (a) 9 − 5 − 4   (b) 9 − (5 − 4)   (c) (9 − 5) − 4

3 (a) 8 + 4 − 1   (b) (8 + 4) − 1   (c) 8 + (4 − 1)

4 (a) $8 \div 2 + 2$ (b) $(8 \div 2) + 2$ (c) $8 \div (2 + 2)$

5 (a) $(6 \times 4) \div 2$ (b) $6 \times (4 \div 2)$ (c) $6 \times 4 \div 2$

6 (a) $8 \div 2 \div 2$ (b) $8 \div (2 \div 2)$ (c) $(8 \div 2) \div 2$

7 (a) $12 \div 6 - 2$ (b) $12 \div (6 - 2)$ (c) $(12 \div 6) - 2$

*8 (a) $4 + 1 + 3$ (b) $7 - 6 - 1$ (c) $8 - 2 - 5$ (d) $4 - 1 + 2$

*9 (a) $6 - 5 + 3$ (b) $8 - 7 + 13$ (c) $17 - 9 + 18$ (d) $3 \times 2 \times 7$

*10 (a) $5 \times 2 \times 6$ (b) $4 \times 3 \times 0$ (c) $3 \times 4 \times 5$ (d) $4 \times 3 \times 5$

*11 (a) $(2 \times 3) + 1$ (b) $2 \times (3 + 1)$ (c) $(2 \times 3) + 1$ (d) $178 \times 99 \times 0$

*12 (a) $(5 \times 4) + 3$ (b) $5 \times (4 + 3)$ (c) $4 \times (1 + 6)$ (d) $(4 \times 1) + 6$

13 Use a calculator, or work in your head, whichever seems easier.
(a) $1 + 2 + 3 + 4 + 5$ (b) $17 - 8$ (c) $1698 - 1375$ (d) 8×7 (e) 16×10
(f) 26×39 (g) 50×10 (h) 16×100 (i) $10 \div 5$ (j) $36 \div 9$
(k) $429 \div 11$ (l) $125 \times 349 \times 189 \times 0$

14 Use a calculator to find:
(a) £7.40 − £3.90 + £0.26   (b) £145 + £1.05 − 56p   (c) £150.10 − £5.45 + 5p
(d) 37p + 192p + £1000.21

---

15 Find, as accurately as you can, a number which gives the answer 6 when it is multiplied by itself.

16 Find, as accurately as you can, the value of the number n if $n \times n \times n = 2$.

17 Make up some questions that your calculator cannot work out, can only work out approximately, or to which it gives the wrong answer.

18 Read your calculator booklet carefully. Aim to find out how to use every key on it. Make up some questions and check your answers by using different models of calculator (swap with your friends).

Using Your Calculator

Symbols for Sets

A set is a collection of things.

In mathematics, a set is represented by a capital letter or by 'curly' brackets.

We use the sign $\in$ to say that something is a member of a set.

$A = \{$multiples of 7$\}$ says 'A is the set of multiples of seven'. Some members of this set are 7, 14, 21, 77 and 700. We write $14 \in A$ to say '14 is a member of set A'. We could also write $10 \notin A$.

1 What does the sign $\notin$ mean?

2 Using your calculator, find five members of set B where $B = \{$multiples of 29$\}$.

3 In this question, $C = \{$multiples of 37$\}$, $D = \{$multiples of 43$\}$ and $E = \{$multiples of 59$\}$. Using your calculator, say whether the following statements are true or false:

(a) $259 \in C$ (b) $250 \in D$ (c) $559 \in D$ (d) $533 \in E$ (e) $629 \notin C$
(f) $1200 \notin D$ (g) $605 \in D$ (h) $3304 \in E$.

4 **Factors of a number are whole numbers that divide exactly into it.**

$A = \{$factors of 756$\}$ and $B = \{$378, 36, 45, 54, 96, 48, 189, 252, 314, 86$\}$.

Using your calculator, find which members of set B are also members of set A.

5 **n(A) means 'the number of elements in set A'.**

Example If $A = \{$a, e, i, o, u$\}$ then n(A) = 5.

(a) If $E = \{$multiples of 8 from 8 to 88$\}$, list set E.   (b) In part (a), what is n(E)?

(c) If $S = \{$multiples of 7 from 7 to 105$\}$, list set S.   (d) In part (c), what is n(S)?

6 **A set with no members is called a null set. We use the signs $\{\}$ and $\emptyset$ to represent it.**

Are the following true or false?

(a) If $M = \{$even numbers that are factors of 91$\}$ then $M = \emptyset$.

(b) If $M = \{$odd numbers that are factors of 91$\}$ then $M = \{\}$.

(c) If $P = \emptyset$ then n(P) = 0.

A Columns

For Discussion

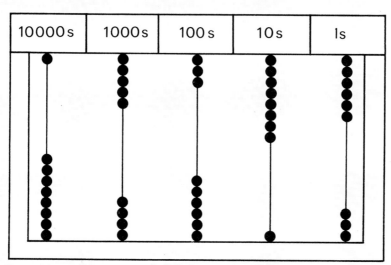

10000s	1000s	100s	10s	Is

Fig. 2:1

The number 15386 is shown at the top of this abacus.

Six beads have been moved up the right-hand rod to show 6 ones, or 6 units.

The three beads moved up the middle rod stand for 3 hundreds.

The left-hand rod shows 1 ten-thousand.

This game will test your understanding of place value.

```
  5  REM "Guess 1"
 10  RAND (Randomize or omit)
 20  PRINT "Guess my number (from 0 to 100)."
 30  LET X = 0
 40  LET N = INT(RND*100)
 50  INPUT G
 60  IF G = N THEN GOTO 110
 70  IF G > N THEN PRINT G;"  is too big."
 80  IF G < N THEN PRINT G;"  is too small."
 90  PRINT "Guess again."
100  GOTO 50
110  PRINT "Correct. Well done."
```

Notes

Line 40 assumes that RND gives a random decimal between 0 and 1. You may have to adjust this for your computer, e.g. RND(1).

You can do a lot to improve this program!

1 Draw another abacus with the same headings but showing 31 059.

2 Think how the number 91 326 would look on the abacus. In 91 326 the figure 3 stands for 3 hundreds. What do the following figures stand for:
(a) the 2   (b) the 1   (c) the 6   (d) the 9?

3 Write in figures the numbers:
(a) forty-six   (b) two hundred and ten   (c) two hundred and one
(d) one thousand, nine hundred and eighty-four   (e) two thousand and one.

4 Write in words, being very careful with spelling:
(a) 40   (b) 113   (c) 209   (d) 1846   (e) 8020.

*5 Draw an abacus, with column headings, showing 60 324.

*6 In the number 8300 the figure 8 stands for 8 thousands. What does the figure 8 stand for in:
(a) 3800   (b) 38   (c) 380   (d) 830   (e) 8   (f) 80?

*7 What does each figure 3 stand for in:
(a) 8300   (b) 3800   (c) 38   (d) 380   (e) 830?

*8 Arrange the five numbers in question 7 in order of size, starting with the smallest.

*9 Write in figures:
(a) seven   (b) eighteen   (c) forty-eight   (d) sixty-five   (e) ninety
(f) two hundred and sixty-eight   (g) one hundred and forty-seven
(h) five hundred   (i) five hundred and forty   (j) one hundred and nine
(k) five hundred and five   (l) two thousand, seven hundred and thirty-nine.

*10 Write in words, being very careful with spelling:
(a) 4   (b) 42   (c) 44   (d) 70   (e) 73   (f) 200   (g) 210
(h) 401   (i) 408   (j) 1941   (k) 2316   (l) 3105   (m) 3016.

11 Increase each number in question 4 by seven, writing the answer in words.

12 How many minutes in:
(a) 3 hours   (b) 1 hour 5 minutes   (c) 3 hours 8 minutes
(d) 4 hours 12 minutes   (e) 9 hours 31 minutes?

13 How many seconds in:
(a) 2 minutes   (b) 9 minutes   (c) 8 minutes 8 seconds
(d) 7 minutes 7 seconds   (e) 5 minutes 57 seconds   (f) 1 hour?

14 This is a Japanese abacus. The beads 'count' when pushed towards the middle bar. This abacus is showing 159.

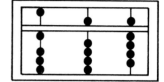

Fig. 2:2

(a) How is the 1 hundred shown?

(b) How are the 5 tens shown?

(c) What is a top bead worth when pushed to the middle bar?

15 Draw a Japanese abacus showing: (a) 345   (b) 806   (c) 397.

---

16 Investigate a number system for counting using only the digits 0 and 1.

17 Use a calculator to find how many seconds there are in:
(a) 1 day   (b) July   (c) 1 year.

18 Work out how to use a Japanese abacus for addition. (You could use dried peas on corrugated cardboard.)

B   Addition and subtraction

For Discussion

TARIFF CODE (see over)	METER READING		UNITS USED	PRICE PER UNIT p	£
	PRESENT	PREVIOUS			
11	83711	82306	1405	5.170	72.63
QUARTERLY CHARGE					7.50
16	51804	47457	4347	2.700	117.36
QUARTERLY CHARGE					1.85

READING DATE For meters read or consumptions estimated during week beginning 7 MAY 84	DATE OF ISSUE OF THIS ACCOUNT 11 MAY 84		AMOUNT DUE NOW 199.34

Fig. 2:3

Find two subtractions and one addition on this electricity bill. Also find: (a) How many units were used altogether. (b) How many more units were paid for on Tariff Code 16 than on Tariff Code 11.

It is wise to always check subtraction answers by addition.

1 Just write the answers to:
(a) 19 − 4   (b) 23 − 8   (c) 52 − 37.

2
(a)   281
  − 120

(b)   486
  − 258

(c)   780
  − 624

(d)   803
  − 221

(e)   306
  − 128

*3 (a) 9 − 5   (b) 29 − 3   (c) 21 − 2   (d) 36 − 8   (e) 42 − 9   (f) 53 − 21
(g) 42 − 33

*4
(a)   319
  − 215

(b)   426
  − 207

(c)   3124
  − 1024

*5
(a)   6031
  − 4120

(b)   8061
  − 1245

(c)   2064
  − 1157

(d)   308
  − 129

(e)   506
  − 218

*6
(a)   303
  − 144

(b)   807
  − 219

(c)   2104
  − 1236

(d)   5210
  − 25

(e)   8006
  − 4

7
(a)   2009
  − 1232

(b)   3007
  − 1357

(c)   300
  − 89

(d)   6005
  − 438

8 (a) 608 − 219   (b) 3001 − 158   (c) 8108 − 6127   (d) 5005 − 4106

9 Copy the following additions and subtractions, replacing the stars by the correct digits:

(a)   3*6
  + *4*
  *111

(b)   96*
  + **7
  *403

(c)   4***
  + *301
  9000

(d)   3*5*
  42*3
  + *710
  *2345

(e)   3*4
  − *8*
  107

(f)   8*6
  − 42*
  *08

(g) ***3* − 80*3 = 1961

Calculators may be used in any of the following questions.

10 (a) Add 612 to 738 then take away 419.
(b) Add 612 to 419 then take away 738.

11 678 + 964 + 2377 + 2647 is a sum with a 'strange' answer. Find this answer, then make up a sum which has four numbers adding to give: (a) 12345   (b) 909090.

12 Obey all the instructions in the flow-chart shown in Figure 2:4.

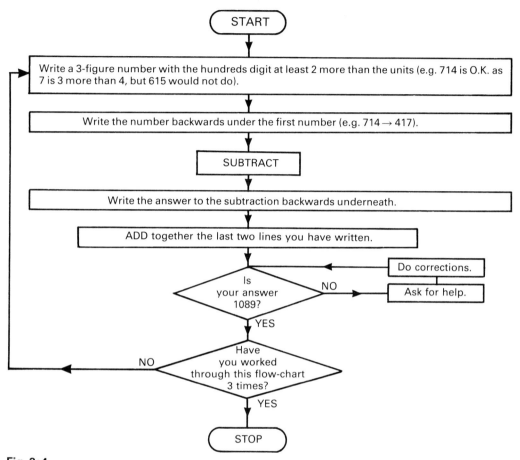

Fig. 2:4

13 (a) In the magic square of Figure 2:5, the numbers add up to 15 in eight ways. Find all eight. There is no need to write anything down.

(b) Copy and complete the magic squares of Figures 2:6 and 2:7. The totals across, down and diagonally will be the same if you have done it correctly.

4	9	2
3	5	7
8	1	6

Fig. 2:5

17	3	
7		
9		5

Fig. 2:6

17		1	8	15
23			14	16
	6	13		
	12	19		3
11	18		2	

Fig. 2:7

14 Remembering that 78 minutes would be written as 1 hour 18 minutes, work out:

(a) | h | min |
     | 3 | 32 |
     | + 2 | 28 |

(b) | days | h | min |
     | | 20 | 41 |
     | + | 5 | 38 |

(c) | days | h | min | s |
     | 1 | 13 | 8 | 41 |
     | + 2 | 19 | 49 | 55 |

(d) | h | min |
     | 4 | 18 |
     | − 2 | 30 |

(e) | h | min |
     | 2 | 27 |
     | − 1 | 53 |

(f) | min | s |
     | 18 | 05 |
     | − 12 | 12 |

(g) | days | h | min |
     | 4 | 2 | 15 |
     | − 1 | 8 | 28 |

15 What is the largest number you can display on your calculator? What happens if you try to add 1 to this number? Do all calculators do the same?

16 Only pressing the equals key once, find:

(a) $16 + 909 − 315$ (b) $67 − 35 + 102 + 96$.

17 Try racing a friend using a calculator. Who wins on $36 + 94$, $7 + 5$ and $312 + 820$? Make up some more.

18 Display 5078 on your calculator. Find the least possible number of key presses that will change 5078 to:

(a) 5278   (b) 5087   (c) 50 780   (d) 50 078.

19 Look back to the flow-chart in question 12.

(a) Try starting with: (i) 320   (ii) 615   (iii) 323   (iv) 324.

(b) You can make 615 'work' if you put an extra figure in your subtraction. How?

20 (a) | WALT |
         | + SAGS |
         | ALAS |

(b) | FRED |
     | + EATS |
     | ADDER |

In these sums each letter stands for a different figure. In (a), S = 1. Work out the other letters.

21 How many different ways of subtracting can you find? Write about them.

A   Turning

Fig. 3:1

1 In Figure 3:2, to which letter will the arrow be pointing if it starts at A each time then turns clockwise through:

(a) a $\frac{1}{2}$ turn (b) a $\frac{1}{4}$ turn (c) 1 turn
(d) a $\frac{3}{4}$ turn (e) $1\frac{1}{2}$ turns (f) $1\frac{1}{4}$ turns?

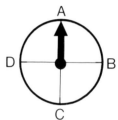

2 Repeat question 1 for anticlockwise turns.

Fig. 3:2

3 In Figure 3:2, a turn from A to B is a **right-angle** turn. Other right-angle turns would be from B to A, and from B to C. Find another five right-angle turns.

*4 In Figure 3:3, to which letter will the arrow be pointing if it starts at W each time then turns clockwise through:

(a) $1\frac{1}{2}$ turns (b) 1 turn (c) a $\frac{1}{4}$ turn
(d) a $\frac{3}{4}$ turn (e) $1\frac{1}{4}$ turns (f) $1\frac{3}{4}$ turns?

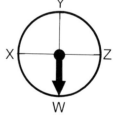

*5 Repeat question 4 for anticlockwise turns.

Fig. 3:3

*6 In Figure 3:3, which of the following are right-angle turns?

W to Z; W to X; X to Y; X to Z; Y to Z; X to W; W to Y.

7 How many turns does the minute hand on a clock make from:

(a) 9 o'clock to 10 o'clock (b) 8 o'clock to 11 o'clock
(c) 7 o'clock to half past 7 (d) half past 2 to half past 3
(e) half past 3 to 5 o'clock (f) 9 o'clock to quarter past 9
(g) quarter past 8 to quarter to 9 (h) quarter past 7 to half past 8
(i) quarter to 2 to quarter to 5 (j) half past 1 to quarter to 12?

8 What is the time if the minute hand turns:

    (a) 1 turn from 8 o'clock   (b) a $\frac{1}{2}$ turn from 1 o'clock
    (c) a $\frac{3}{4}$ turn from 2 o'clock   (d) $1\frac{1}{2}$ turns from $\frac{1}{2}$ past 3
    (e) $2\frac{1}{4}$ turns from $\frac{1}{4}$ past 5   (f) $1\frac{3}{4}$ turns from $\frac{1}{4}$ to 8?

Fig. 3:4

9 On the clock face shown in Figure 3:4 the lines drawn from 8 and 11 to the centre make a right angle. Note the special 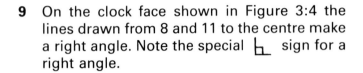 sign for a right angle.

Copy and complete the table to show other numbers that make a right angle when joined to the middle.

1st number	8	8	9	9	10	10	11	11	4	4
2nd number	11	5								

10 The dial in Figure 3:5 has eight divisions. The pointer turns clockwise only, but it can start from any number. From 0 to 1 is $\frac{1}{8}$ (say 'one-eighth') of a turn. From 5 to 6 is also $\frac{1}{8}$. Copy and complete the tables.

Fig. 3:5

TO

FROM	1	3	5
0	$\frac{1}{8}$		
1	1	$\frac{1}{4}$	$\frac{1}{2}$
2	$\frac{7}{8}$		

TO

FROM	0	4	6	7
3				
5			$\frac{1}{8}$	
7				

11 Are the hands of a clock at right angles at half past three? If not, why not?

12 At what times *will* the hands of a clock be at right angles?

13 Look around you for things that turn, like doors turning on hinges. List at least ten, then find how much of a turn they will turn through. You may need to approximate, like: 'about a $\frac{1}{2}$ turn'; 'between a $\frac{1}{4}$ and a $\frac{1}{2}$ turn'; '3 and a bit turns'; and so on.

B   Using a protractor

A whole turn is 360° (say '360 degrees').

A half turn is 180°. A quarter turn is 90°.

Fig. 3:6   This angle is 1 degree.

1   Fit a protractor on Figure 3:7 as instructed.

(a) Write the number of degrees turned clockwise from 0 when the arrow reaches A, B, C, D, E and F. Write your answers: A = ...°; B = ...°; etc.

(b) The arrow turns on past 90°. How many degrees has it turned when it reaches G, H, I, J, K and L?

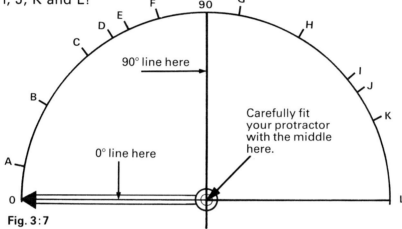

90° line here

0° line here

Carefully fit your protractor with the middle here.

Fig. 3:7

2   (a) Copy Figure 3:7, including the letters A, B, C, etc., *but* point the arrow to L instead of 0. (The easiest way to copy the figure is to draw round a protractor, but you must mark the middle point *first*.)

(b) We are now going to imagine the arrow turns from L back to A. Fit a protractor on your diagram. Find the 0 (zero) on your protractor that is nearest to L. It is on the inside set of figures. You use this inside set when turning anticlockwise. You will not go wrong if you *always* look for the 0 first to decide which set of figures to use. Then make sure the answer you give is sensible for the angle you are measuring. Write the number of degrees turned from L for each of the letters back to A. Start your answers: K = 25°; J = 35°.

3   Measure each of the angles in Figure 3:8.

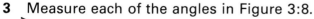

(a)

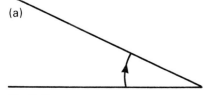

(b)

(c)

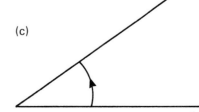

Fig. 3:8

*4 Fit your protractor correctly onto each of the angles in Figure 3:9 to find the number of degrees turned. (The arrow sign shows you where to put the middle of the protractor. Make sure you read from the correct 0 and think of the line turning clockwise to make the angle.)

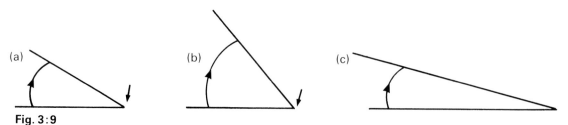

Fig. 3:9

*5 For the angles in Figure 3:10 the turn is anticlockwise. Think from which 0 you should start and which set of figures you should use, then find the number of degrees in each angle turned.

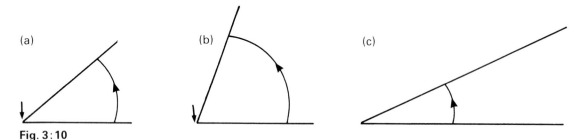

Fig. 3:10

*6 For the angles in Figure 3:11 the turn is more than a quarter turn. Measure each angle, thinking carefully about which 0 you should start from.

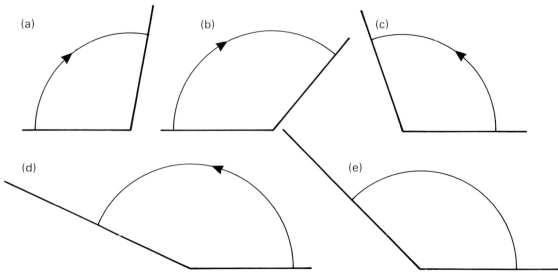

Fig. 3:11

7 Figure 3:12 shows a protractor being used in two ways to measure a 30° angle. Decide which 0 is used, inside or outside, in (a) and (b). (Written answers not required.)

Now measure each angle in Figures 3:8, 3:9, 3:10 and 3:11 in two ways, once turning clockwise and once turning anticlockwise.

There is no need to write down any answers, but make sure the angle reads the same whichever way you turn. This is very important, so do not cheat!

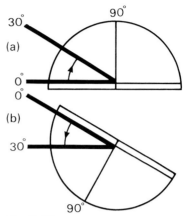

Fig. 3:12

8 Measure the angles in Figure 3:13. Make sure the 0 line on your protractor is along one of the angle lines and the centre of the protractor is at the point of the angle. Then decide which 0 to start from and which set of figures to use. Write your answers: $a = \ldots°$; etc.

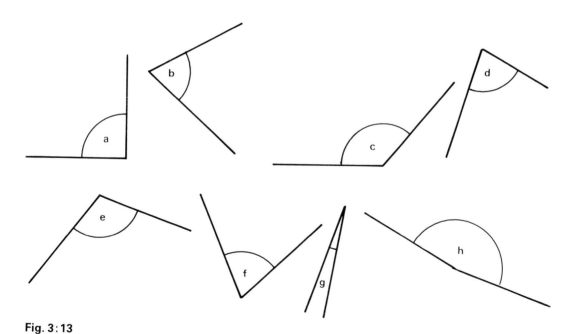

Fig. 3:13

9 A fly is sitting on the end of the big hand of a clock face on a church tower. A spider is sitting half-way along the hand.

(a) Which travels further in an hour, the spider or the fly?

(b) Which travels faster?

3

10 Figure 3:14 shows how you can draw a circle using a protractor.

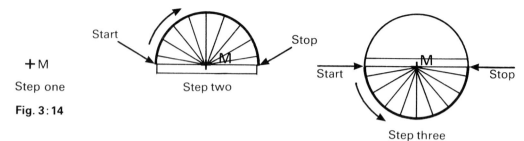

Step one   Mark the middle, M.

Step one   Mark the middle, M.

Step two   Draw round the protractor from 0 to 180 *only* (*not* right to the bottom).

Step three   Turn the protractor upside down. Keep the middle at point M. Complete the circle from 0 to 180 again.

Draw three circles, then copy Figures 3:15, 3:16 and 3:17. The degrees to mark are shown around the circumference.

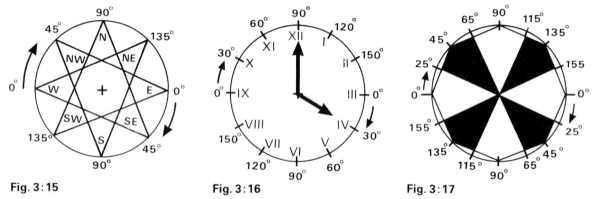

Fig. 3:15   Fig. 3:16   Fig. 3:17

11 Draw the following angles exactly, then swop with a friend and check each other's. Correct any you had wrong. Remember to mark an angle as in Figure 3:18.

128°   72°   108°   36°
144°   91°   90°   89°

Fig. 3:18

12 A turn of 180° makes an angle into a straight line. Work out the value of each letter in Figure 3:19. (Do *not* measure them; they are drawn the wrong size!)

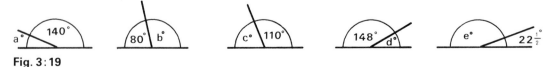

Fig. 3:19

13 Fold two pieces of paper as shown in Figure 3:20. What two angles do you make? Can you make 60° with (a) and 45° with (b)?

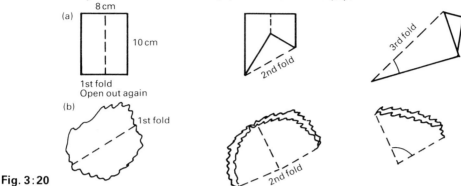

Fig. 3:20

C   Kinds of angles

An acute angle is less than a quarter turn.

A right angle is a quarter turn.

An obtuse angle is between a quarter turn and a half turn.

Fig. 3:21

A reflex angle is more than a half turn.

Fig. 3:22

1 Write the names of the angles in Figure 3:23, choosing from acute, right, obtuse and reflex.

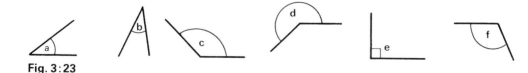

Fig. 3:23

*2 Look back to exercise 3B, question 8. Say what kind of angle each is.

*3 Draw small diagrams, as in Figure 3:23, of three acute angles, three obtuse angles and three reflex angles. Ask your teacher to check them.

4 A quarter turn is 90° (ninety degrees). A half turn is 180°. A whole turn is 360°. How many degrees is three-quarters of a turn?

5 On a compass, north (N) is taken as 0°. East (E) is 90°, south (S) is 180° and west (W) is 270°.

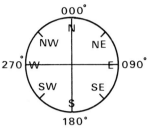

Fig. 3:24

How many degrees is:
(a) NE   (b) SE   (c) SW   (d) NW?

6 Figure 3:25 shows how to draw an angle if the arms are to be less than the radius of your protractor.

Making the arms 3 cm long, draw an angle of: (a) 30°   (b) 80°   (c) 45°.

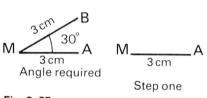

Angle required

Step one

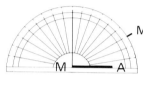

Mark 30°

Step two

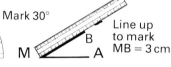

Line up to mark MB = 3 cm

Step three

Fig. 3:25

7 Using a protractor and a ruler, draw Figures 3:26 to 3:31 full size.

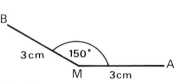

Fig. 3:26

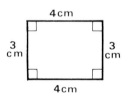

Fig. 3:27

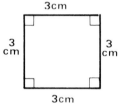

Fig. 3:28

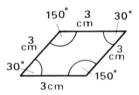

Fig. 3:29

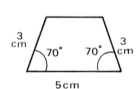

Fig. 3:30

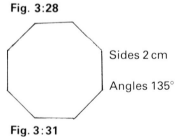

Sides 2 cm

Angles 135°

Fig. 3:31

8 Use a protractor to draw a circle (as in Figure 3:14). Mark every 10° as accurately as you can, writing outside the circle the number of degrees turned from 0 right round to 350. Join every mark to all the other marks, using a ruler and a sharp pencil or a fine-point ballpen. The resulting pattern is called a Mystic Rose.

4 Decimals: addition; subtraction

A Tenths and hundredths

Ten 10p's = £1 or 10p = £0.1

100p = £1 or 1p = £0.01

Fig. 4:1

1

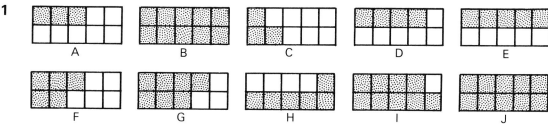

Fig. 4:2

In rectangle A, 0.3 (3 tenths) is shaded.

B + A total 1.3 (1 whole and 3 tenths) rectangles shaded.

Write as a decimal, like 0.3 and 1.3, the amount shaded in:
(a) C   (b) D   (c) E   (d) G   (e) I   (f) B + G
(g) B + H   (h) B + J + A   (i) C + D.

Fig. 4:3

2 (a) How many small squares, the size of K, are there in Figure 4·4?

(b) In Figure 4:4 one small square is one hundredth or 0.01 of the big square, so K = 0.01 of the big square.

Shape L contains 10 squares, so it is ten hundredths or 0.10 of the big square.

Which shape is 0.03 of the big square?

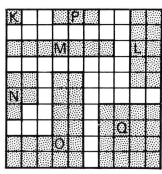

Fig. 4:4

3 Write as a decimal fraction of the big square in Figure 4:4 (like 0.03 and 0.10) shape:
(a) M   (b) N   (c) O   (d) Q.

4 What decimal fraction of Figure 4:4 is *not* shaded?

25

5 Write the value of each figure in 173.24. Start your answer: The 1 stands for ...

6 Write in figures, using a decimal point:
(a) 5 units and 6 tenths   (b) 9 tenths
(c) 3 tens, 6 units, 1 tenth and 8 hundredths   (d) 7 hundredths
(e) 15 hundredths.

*7 Write in figures:
(a) three hundred and ninety-one point five
(b) two hundred and eighteen point seven
(c) fifty point three
(d) seven thousand and sixty-eight point nine.

*8 Example 302.6 is 3 hundreds, 0 tens, 2 units and 6 tenths.

Write in a similar way:
(a) 193.8   (b) 271.4   (c) 40.2   (d) 13.6   (e) 1476.9

*9 Write as a decimal:
(a) 1 hundredth   (b) 8 hundredths   (c) 19 hundredths   (d) 3 hundredths
(e) 40 hundredths   (f) 30 hundredths.

*10 Example 38.07 is 3 tens, 8 units, 0 tenths, 7 hundredths.

Write in a similar way:
(a) 46.02   (b) 83.51   (c) 17.67   (d) 40.04

*11 Examples 38.07 is read 'Thirty-eight point nought seven' (or 'point oh seven' or 'point zero seven').

3.15 is read 'Three point one five' (*not* 'Three point fifteen').

Write in words:
(a) 16.05   (b) 82.17   (c) 16.39   (d) 40.14   (e) 40.01   (f) 40.38

*12 State the value of the figure 9 in:
(a) 96   (b) 29   (c) 3.9   (d) 3.09   (e) 3.129

13 Copy and complete this table:

hundreds					thousandths
100s			$\bullet$		$\dfrac{1}{1000}$ s

14 In Figure 4:5 each figure is drawn to the size representing how much it is really worth. The 1 unit is 10 cm high; the 1 tenth is therefore a tenth of this, 1 cm high; the 1 hundredth is 1 mm high.

(a) Draw 1.64 to show how much each figure is really worth. Make the one unit 10 cm high, the six tenths 6 cm high and the four hundredths 4 mm high.

(b) Draw pictures of 1.68 and 1.19 in the same way.

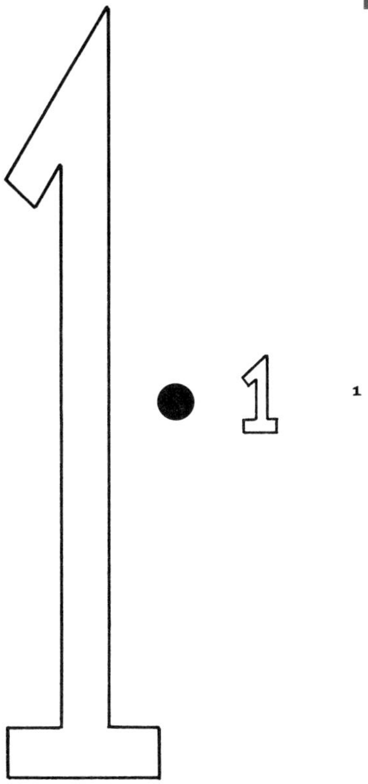

15 Draw a line of length:
(a) 10 cm   (b) 1 cm   (c) 0.1 cm   (d) 0.01 cm.

16 The following sentences contain numbers with too many places of decimals. Rewrite them with a sensible number of decimal places (or none at all).

(a) The man was 186.1243 cm tall.

(b) The paper is 25.1437 cm long and 20.312 cm wide.

(c) Jim ran 300.341 metres in 45.3099 seconds.

(d) I need to buy 6.38 tins of paint for a wall of area 50.314 square metres.

Fig. 4:5

17 Examples $\frac{1}{2} = \frac{5}{10} = 0.5$; $\frac{1}{4} = \frac{25}{100} = 0.25$

Copy and complete:
(a) $\frac{2}{5} = \frac{}{10} = 0.$ (b) $\frac{4}{5} = \frac{}{10} = 0..$ (c) $\frac{3}{4} = \frac{}{100} = 0.$

(d) $\frac{7}{20} = \frac{}{100} = 0.$ (e) $\frac{9}{20} = \frac{}{100} = 0.$ (f) $\frac{8}{25} = 0.$

18 Choose a suitable size rectangle and divide it into 100 centimetre squares. Choose a fraction of the rectangle, e.g. 0.24, and draw a pattern with this area so that its perimeter is as small as possible. Then try again, but make the perimeter as long as possible. Repeat for other fractions. Write about any discoveries you make.

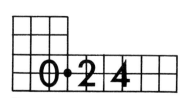

Fig. 4:6

B Addition and subtraction

Decimal points must be lined up, with all the units figures in the same column.

Remember that it is wise to check subtraction by addition.

1 (a) $\quad 4.38$ (b) $\quad 16.05$ (c) $\quad 4.61$ (d) $\quad 7.9$
$\qquad -1.69 \qquad\qquad -8.33 \qquad\qquad -1.8 \qquad\qquad -1.61$

2 (a) $8.37 + 6.19$ (b) $42.3 + 87$ (c) $16.6 - 3.15$

*3 (a) $\quad 5.24$ (b) $\quad 16.06$ (c) $\quad 72.43$ (d) $\quad 123.45$
$\qquad +7.38 \qquad\qquad +23.59 \qquad\qquad +8.57 \qquad\qquad +67.89$

*4 (a) $\quad 8.34$ (b) $\quad 3.91$ (c) $\quad 5.05$ (d) $\quad 4.03$
$\qquad -2.79 \qquad\qquad -1.82 \qquad\qquad -3.14 \qquad\qquad -1.72$

*5 (a) $\quad 15.09$ (b) $\quad 23.08$ (c) $\quad 4.0$ (d) $\quad 5.0$
$\qquad -13.81 \qquad\qquad -7.77 \qquad\qquad -3.2 \qquad\qquad -1.8$

*6 (a) $\quad 6$ (b) $\quad 7$ (c) $\quad 6.1$ (d) $\quad 4.2$
$\qquad -1.2 \qquad\qquad -2.5 \qquad\qquad -1.78 \qquad\qquad -3.69$

*7 (a) $7.6 + 8.9$ (b) $8.3 - 4.2$ (c) $18.7 - 6.9$ (d) $20.5 - 1.9$

*8 (a) $30.4 - 2.7$ (b) $13 + 42.9$ (c) $29 + 17.6$ (d) $16.2 + 39$

*9 (a) $142.4 + 16.38$ (b) $76.2 + 8.39$ (c) $51.03 - 2.6$

10 (a) $38.6 - 3.82$ (b) $51.2 - 4.67$ (c) $30.1 - 5.97$ (d) $900.9 - 76.31$

11 (a) $163 + 8.2 + 17.69$ (b) $3012 + 16.4 + 8.03 + 0.152$ (c) $0.412 + 0.03 + 17 + 0.9$

12 (a) Add 31.82 to 0.95 then subtract 12.6
     (b) Add 31.82 to 12.6 then subtract 0.95

13 (a) Add 9.8 to 130.3 then subtract 0.53
     (b) Add 130.3 to 0.53 then subtract 9.8

14 Do the work in brackets first:
  (a) $(7.6 + 3.2) + 8.15$ (b) $7.6 + (3.2 + 8.15)$
  (c) $(9.2 - 1.5) + 4.71$ (d) $9.2 - (1.5 + 4.71)$

For questions 15 to 18 use these sets:

$A = \{19.2, 27.8, 0.4, 0.1, 3.9, 0.9, 9.9, 4.0, 5, 10\}$

$B = \{6.52, 0.64, 4.29, 7.30, 8.01, 9.09, 5.3, 18, 9.99, 0.99\}$

15 Copy sets A and B carefully, then rewrite them in increasing order of size. You can cross out each element on your copy as you make the ordered set.

16 (a) List set C, made by increasing each element in set A by 1 tenth (in the same order as printed above).

  (b) List set D, made by increasing each element in set A by 1 hundredth.

  (c) List set E, made by decreasing each element in set A by 1 tenth.

  (d) List set F, made by decreasing each element in set A by 1 hundredth.

17 Repeat question 16 using the elements of set B instead of set A. Name your new sets G, H, I and J.

18 Do all this question in your head, writing down the answers only.

  (a) List set K, made by adding pairs of elements in set A (above question 15), that is, $19.2 + 27.8 + ...$

  (b) List set L, made from set B in the same way.

  (c) Find the sum of the first half of the elements in set A and the sum of the last half, then find the difference between these sums.

  (d) Repeat (c) for set B.

  (e) List set M, made by finding the difference between each pair of elements in set A.

  (f) List set N, made from set B in the same way.

19 Use a calculator to find:
  (a) $(1763.981 - 71.614) + 81.7302$ (b) $(167.26 - 273.98) + 197.003$
  (c) $80.074 - 93.081$ (d) 0.25×0.38 (e) $1 \div 3$ (f) $1 \div 7$

C Money: addition and subtraction

CUSTOMER ORDER NUMBER 512001 July, 1984		OUR REFERENCE BJ 136751		VAT REG NO. 200 5127					
CODE	DESCRIPTION SALES/SERVICE		QTY	UNIT PRICE	DISC. RATE	VAT RATE	GOODS AMOUNT		
	PROJECTOR Service; replace worn parts; lubricate and adjust.								
	Cam		1	9	30	Nett	15%	9	30
	Bearings		2	–	90	Nett	15%	1	80
	Pilot lamp cover		1	–	62	Nett	15%	–	62
	Pilot lamp		1	12	40	Nett	15%	12	40
	Projector lamp A1/252		1	5	38	Nett	15%	5	38
321								29	50
301	Labour Charge		4½h	14	50	Nett	15%	65	25
						GOODS TOTAL		94	75
						VALUE ADDED TAX		14	21
						TOTAL NOW DUE		108	96

Fig. 4:7

1 How many pence make: (a) £1   (b) £2   (c) £0.65   (d) £1.78?

2 Write the following amounts using a £ sign: (a) 300p   (b) 69p   (c) 264p.

3 Mrs Lawson runs a mail-order club. Last week her customers paid her £18.46, £5.93, £12 and £100.06. Add these four payments together.

4 Work out: £5.00 take away £3.87

5 The sale price of a jacket is £68. The usual price is £80. What is the reduction?

6 Milk-pan: usual price £14.45; bargain price £12.70
Frying-pan: usual price £16.30; bargain price £14.50
Chip-pan: usual price £20.95; bargain price £19.20

Find:

(a) the total cost of the three pans at the bargain prices

(b) the reduction on the milk-pan (work out £14.45 − £12.70)

Fig. 4:8

(c) the reduction on the frying-pan

(d) the reduction on the chip-pan.

*7 Example

£	p
18	23
7	46
15	00
0	02
40	71

Write the following amounts in columns, as in the example, then add them.
Check each one.
(a) £16.25, £8.41, £6.21   (b) £2.33, £8.46, £12.17   (c) £31.16, £41.05, £18
(d) £4, £3.06, £2.18   (e) £13, £27.16, £14.32, £38   (f) £6, 36p, £8.19
(g) £5, £4.16, 93p, 12p, £7.09   (h) £14, 3p, 18p, 6p, £3.62

*8 Write the following amounts under each other, then subtract. Make sure you put the larger amount at the top, and remember to check by adding.
(a) £16.24 − £9.36   (b) £18.16 − £7.09   (c) £20.15 − £5.03
(d) £5 − £3.27 (write £5 as £5.00)   (e) £5 − £2.81   (f) £6 − £3.16
(g) £7 − £2.28   (h) £4 − £3.18

9 Mardi used her calculator to add the costs of the blouse and the skirt (see Figure 4:9). She was not quite sure what the answer meant. Why do you think that was? How would you explain the calculator's answer to Mardi?

£23·58   £16·92

Fig. 4:9

10 Use a calculator to find the answer to £2.50 + £30 − £0.68. You should be able to do this using only eleven key presses. Can you?

11 A pupil made a mistake in each of the following. Find out what he did wrong, then work out the correct answer.

(a) £6.25 + £5

£6·25
+£   5
£6·30 ✗

(b) £7.28 + £16

£7·28
+£   16
£7·44 ✗

(c) £5.43 + £8.29

£5·43
+ £8·29
£13·81 ✗
       2

(d) £6.32 − £4.88

£4·88
−£6·32
£2·56 ✗

(e) £4 − £3.26

£4·00
−£3·26
£1·26 ✗

(f) £3.62 + £8 + 3p

£3·62
8
+   3
£3·73 ✗

31

12 Freda has £1.86; Anna has 92p; Julie has £2.00; Tara has 6p.

(a) Write the girls' names in the order of how much they have, Tara first.

(b) How much have they altogether?

(c) How much more has Julie than each of the others? (*three answers*)

(d) How much more has Freda than Anna?

(e) How much more has Freda than Tara?

(f) How much more has Anna than Tara?

13 If you have £1.00 and spend 60p, you will have 40p left. The 40p is called the **balance**. What is the balance if you have 80p and spend 30p?

14 Figure 4:10 shows a page from an Account Book. Copy it, work out how the first two balances were found, then find the other five balances.

Details	+/-	£	P
From last page		15	62
Sales	+	50	00
Balance		65	62
Rent	−	33	42
Balance		32	20
Sales	+	27	80
Balance			
Stamps	−	3	00
Balance			
Sales	+	15	38
Balance			
Sales	+	19	24
Balance			
Electricity	−	16	18
Balance to next page			

Fig. 4:10

15 Just write down the answers to the following. Do no written working out. Check each one twice and remember that you can check subtraction by addition.

(a) What is the change from £5 if you spend:
(i) 26p (ii) 57p (iii) £1.18 (iv) £2.97 (v) £3.01?

(b) What is the balance if you start with £100 each time and spend:
(i) 97p (ii) £18 (iii) £27 (iv) £2.53 (v) £8.47 (vi) £16.21
(vii) £57.67 (viii) £83.09 (ix) £60.04?

16 Figure 4:11 shows Jane's Pocket-money Account. Copy it, then fill in the missing amounts. (For instance, on 1st January she must have been given £5 pocket-money, as when she spent £4 the balance was £1.)

Week beginning	Details	+/-	£	P
1st January	Pocket Money / Spent	−	4	00
8th January	BALANCE / Pocket Money	+	1	00
	BALANCE / Spent	−	6	50
15th January	BALANCE / Pocket Money		1	25
	BALANCE / Spent		4	75
22nd January	BALANCE / Pocket Money		2	50
	BALANCE / Spent		3	75
29th January	BALANCE		1	80

Fig. 4:11

17 When you go abroad you change British £'s into foreign currency. On July 27th, 1979, £1 bought 9,72 francs, or 4,19 marks, or 1850 lire. How many francs, marks or lire would you have received for £2?

18 In 1979 there were roughly 10 francs, or 4 marks, or 2000 lire to the pound.

(a) About how much in pence was:
(i) 1 franc   (ii) 1 mark   (iii) 200 lire?

(b) About how much in pounds was:
(i) 100 francs   (ii) 30 francs   (iii) 70 francs   (iv) 20 marks
(v) 48 marks   (vi) 10000 lire?

19 Use a calculator to work out the answers to question 18 using up-to-date exchange rates. You will find these in most newspapers.

5 Circles: naming parts

A Centre and radius

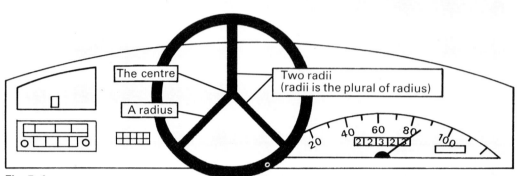

Fig. 5:1

1 Draw a circle of radius 5 cm. Then, using the same centre, draw four more circles of radii 4 cm, 3 cm, 2 cm, and 1 cm.

2 (a) Copy Figure 5:2 exactly, leaving at least a 3 cm space above and below it.

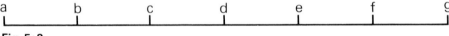

Fig. 5:2

    (b) Draw five circles, each of radius 2 cm, with centres on the line at the points b, c, d, e and f.

    (c) Repeat part (b), but use a radius of $1\frac{1}{2}$ cm.

    (d) Colour or shade the rings to make your diagram look like a chain, as in Figure 5·3.

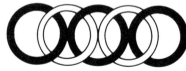

Fig. 5:3

*3 Draw a target of five circles with radii $1\frac{1}{2}$ cm, $2\frac{1}{2}$ cm, $3\frac{1}{2}$ cm, $4\frac{1}{2}$ cm and $5\frac{1}{2}$ cm.

*4 Copy Figure 5:4 exactly, leaving at least a 2 cm space above and below it. Draw seven circles of radii $1\frac{1}{2}$ cm, with centres on the line at points b, c, d, e, f, g and h.

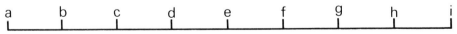

Fig. 5:4

Colour or shade your circles to look like a row of overlapping coins or counters.

34

*5

a   b   c   d   e   f   g   h   i

Fig. 5:5

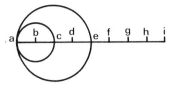

Fig. 5:6

Copy Figure 5·5 exactly, leaving at least a 4 cm space above and below it. Draw four circles, centres at b, c, d and e, all passing through the point a. The first two are shown in Figure 5:6.

Then draw three circles, centres f, g and h, all passing through the point i.

6   Copy Figures 5:7 to 5:11, but make them twice as big. Use compasses for all circles and parts of circles. Centres are marked with dots. Always start with the biggest circle.

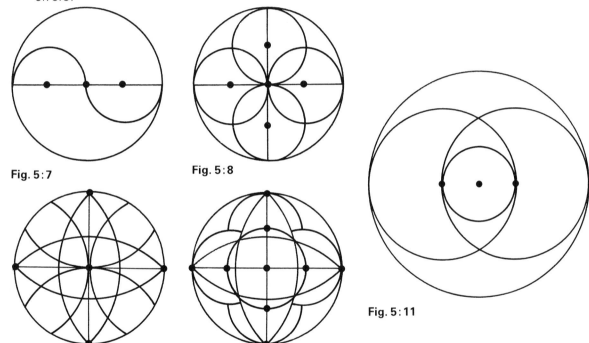

Fig. 5:7

Fig. 5:8

Fig. 5:9

Fig. 5:10

Fig. 5:11

7   Draw two 2 cm-radius circles, the centre of one being on the circumference of the other. Now extend the pattern by drawing more 2 cm-radius circles, each centre being at the point where two other circles cross.

8   Copy the spiral shown in Figure 5:12 exactly, using centres 1, 2 and 3 in order. Then, using centre 4 and at least one more centre, continue the spiral.

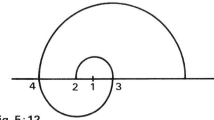

Fig. 5:12

9 Figure 5:13 represents a virus, Z, about to invade a cell, A.

Copy the diagram using radii of $1\frac{1}{2}$ cm and 2 cm.

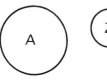

Fig. 5:13

Then draw a series of four pictures showing Z just touching A, Z partly inside A, Z *just* completely inside A, and Z in the middle of A. Measure and write down the distances between the centres in each of these four stages.

---

10 Draw a circle of radius 2 cm, leaving a 4 cm space below it. Mark a point A on the circumference, at the top. Now draw more circles of different sizes, each with its centre on the circumference of the first circle, and each passing through point A. You should have drawn a heart shape called a **cardioid**.

11 Copy Figure 5:14. Leave a 4 cm space above and below the circle. Then draw about twenty circles with centres on the first circle, each passing through point A. The curve drawn this time is called a **limaçon**.

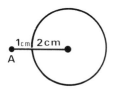

Fig. 5:14

Fig. 5:15

12 Copy Figure 5:15. The size is up to you. Each circle must now have its centre on the thicker circle and touch the straight line. The curve is called a **nephroid**.

B Diameter; circumference; arc; chord

Diameter: the distance (or line) across a circle through the centre.

Circumference: the distance (or line) round a circle.

Arc: part of the circumference.

Chord: any straight line joining two points on the circumference.

1 (a) In Figure 5:16, what do we call the following lines:
(i) OA   (ii) OA, OE and OB
(iii) AOB   (iv) AC   (v) BC
(vi) BE   (vii) CD (straight)
(viii) CD (curved)?

(b) In Figure 5:16, how long would radius OE be if the diameter AB was 18 cm?

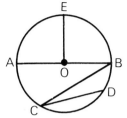

Fig. 5:16

2 A circle has a radius of 4 cm. What is the length of its diameter?

3 Figure 5:17 illustrates a coin being rolled through one complete turn. What is the length of the circumference of this coin?

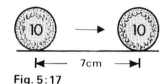

Fig. 5:17

***4** (a) Write the names of the following lines in Figure 5.18:
(i) OP   (ii) QS (straight)   (iii) RS
(iv) QO   (v) OR, OS and OP
(vi) PQ   (vii) POS   (viii) PR (straight)
(ix) QOR   (x) OS and OQ.

(b) In Figure 5:18, is PO + OQ longer, shorter, or the same distance as POS?

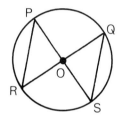

Fig. 5:18

***5** State the values of (a) to (j) in the table.

Radius	13 cm	17 cm	(c)	(d)	$6\frac{1}{2}$ cm	$8\frac{1}{2}$ cm	$16\frac{1}{2}$ cm	(h)	(i)	(j)
Diameter	(a)	(b)	88 cm	48 cm	(e)	(f)	(g)	11 cm	23 cm	92 cm

***6** Draw any picture (not a pattern) using only straight lines, circles and arcs.

7 Draw a circle of diameter 6 cm, drawing on it one diameter AB. Mark a point C anywhere on the circumference.
(a) Join A to C and join B to C. Measure angle ACB.
(b) Mark a point D on the circumference. Measure angle ADB.

8 Draw a circle with diameter AB 6 cm long. Figure 5:19 shows a piece of paper, right-angled at P, with its edges passing through A and B. At how many different places could point P be? Could P be anywhere?

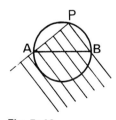

Fig. 5:19

37

9 (a) Draw a right-angled triangle. Draw a circle through the three corners.

(b) Repeat part (a) for three different right-angled triangles.

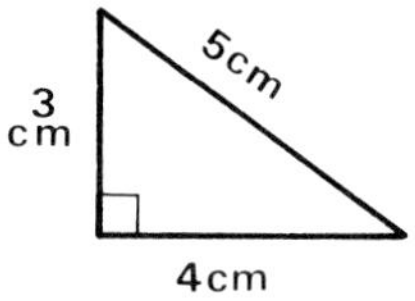

Fig. 5:20

10 The ball (or sphere) in Figure 5:21 has a set of parallel lines painted on it. Draw a picture of the sphere seen from directly above it.

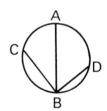

Fig. 5:21

11 Figure 5:22 represents a sphere of plasticine which is to be sliced through AB, BC and BD.

(a) Into how many pieces will the sphere be cut?

(b) What shape will the flat parts of the pieces be?

Fig. 5:22

12 A point moves so that it stays the same distance from a fixed point. What shape does the moving point make?

---

13 Draw a circle of radius 3 cm. Draw a diameter. Label it AB. From A draw two chords of length 5 cm. Now draw, still from A, two chords of length: (a) 4 cm (b) 3 cm (c) 2 cm (d) 1 cm. Draw ten similar chords starting from B. Colour your pattern.

14 Draw a set of concentric (same-centred) circles of radii 1 cm, 2 cm, 3 cm, 4 cm, 5 cm and 6 cm. Draw a diameter of the 6 cm circle. Draw ten chords parallel (like exercise-book lines) to the diameter and spaced 1 cm apart. Colour every other section of your pattern black.

15 Investigate the movement of the centre point of a ladder as it slides from vertical to horizontal, with one end remaining against a wall and the other remaining on horizontal ground.

16 Investigate how a set-square and two drawing-pins (pushed point-up through a piece of paper) can be used to draw circles of different size.

17 Make a cylindrical box.

6 Metric system: length

A Centimetre and millimetre

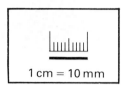
1 cm = 10 mm

1 mm = 0.1 cm

Fig. 6:1

A **centimetre** is a hundredth part of a metre. It is usually written as **cm**.

A **millimetre** is a thousandth part of a metre. It is usually written as **mm**.

1 (a) In Figure 6:2, how many cm is it from:
   (i) A to C   (ii) B to E?

   (b) How many mm is it from:
   (i) A to C   (ii) B to E?

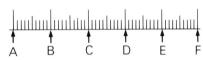
A   B   C   D   E   F

Fig. 6:2

2 In Figure 6:3, check the length of the $3\frac{1}{2}$ cm line, then write the lengths of (a) and (b) in cm.

   $3\frac{1}{2}$ cm   (a) └─────────┘   (b) └───┘

Fig. 6:3

3 In Figure 6:4, check the length of the 23 mm line, then write the lengths of (a), (b) and (c) in mm.

   23 mm   (a) └──────┘   (b) └─────┘   (c) └──┘

Fig. 6:4

4 How many mm make: (a) 1 cm 2 mm   (b) 4.6 cm   (c) 18.5 cm?

5 Write in cm and mm, like question 4(a): (a) 24 mm   (b) 342 mm   (c) 160 mm.

6 Write the lengths in question 5 in cm, as a decimal, like question 4(b) and (c).

*7 (a) In Figure 6:5, measure in cm:
   (i) A to B   (ii) B to C   (iii) C to E
   (iv) E to D.

   (b) Measure in mm:
   (i) A to D   (ii) A to F   (iii) A to E
   (iv) F to E   (v) B to E.

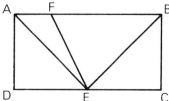
Fig. 6:5

6

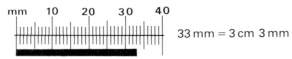

33 mm = 3 cm 3 mm

Fig. 6:6

*8 Using Figure 6:6 to help you, copy and complete:
(a) 14 mm = 1 cm ... mm   (b) 47 mm = ... cm ... mm
(c) 123 cm = 12 cm ... mm   (d) 268 mm = ... cm 8 mm
(e) 317 mm = ... cm ... mm   (f) 261 mm = ... cm ... mm
(g) 100 mm = ... cm 0 mm   (h) 200 mm = ... cm ... mm.

*9 **Example**   2 cm 3 mm = 23 mm.

Write in a similar way:
(a) 1 cm 7 mm   (b) 7 cm 6 mm   (c) 16 cm 8 mm   (d) 19 cm 3 mm.

*10 **Example**   10 mm = 1 cm, so 1 mm = $\frac{1}{10}$ cm.

Remember that $\frac{1}{10}$s (tenths) is the first column after the decimal point, so
1 mm = $\frac{1}{10}$ cm = 0.1 cm.

Write in centimetres, using a decimal point:
(a) 2 mm   (b) 4 mm   (c) 7 mm.

*11 **Example**   37 mm = 3.7 cm; 184 mm = 18.4 cm.

Write in centimetres, using a decimal point:
(a) 14 mm   (b) 47 mm   (c) 123 mm   (d) 268 mm   (e) 317 mm
(f) 261 mm.

*12 How many millimetres altogether make:
(a) 6.9 cm   (b) 4.3 cm   (c) 16.9 cm   (d) 18.2 cm   (e) 20.4 cm
(f) 30.5 cm?

13 **Example**   In Figure 6:7, A to B = 12 mm = 1 cm 2 mm = 1.2 cm.

Write a statement like the one above about:
(a) A to C   (b) A to D   (c) A to E   (d) A to F   (e) A to G
(f) B to E   (g) C to G   (h) C to E   (i) B to F   (j) C to F.

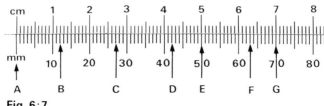

Fig. 6:7

40

14 Figure 6:8 is not the correct size. Use a ruler and a protractor to draw it the correct size. Measure the length of BD.

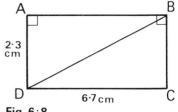

Fig. 6:8

15 Use a ruler and protractor to draw Figure 6:9. Measure the length of XY to the nearest 0.1 cm.

16 Write as a decimal, in cm:
(a) 16 cm 3 mm   (b) 29 mm
(c) 119 mm   (d) 2 cm 2 mm.

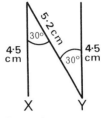

17 Write in order of size, smallest first:
(a) 22 cm, 2 mm, 20 mm, 2.4 cm, 180 mm
(b) 14 cm, 12 mm, 9 mm, 3.6 cm, 111 mm.

Fig. 6:9

18 (a) 18.3 cm + 3.8 cm   (b) 17.4 cm + 16.9 cm   (c) 19.8 cm − 6.3 cm
(d) 15.5 cm − 7.6 cm   (e) 20.7 cm − 18.8 cm
(f) (3.4 cm + 2.8 cm) − 2.1 cm (Do the bracket sum first.)
(g) (19.3 cm − 7.8 cm) + 3.6 cm

19 A goldfish, 4 cm long now, grows 3 mm per year.

(a) How long should it be in:
(i) 1 year from now   (ii) 2 years   (iii) 3 years   (iv) 4 years
(v) 5 years?

(b) How old is the goldfish in Figure 6:10, approximately?

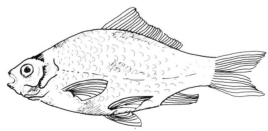

Fig. 6:10 Full size

20 A match is 43 mm long.

(a) Write this in cm, as a decimal.

(b) After the match is struck, 1.8 cm burns away. What length in mm is left?

(c) Draw the match before and after use, full size.

21 To enter 6 cm 9 mm on a calculator you need to change it to 6.9 cm. Use a calculator to find:
(a) 16 cm 9 mm × 28   (b) 18 cm 7 mm × 36   (c) 17 cm 6 mm × 263.

22 Measure:
(a) your little finger   (b) your hand-span (fingers outstretched)
(c) the length of your foot
(d) the distance round your thumb and round your wrist.

B   Metre and centimetre

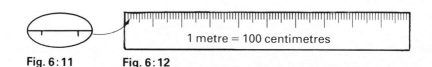

1 metre = 100 centimetres

Fig. 6:11   **Fig. 6:12**

1 Would you use metres, centimetres or millimetres to measure:
(a) the height of a daffodil   (b) the thickness of a piece of glass
(c) the length of a garden?

2 How many cm make:
(a) 2 m   (b) 12 m   (c) $\frac{1}{2}$ m   (d) 6 m 17 cm?

3 Write in metres and centimetres:
(a) 128 cm   (b) 160 cm   (c) 6.34 m.

4 Write 4 m 25 cm as a decimal, in metres.

*5 $A = \{7 \text{ mm}, 7 \text{ cm}, 7 \text{ m}\}$

Which length in set A could be correct for:
(a) the length of a pea-pod   (b) the diameter of a pencil
(c) the height of a flag-pole?

*6 $B = \{15 \text{ mm}, 15 \text{ cm}, 15 \text{ m}\}$

Which length in set B could be correct for:
(a) the width of a rubber   (b) the length of a swimming-pool
(c) the length of a ruler?

* **7 Example**   1 m = 100 cm; $2\frac{1}{2}$ m = 250 cm

Write in a similar way:
(a) 3 m   (b) 5 m   (c) 9 m   (d) $1\frac{1}{2}$ m   (e) $3\frac{1}{2}$ m   (f) $5\frac{1}{2}$ m
(g) $\frac{1}{2}$ m   (h) 10 m   (i) $10\frac{1}{2}$ m.

* **8** How many cm make:
(a) 3 m 14 cm   (b) 3 m 4 cm   (c) 10 m 6 cm   (d) 10 m 10 cm?

9 Example   192 cm = 1 m 92 cm = 1.92 m

Copy and complete:
(a) 239 cm = ... m ... cm = 2.39 m   (b) 172 cm = ... m ... cm = ... m
(c) 638 cm = ... m ... cm = ... m   (d) ... cm = ... m ... cm = 4.36 m.

10 How many cm make:
(a) 6.14 m   (b) 12 m 13 cm   (c) 12 m 3 cm   (d) 8 m 9 cm   (e) 7.01 m
(f) 18.08 m   (g) 6.80 m   (h) 9.10 m   (i) 4.7 m   (j) 8.2 m
(k) 9.6 m   (l) 4.5 m?

11 (a) Figure 6:13 shows a street lamp, 4 m 18 cm high. How many centimetres is this?

(b) The lampshade is 35 cm high. How tall, in cm, is the post under it?

(c) A boy climbs up 3.05 m. How many metres from the top is he?

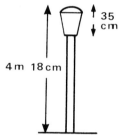

Fig. 6:13

12 Each of the triangles in Figure 6:14 is made from 20 m of string. State the length of the third side in metres.

(a)   (b) 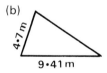   (c)   (d)

Fig. 6:14

13 To enter 3 m 8 cm on a calculator you need to change it to 3.08 m. Use a calculator for:
(a) 5 m 18 cm × 35   (b) 19 m 6 cm × 22
(c) 8 m 5 cm × 162   (d) 9 m 4 cm × 39.

14 Make a chart showing objects you would measure in metres, or centimetres, or millimetres. Write a size for each object.

6

C Kilometre

A kilometre (km) = 1000 metres.

To convert from miles to kilometres use the rule: **5 miles is about 8 km.**

Kilo means 1000.
Centi means $\frac{1}{100}$.
Milli means $\frac{1}{1000}$.

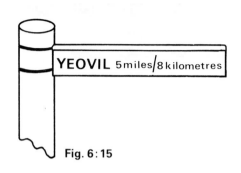

YEOVIL 5 miles / 8 kilometres

Fig. 6:15

1 Write in metres:
(a) 3 km   (b) $1\frac{1}{2}$ km   (c) 4 km 419 m   (d) 5 km 500 m   (e) 6.5 km.

2 Write in kilometres:
(a) 6000 m   (b) 8500 m.

*3 Remember that 1 km = 1000 metres. How many kilometres is a 5000-metre race?

*4 (a) How many metres is 7 km?

(b) How many metres high is a plane at 10 km?

*5 (a) A hot-air balloon reaches a height of $1\frac{1}{2}$ km. How many metres is this?

(b) The balloon travels a distance of $6\frac{1}{2}$ km. How many metres is this?

(c) The balloonist enters for a 8500-metre race. How many kilometres is this?

Fig. 6:16

*6 **Example**   0.5 km = $\frac{1}{2}$ km = 500 m; 2.5 km = 2500 m

Copy and complete:
(a) 1.5 km = ... m   (b) 3.5 km = ... m   (c) 2000 m = ... km
(d) 3500 m = ... km   (e) 4500 m = ... km

44

7 **Examples** You know that 7 km = 7000 metres,
so 7 km 26 m = 7000 m + 26 m = 7026 m.

Similarly, 6 km 41 m = 6041 m
and 7 km 3 m = 7003 m.

Write in a similar way:
(a) 7 km 36 m   (b) 8 km 62 m   (c) 9 km 15 m   (d) 4 km 8 m
(e) 5 km 7 m   (f) 7 km 9 m   (g) 12 km 3 m.

8 **1 km = 1000 m; $\frac{1}{2}$ km = 500 m; $\frac{1}{4}$ km = 250 m**

How many metres is:
(a) $1\frac{1}{4}$ km   (b) $2\frac{1}{4}$ km   (c) $3\frac{3}{4}$ km   (d) $4\frac{3}{4}$ km   (e) $\frac{1}{8}$ km?

9 **Centi means** $\frac{1}{100}$; There are 100 **centi**metres in 1 metre.

Milli means $\frac{1}{1000}$; There are 1000 **milli**metres in 1 metre.

Kilo means 1000; There are 1000 metres in 1 **kilo**metre.

Some other units used in the metric system are grams, litres and volts.

Copy and complete:
(a) 1 volt = ... millivolts   (b) 8 volts = ... millivolts
(c) 1 kilovolt = ... volts   (d) 10 kilovolts = ... volts
(e) 4 grams = ... milligrams   (f) 1 gram = ... centigrams
(g) 6 grams = ... centigrams   (h) 1 kilogram = ... grams
(i) 3 kilograms = ... grams   (j) ... litres = 4000 millilitres
(k) ... litres = 800 centilitres.

---

10 **5 miles is about 8 kilometres.**

About how many km is:
(a) 10 miles   (b) 15 miles   (c) 30 miles?

11 About how many miles is:
(a) 32 km   (b) 40 km   (c) 72 km   (d) 4 km   (e) 2 km
(f) 1 km?

12 Draw a signpost near to your home. Write the distances in miles and kilometres.

13 Make a leaflet about 'The History of the Metric System'.

Using Your Calculator

What £7 Million Could Buy

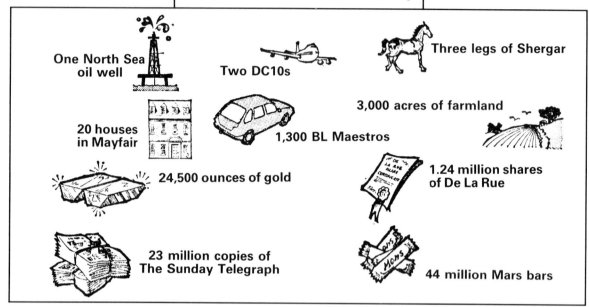

What £7 million could buy

One North Sea oil well

Two DC10s

Three legs of Shergar

20 houses in Mayfair

1,300 BL Maestros

3,000 acres of farmland

24,500 ounces of gold

1.24 million shares of De La Rue

23 million copies of The Sunday Telegraph

44 million Mars bars

This illustration was printed in The Sunday Telegraph in 1983, following a large robbery.

Use your calculator and the above information to find the cost in 1983 of the following items.

(a) One North Sea oil well.

(b) A DC10.

(c) Shergar (a racehorse that was stolen in the same year).

(d) A house in Mayfair.

(e) A BL Maestro.

(f) An acre of farmland.

(g) An ounce of gold.

(h) One share in De La Rue (the firm that was robbed).

(i) One copy of The Sunday Telegraph.

(j) A Mars bar.

7 Constructions: 60°

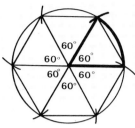

Fig. 7:1

Figure 7:1 shows that the radius of a circle can be stepped round the circumference six times exactly, giving angles of 60° at the centre. The thicker lines show you the part used to construct a 60° angle, as in Figure 7:2.

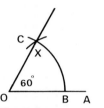

Fig. 7:2

1 Construct Figure 7:3 accurately. Start with angle A, then construct angles B, C and D in order. All angles are 60°.

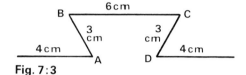

Fig. 7:3

2 (a) Draw a line, AB, 4 cm long. Construct angles of 60° at A and B to make a triangle.

  (b) Measure the top angle of your triangle with a protractor.

  (c) What is the sum of the three angles in degrees?

  (d) This kind of triangle is called **equilateral**. What do you think the word equilateral means?

3 Use constructed 60° angles to draw Figure 7:4.

  (a) What do we call lines that go in the same direction?

  (b) Copy: **AB//CD is short for 'AB is parallel to CD'.**

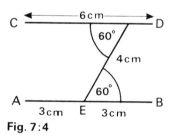

Fig. 7:4

---

4 Without using a protractor, construct angles of 120°, 240° and 300°.

5 Draw some designs based on 60° angles, equilateral triangles and hexagons.

6 Find out about wasps and hexagons. Write a report or draw a chart about them.

A Multiplication by single integers

×	2							
2	4	**3**						
3	6	9	**4**					
4	8	12	16	**5**				
5	10	15	20	25	**6**			
6				30		**7**		
7				35			**8**	
8				40				**9**
9				45				

Fig. 8:1 Table triangle

1 Carefully copy Figure 8:1. Squared paper will make it easier to do, and it will be easier to use if you write both sets of 2, 3, 4, 5, 6, 7, 8, 9 in a different colour. Fill in the missing numbers, then work out how to use the triangle.

2 (a) 16 × 3   (b) 87 × 7   (c) 105 × 7   (d) 60 × 4

*3 (a) 15 × 5   (b) 18 × 2   (c) 19 × 3   (d) 23 × 2

*4 (a) 123 × 3   (b) 386 × 2   (c) 127 × 4   (d) 216 × 4

*5 (a) 27 × 7   (b) 78 × 7   (c) 83 × 7   (d) 98 × 7

*6 (a) 89 × 8   (b) 99 × 9   (c) 187 × 8   (d) 198 × 9

*7 (a) 206 × 3   (b) 308 × 2   (c) 406 × 4   (d) 103 × 5

*8 (a) 70 × 2   (b) 60 × 3   (c) 80 × 4   (d) 90 × 5

Fig. 8:2

Fig. 8:3

48

9 (a) 97×8 (b) 88×7 (c) 970×7 (d) 806×7

10 $7 + 9 \times 9$ has two answers, depending which you do first, $\times$ or $+$. Because of this we have a rule: $\times$ before $+$. Find out if your calculator knows this rule.

11 Copy and complete the three lines given, then work out the next two lines of the pattern.

$$9 \times 9 + 7 =$$
$$98 \times 9 + 6 =$$
$$987 \times 9 + 5 =$$

12 Write down the last possible line of the pattern in question 11.

13 (a) Multiply 12345679 (note that there is no 8) by 2, then multiply your answer by 9.

(b) Repeat (a) but multiply first by 3 instead of by 2.

14 Copy and complete the following. Just write down the answers, without written working. Use your answers to question 13 to help you.

(a) $12345679 \times 4 \times 9 =$

(b) $12345679 \times 5 \times 9 =$

Now work out the next four lines of the pattern.

Try to check your answers with a calculator.

15 (a) $12345 \times 8 + 5$ (Remember: $\times$ before $+$)

(b) Copy and complete the number pattern up to the last line, which has $+ 9$ before the equals sign.

$$1 \times 8 + 1 =$$
$$12 \times 8 + 2 =$$
$$123 \times 8 + 3 =$$

---

16 $5 \times 7 \times 8$ can be worked out in three ways:

35×8 or 5×56 or 40×7.

All give the same answer, but the last way is easiest.

Find the easiest way to work out:

(a) $5 \times 9 \times 6$ (b) $7 \times 5 \times 4$ (c) $8 \times 2 \times 15$
(d) $9 \times 2 \times 9$ (e) $31 \times 8 \times 5$ (f) $1.5 \times 8 \times 2$
(g) $2.6 \times 5 \times 5$ (h) $2.5 \times 16 \times 4$ (i) $0.25 \times 7 \times 8$
(j) $6.5 \times 25 \times 4$ (k) $4 \times 9 \times 2.5$ (l) $7.5 \times 4 \times 17$

17 A cube is a number multiplied by itself, then multiplied by itself again.

Number	1	2	3	4	5	6	7	8	9	10	11	12	13	14	15	16	17	18	19	20
Cube	1	8	27																	

(a) Copy and complete the table.

(b) Can you find the number whose cube is 100? The table shows you it is more than 4 but less than 5. Try 4.5 cubed. Is the answer too big or too small? What shall we try next? When shall we stop trying? (Not yet!)

(c) Make a table of the numbers that cube to give 10, 20, 30, ... 90, 100.

B Multiplication by powers of ten

Silly Sam's way

Sensible Sue's way

Fig. 8:4

1 Copy and complete this table. Make the columns 2 cm wide.

Number	6	16	20	100
× 10				
× 100				
× 1000				

2 (a) 60 × 40   (b) 700 × 80   (c) 600 × 900   (d) 80 × 9000   (e) 500 × 20

*3 State the missing numbers (marked ∗) in:

(a) ∗ × 10 = 70   (b) ∗ × 100 = 500   (c) ∗ × 10 = 360
(d) ∗ × 100 = 2700   (e) 6 × ∗ = 60   (f) 17 × ∗ = 170
(g) 36 × ∗ = 3600   (h) 48 × 100 = ∗   (i) 360 × 10 = ∗

*4 (a) 50×30 (b) 40×70 (c) 60×50 (d) 400×500

5   6000 can be written 6×10^3. This is called **standard form**. The first number is always between 1 and 10, and the small raised 3 after the 10 shows there are 3 zeros after the 6.

Copy the following, replacing the stars with the correct numbers:
(a) $5000 = 5 \times 10*$ (b) $400 = 4 \times 10*$
(c) $3000 = * \times 10*$ (d) $200 = * \times 10*$
(e) $3\,000\,000 = * \times 10*$ (f) $* = 6 \times 10^5$
(g) $* = 8 \times 10^4$ (h) $* = 1 \times 10^6$

---

6   A *million* $= 1 \times 10^6 = 1\,000\,000$.

A thousand million, $1\,000\,000\,000$ is usually called a *billion*.

Write the names of:
(a) 1000   (b) 10000   (c) 100000   (d) 1000000   (e) 10000000
(f) 100000000   (g) 1000000000.

7   A **googol** is 1×10^{100}. Write a googol in full!

C   Multiplication by two-digit numbers

64×78 can be thought of as
64×8 plus 64×70.

```
              64
          ×   78
This is 64×8  ... 512
This is 64×70 ... 4480
              4992
```

1 (a)   63   (b)   42   (c) 49×78
        $\times 20$ $\times 38$

*2 (a)   16   (b)   18   (c)   19   (d)   26   (e)   36   (f)   42   (g)   34
         $\times 20$ $\times 30$ $\times 40$ $\times 20$ $\times 30$ $\times 50$ $\times 50$

*3 (a)   36   (b)   63   (c)   42   (d)   33   (e)   52
         $\times 23$ $\times 32$ $\times 31$ $\times 44$ $\times 43$

*4 (a) 27×32 (b) 46×18 (c) 39×15 (d) 46×58
(e) 40×57 (f) 60×38 (g) 102×12 (h) 706×27

5 (a) 11×11 (b) 26×11 (c) 34×11 (d) 59×11 (e) 68×11

6 (a) Work out 45×11 and 76×11.

(b) Look at Figure 8:5. Find how it shows a way of working out the multiplications in part (a).

(c) Check the answers to question 5 using this method.

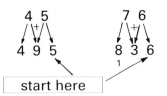

start here

Fig. 8:5

7 Figure 8:6 shows the quick method for 879×11.

Find in a similar way:

(a) 721×11 (b) 342×11 (c) 156×11

(d) 248×11 (e) 397×11 (f) 869×11

(g) 1032×11 (h) 4937×11 (i) 6008×11

(j) 7009×11 (k) 123456789×11.

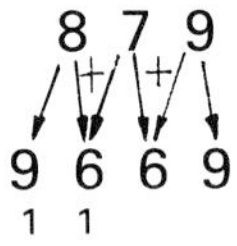

Fig. 8:6

8 (a) (i) 25×25 (ii) 35×35 (iii) 45×45 (iv) 55×55

(b) What are the last two figures of each answer?

9 Follow the method shown in Figure 8:7 to find 25×25 and 195×195 without long multiplication.

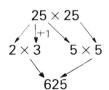

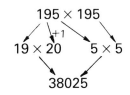

Fig. 8:7

(a) Check the answers to question 8 using the method shown in Figure 8:7.

(b) 75×75 (c) 85×85 (d) 95×95

(e) 105×105 (f) 295×295 (g) 285×285

10 How could you find 318674×739929 exactly, using a calculator?

D Multiplication by decimal fractions

Most mathematicians use the method shown in the example. Your teacher will explain why the method works.

Example To find 6.4×0.78

Work out 64×78, giving 4992. As there are three figures after the decimal points in 6.4 and 0.78 there will be three figures after the decimal point in the answer, giving: *Answer* 4.992

1 (a) 1.6×2 (b) 3.8×3 (c) 0.6×4 (d) 0.8×5 (e) 4.2×3.8 (f) 7.62×0.35

*2 (a) 2.7×3 (b) 8.1×2 (c) 4.6×5 (d) 3.8×5

*3 (a) 0.8×2 (b) 0.7×3 (c) 0.5×4 (d) 0.6×5

*4 (a) 2.3×8.1 (b) 2.32×1.6 (c) 4.32×12 (d) 2.15×0.3 (e) 1.32×0.15

5 Remember the rule: Multiply before you add or subtract.

(a) $7.6 \times 3.4 + 1.9$ (b) $7.6 + 2.9 \times 8.3$
(c) $0.3 \times 0.15 + 0.39$ (d) $0.821 + 18 \times 0.56$
(e) $0.6 \times 0.5 - 0.3$ (f) $0.7 \times 0.9 - 0.321$

6 Numbers multiplied by themselves are called *squares*.

Examples   49 is the square of 7, as $7 \times 7 = 49$.
The square of 0.1 is $0.1 \times 0.1 = 0.01$
The square of 0.2 is $0.2 \times 0.2 = 0.04$

Copy and complete the table of squares.

Number	0.1	0.2	0.3	0.4	0.5	0.6	0.7	0.8	0.9
Square									

Fig. 8:8

7 Use a calculator to find the number which squares to make:
(a) 0.3   (b) 0.4   (c) 0.5

8 Make a table for the numbers that square to make the sets:
{0.1, 0.2, 0.3, ... 0.9} and {0.01, 0.02, 0.03, ... 0.09}.

E   Decimal fractions × powers of 10

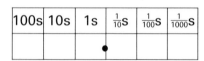

100s	10s	1s	$\frac{1}{10}$s	$\frac{1}{100}$s	$\frac{1}{1000}$s
		•			

Moving figures one column to the left makes them worth ten times as much.

0.809 $\xrightarrow{\text{move figures one place to the left}}$ 8.09
This shows that $0.809 \times 10 = 8.09$

Note that the first zero is not needed when you write the answer.

1.2 $\xrightarrow{\text{move the figures two places to the left}}$ 120
This shows that $1.2 \times 100 = 120$

Note that you need a zero to show the empty units column.

1 Copy and complete this table.

Number	6	6.1	6.12	61	61.2	0.6	0.61	0.612
× 10								
× 100								

2 Copy the following, replacing the stars by the correct numbers.

(a) $6.4 \times * = 64$ (b) $8.32 \times * = 83.2$ (c) $7.16 \times * = 716$
(d) $4.69 \times * = 46.9$ (e) $0.412 \times * = 41.2$ (f) $4.12 \times * = 4120$
(g) $* \times 10 = 61.2$ (h) $* \times 10 = 7.85$ (i) $* \times 10 = 97.4$
(j) $* \times 100 = 33.1$ (k) $* \times 100 = 1.6$ (l) $4.7 \times 1000 = *$

---

3 7.6×10^2 is a number in **standard form**.

10^2 is the shorthand for 10 squared, which means 10×10.
So $7.6 \times 10^2 = 7.6 \times 100 = 760$.

Find:
(a) 8.9×10^2 (b) 5×10^2 (c) 3.71×10^2
(d) 3.2×10^3 (e) 4.73×10^3 (f) 3.16×10^3

4 Put into standard form:
(a) 713   (b) 678   (c) 75   (d) 9000   (e) 8761

5 Some calculators use standard form to show very large or very small numbers. If yours does it will have an EE (or EXP) key. Your instruction booklet will tell you how to use it.

A Naming polygons

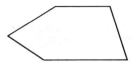

Fig. 9:1

A **polygon** is a plane (flat) shape with any number of straight sides.
Figure 9:1 is a **convex** polygon.
Figure 9:2 is a **concave** polygon.

Fig. 9:2

A **triangle** has 3 sides. A **quadrilateral** has 4 sides. A **pentagon** has 5 sides.
A **hexagon** has 6 sides. A **heptagon** has 7 sides. An **octagon** has 8 sides.
A **nonagon** has 9 sides. A **decagon** has 10 sides.

1 Name the following polygons in Figure 9:3.

(a) The spire of the clock tower.
(b) The window with the bell, in the spire.
(c) The door in the clock tower.
(d) The clock.
(e) The windows on the side.
(f) The window in the small tower.
(g) The whole shape (right round the outside).

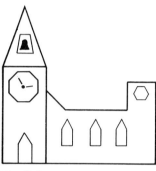

Fig. 9:3

2 Copy each shape in Figure 9:4. You can make them bigger, but keep them as nearly the same shape as you can. Write the correct name under each one, chosen from the following list.

Triangle; Concave quadrilateral; Convex quadrilateral; Concave pentagon; Convex pentagon; Concave hexagon; Convex hexagon; Concave octagon; Convex octagon; Concave decagon.

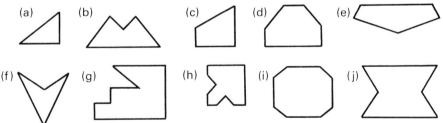

Fig. 9:4

3 Design a picture made up of polygons, like the church. List each polygon you use and say where it is in your picture.

B   Drawing regular polygons

As all regular polygons have their corners on a circle, they can be drawn by dividing the circumference into the same number of equal parts as the polygon has sides. It is easiest to make the circle the same diameter as your protractor.

For a regular hexagon, mark every 60° (because 360° ÷ 6 = 60°).
For a regular octagon, mark every 45° (because 360° ÷ 8 = 45°).

1 Draw:
(a) a regular hexagon   (b) a regular octagon   (c) a regular decagon
(d) a regular quadrilateral   (e) a regular pentagon.

2 Follow the steps of Figure 9:5 to draw a six-pointed star. (It is the symbol of the Jewish people, who call it the Star of David.) Use circles of radii about 4 cm and 5 cm.

Step one 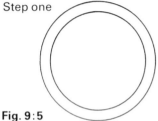   Step two 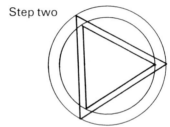   Step three

Fig. 9:5

3 Draw a pentagram (Figure 9:6) and the star based on it (Figure 9:7). The pentagram is a symbol used in magic rites.

Fig. 9:6

Fig. 9:7

4 Cut out ten strips of card, 8 cm long and 1½ cm wide. Make holes 1 cm from each end of the strips and, using 'point-up' drawing pins, join them to make each polygon from triangle to decagon.

5 Is a polygon certain to be regular if its sides are the same length?

10 Integers: division

A Sharing

Fig. 10:1

1 How many 7s make:
(a) 7   (b) 21   (c) 56   (d) 49   (e) 70?

2 Divide (or share) the following sums of money equally between 9 friends, saying how much each will receive.
(a) £9   (b) £27   (c) £45   (d) £63

3 How much will each person receive if £100 is shared equally between:
(a) 100 people   (b) 10 people   (c) 50 people   (d) 25 people?

4 If the answer to the questions following is 'Yes', say how much each. All shares are to be equal.

(a) Can 32 eggs be shared among 4 people?   (b) Can 9 girls share 36 sweets?

(c) Is 56 days a whole number of weeks?   (d) Can 8 boys share 72 tadpoles?

(e) Will 81 plants make 9 equal rows?   (f) Can 9 farmers share 64 sheep?

(g) Is 45 days a whole number of weeks?   (h) Can 7 men share 42 bottles?

(i) Can 48 eggs be packed 6 to a box?   (j) Will 6 divide exactly into 40?

(k) Is there a whole number of sixes in 24?   (l) Will 9 go into 35 exactly?

(m) Can you divide 30 by 6 exactly?   (n) Will 58 divide exactly by 9?

5 **Digit-add** is the trick of adding up the digits (figures) of numbers until you end with a single digit.

Example $4128 \rightarrow 4 + 1 + 2 + 8 \rightarrow 15 \rightarrow 1 + 5 \rightarrow 6$

           (**Note:** Read the arrow sign as 'becomes')

Find the digit-add of:
(a) 63   (b) 315   (c) 210   (d) 9243   (e) 3309   (f) 6132.

6 (a) Does each digit-add in question 5 divide exactly by 3?

(b) Does each number in question 5 divide exactly by 3?

7 The following numbers divide exactly by 9. Find their digit-adds.
(a) 963   (b) 8766   (c) 3123   (d) 18 945

8 A number will divide exactly by:

2 if it is even.   **3** if its digit-add is 3, 6 or 9.
5 if it ends in 0 or 5.   **6** if its digit-add is 3, 6 or 9, and it is even.
9 if its digit-add is 9.   **10** if it ends in 0.

(a) Copy the table and show if the numbers divide by 2, 3, 5, 9 or 10.

(b) Which numbers divide by 6?

÷	36	48	60	72	90	108	125	150	180	209
2	√									
3	√									
5	×									
9	√									
10	×									

9 In the following, say what sign, (+, −, × or ÷) should be written instead of the star.

(a) John has £12. He gives £8 to Ann. John now has £(12 * 8).

(b) Ann gives half her £8 to Pat. She gives Pat £(8 * 2).

(c) Fred owes 8 people £15 each. He needs £(8 * 15) to pay them.

(d) 9 toys cost £63. Each toy costs the same. The price of one toy is £(63 * 9).

(e) There are 50 nuts in a box. To buy 1000 nuts I need (1000 * 50) boxes.

(f) I am driving at 48 km/h. In 6 hours I shall have gone (48 * 6) km.

(g) My tank holds 40 litres of petrol. At 10 km a litre I can go (40 * 10) km.

(h) At 40 km/h it will take me (400 * 40) hours to go 400 km.

(i) A quarter of my garden is lawn. My garden has an area of 1 hectare. My lawn has an area of (1 * 4) hectares.

10 Now work out the answers to question 9. For example, the answer to (a) is £4.

11 Do the work in brackets first:
(a) $(17 + 9) \div 2$ (b) $(123 - 57) \div 6$
(c) $(115 \times 3) - (145 \div 5)$ (d) $(18 \times 3) \div (27 \div 3)$.

12 Copy and complete this table.

2	4	8	16	32	64			
1	2	3	4	5	6	7	8	9	10

In 1614, John Napier found that he could use a table like this to avoid division!

Example To find $32 \div 4$.

$$32 \div 4 = 8$$
$$5 - 2 = 3$$

The arrows show the order of working.
① 32 gives 5 from the table
② 4 gives 2 from the table
③ subtract
④ 3 gives 8 from the table

Example To find $64 \div 16$.

$$64 \div 16 = 4$$
$$6 - 4 = 2$$

Use Napier's table (called 'logarithms') to find:
(a) $32 \div 8$ (b) $64 \div 8$ (c) $64 \div 2$ (d) $128 \div 8$ (e) $512 \div 64$
(f) $256 \div 32$ (g) $1024 \div 128$.

B Short division

Example $5604 \div 6$ $6 \overline{) 5\ 6^20^24}$ with quotient $9\ 3\ 4$

1 (a) $4734 \div 6$ (b) $5121 \div 9$

2 (a) $735 \div 7$ (b) $21606 \div 6$

3 Give the remainder in the form 17 r 2 for: (a) $3743 \div 6$ (b) $3534 \div 7$.

4 Give the answer in the form $17\frac{1}{6}$ for: (a) $2603 \div 6$ (b) $45070 \div 9$.

*5 (a) $783 \div 9$ (b) $3633 \div 7$ (c) $2496 \div 6$ (d) $9675 \div 5$

*6 (a) $1216 \div 4$ (b) $1254 \div 6$ (c) $6464 \div 8$ (d) $4942 \div 7$

*7 Give the answer in two ways, e.g. 17 r 2 and $17\frac{2}{3}$, for:
(a) $1069 \div 3$ (b) $369 \div 7$ (c) $3751 \div 6$ (d) $3842 \div 7$
(e) $2011 \div 4$ (f) $1821 \div 8$ (g) $4543 \div 9$ (h) $3977 \div 6$.

8 (a) $21\,014 \div 7$ (b) $360\,636 \div 6$

9 **$276 \div 5 = 55$ r 1.** However, if you write a decimal point after the 6, and then a 0, you can divide again. You can keep doing this for as long as you like, or until the division works out exactly.

Examples

$$5 \overline{) \, 2 \ 7^{2}6 \ . \ ^{1}0} \quad = \quad 5 \ 5 \ . \ 2$$

$$4 \overline{) \, 4 \ 2^{2}1 \ . \ ^{1}0^{2}0} \quad = \quad 1 \ 0 \ 5 \ . \ 2 \ 5$$

Write 0s as necessary until the division works out for:

(a) $326 \div 5$ (b) $8134 \div 4$ (c) $121 \div 4$ (d) $1002 \div 8$ (e) $4 \div 5.$ (f) $3 \div 5$

10 Divisions that do not work out exactly always start to repeat or **recur**. For example, $1 \div 3 = 0.333333\ldots$ and $1 \div 7 = 0.142857\,142857\,142857\ldots$

We write a dot over the 3 to show it recurs, so $1 \div 3 = 0.\dot{3}$ and we write a dot over the 1 and the 7 to show the pattern 142857 recurs, so $1 \div 7 = 0.\dot{1}42857\dot{7}$

Similarly, $0.16666\ldots$ would be written as $0.1\dot{6}$

Work out the following until they start to recur, then write the answers with dots:

(a) $2 \div 3$ (b) $5 \div 6$ (c) $184 \div 9$ (d) $2 \div 7$ (e) $456 \div 7.$

11 Follow these patterns:

$348 \xrightarrow{3 \times 4 \times 8} 96 \xrightarrow{9 \times 6} 54 \xrightarrow{5 \times 4} 20 \xrightarrow{2 \times 0} 0$

$243 \xrightarrow{2 \times 4 \times 3} 24 \xrightarrow{2 \times 4} 8$

348 reduced to a single figure after four steps. 243 only needed two steps. Investigate the number of steps needed for some other numbers. What is the smallest number that needs two steps? What about 3 steps, 4 steps, etc?

12 **Example** 24 will divide exactly by $\{2, 3, 4, 6, 8\}$

List the sets of numbers from 2 to 10 that will divide exactly into the following.

(a) 20 (b) 25 (c) 32 (d) 36 (e) 41 (f) 45 (g) 49 (h) 54

13 To divide into a decimal fraction, divide as usual but put a point in the answer before starting to divide into the tenths figure.

Example

$$7 \overline{) \, 1 \ 4 \ . \ 7} \quad = \quad 2 \ . \ 1$$

Find: (a) $106.4 \div 7$ (b) $50.58 \div 9$ (c) $35.21 \div 7$ (d) $15.08 \div 6$
(e) $0.23 \div 8$ (f) $0.145 \div 7.$

14 Until 1971, pounds sterling (£) were divided into shillings (s) and pence (d).

12d = 1s and 20s = £1.

Try these divisions:
(a) £16 : 8s : 6d ÷ 2   (b) £9 : 6s : 8d ÷ 2
(c) £1 : 1s : 8d ÷ 2   (d) £5 : 17s : 6d ÷ 2.

Make up some more of your own. Ask your teacher to check them. Your teacher may have an old arithmetic book with lots of questions like these!

Project

Tessellations

A tessellation is made up of shapes that join together without leaving any gaps between them.

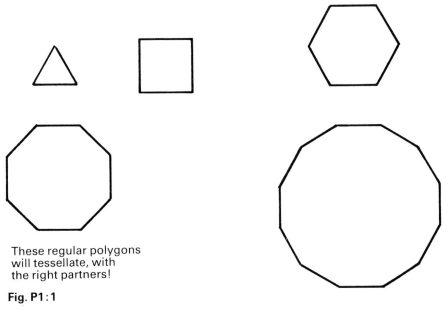

These regular polygons will tessellate, with the right partners!

Fig. P1:1

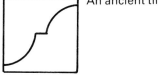

An ancient tile

Fig. P1:2

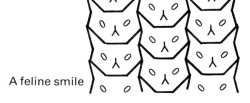

A feline smile

A Topological equivalence

Topology is the study of the effect of distorting a shape.

The shape must not be torn and no two points must be joined together. Figure 11:1 shows some **topological transformations** of a pin-man, except for the last one, which breaks both rules.

Fig. 11:1

For Discussion

GEOGRAPHICAL MAP

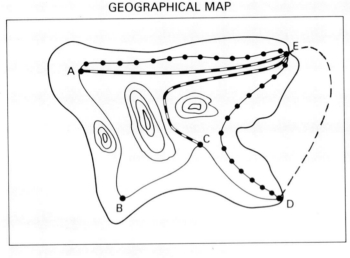

TOPOLOGICAL MAP

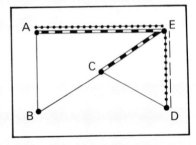

KEY

■■■ RAIL
— BUS
••••• COACH
--- BOAT

Fig. 11:2

1 ⇒ STARTS FROM OR PASSES THROUGH

	A	B	C	D	E
RAIL	1	0	1	0	1
BUS					
COACH					
BOAT					

1 A simple closed curve is any topological transformation of a circle. All the shapes in Figure 11:3 are simple closed curves. Copy those shapes in Figure 11:4 which *are* simple closed curves. Do *not* copy those which are *not* simple closed curves.

Fig. 11:3

Fig. 11:4

2 In Figure 11:5 shapes (a) and (h) are topologically equivalent. Name three other pairs of topologically equivalent shapes in Figure 11:5.

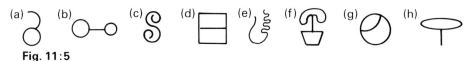

Fig. 11:5

---

3 Look at the maps at the start of this exercise. State all the ways of getting from A to D. Say what transport you would use each time, and where you would change transport.

4 Cut out a strip of paper as shown in Figure 11:6. Give it a half twist and glue it together so that the two stars are stuck together. You have made a Möbius Strip (August Möbius was a German mathematician).

About 30 cm long

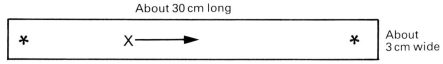

About 3 cm wide

Fig. 11:6

Put your pen on × and draw a line in the direction of the arrow. Have you drawn on the inside or the outside of the strip? What happens if you cut along this line? What happens if you cut the resulting strip again? What if you cut along a line a third of the distance from one edge, using a new strip? What if you give the strip two twists before you glue it? Keep experimenting!

B Nodes; regions; arcs

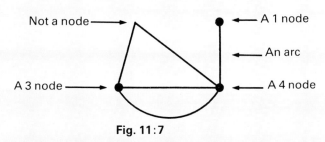

Fig. 11:7

A **node** is a junction. All nodes are marked with a big dot.

A **region** is an area enclosed by **arcs**.

Do not forget the outside region!

Figure 11:7 has 3 nodes, 4 arcs and 3 regions.

1 (a) Copy the eight letters shown in Figure 11:8, but make each one 3 lines of your exercise book high.

(b) By each node write its order, as shown in Figure 11:9.

Fig. 11:8

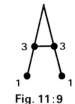

Fig. 11:9

2 Copy the networks in Figure 11:10. Write by each network the number of nodes, regions and arcs, as in Figure 11:11.

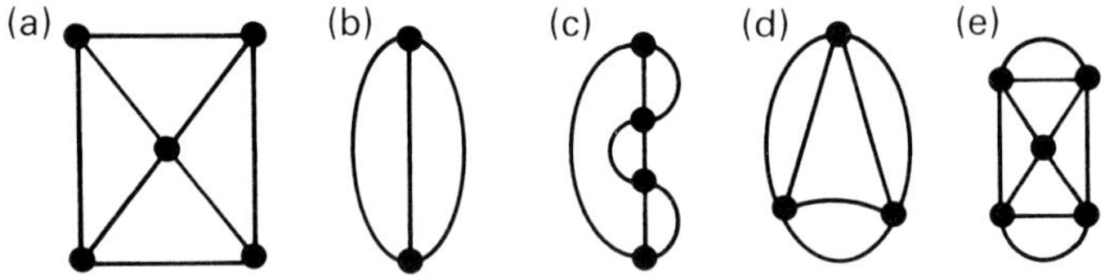

(a) (b)  (c) (d) (e)

Fig. 11:10

Example
Nodes 4
Regions 4
Arcs 6

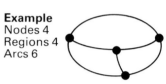

Fig. 11:11

3 Copy the table and fill in the answers for the diagrams in Figure 11:10. Then add the number of nodes and regions for each diagram and compare the total with the number of arcs. Write down any connection you can find.

	Nodes (N)	Regions (R)	Arcs (A)
(a)	5	5	8
(b)			
etc.			

4 (a) Copy the nodes in Figure 11:12, but make them about twice as far apart. Then draw the networks with the given number of arcs.

(i) Four arcs (ii) Five arcs (iii) Four arcs (iv) Six arcs

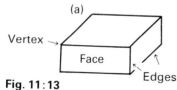 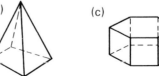

Fig. 11:12

(b) Does $N + R = A + 2$ for each diagram? (See the table in question 3 for the meaning of N, R and A.)

5 Copy the sketches in Figure 11:13. List the number of faces, vertices and edges. Find a rule connecting your answers. Try the rule on other solids, e.g. a desk, a ruler, a dodecahedron.

(a) Vertex → Face Edges (b) (c) (d)

Fig. 11:13

C   Traversable networks

A **traversable network** is a diagram which can be drawn with one pencil stroke without lifting the pencil or going over any line twice.

1   Which of the networks in Figure 11:14 are traversable?

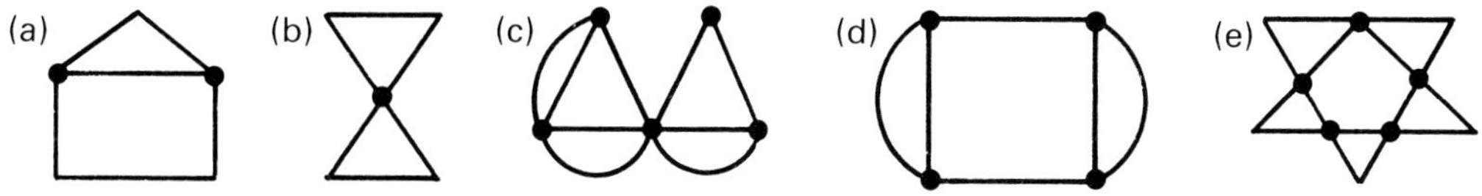

(a)   (b)   (c)  (d) 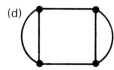 (e)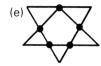

Fig. 11:14

2   Copy Figure 11:15. Draw traversable networks using the given nodes. The numbers tell you how many arcs are to leave that node. Be very careful not to make any *extra* nodes.

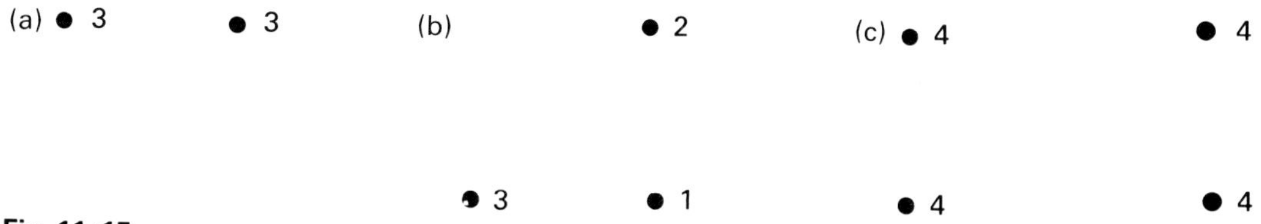

   (a) ● 3   ● 3   (b)   ● 2   (c) ● 4   ● 4

                             ● 3   ● 1   ● 4   ● 4

Fig. 11:15

3   Copy the networks in Figure 11:16. By each node write its order. Which of the networks are traversable?

(a)  (b)   (c)   (d)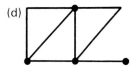

Fig. 11:16

4   Copy the networks in Figure 11:14. By each node write its order.

5   (a) Copy the table and fill in your answers to questions 1, 2 and 3. You will need 9 lines of your book, plus the headings. An odd node is one with order 1, 3, 5, etc.

	Number of odd nodes	Number of even nodes	Traversable?
1(a)	2	0	Yes
1(b)			
etc.			

   (b) Can you say which networks are traversable by the number of odd nodes that they have?

6 Test out your answer to question 5(b) with networks of your own design.

7 Find out about Leonard Euler and the Könisberg bridges.

D Route matrix

A **matrix** is a table of numbers. A **route matrix** describes a network. The plural of matrix is **matrices**.

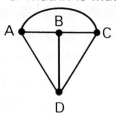

		To			
		A	B	C	D
F	A	0	1	1	1
r	B	1	0	1	1
o	C	1	1	0	1
m	D	1	1	1	0

Fig. 11:17

The loop at A counts as 2 (clockwise/anti-clockwise).

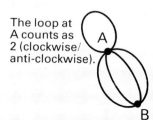

		To	
		A	B
F	A	2	4
r	B	4	0
o			
m			

Fig. 11:18

1 Write the route matrix for each diagram in Figure 11:19.

(a) 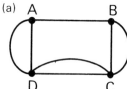   (b) 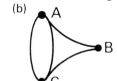   (c) 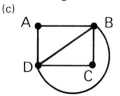   (d)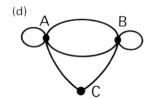

Fig. 11:19

2 Copy the two sets of nodal points in Figure 11:20, making them about twice as far apart. Draw the networks given by the route matrices. Take care not to make extra nodes.

(a)

		To		
		A	B	C
F	A	0	2	1
r	B	2	0	1
o	C	1	1	0
m				

•A   •B

•C

(b)

		To			
		A	B	C	D
F	A	0	1	2	1
r	B	1	0	2	1
o	C	2	2	0	1
m	D	1	1	1	0

•A   •B

•C   •D

Fig. 11:20

*3 Write the route matrix for each network in Figure 11:21.

(a) 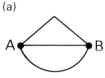   (b) 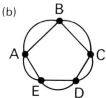   (c)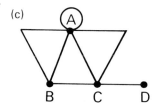

Fig. 11:21

*4 Repeat question 2 for the networks described in Figure 11:22.

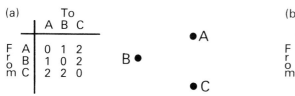

(a)

		To		
		A	B	C
F A		0	1	2
r B		1	0	2
o m C		2	2	0

•A

B•

•C

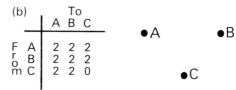

(b)

		To		
		A	B	C
F A		2	2	2
r B		2	2	2
o m C		2	2	0

•A   •B

•C

Fig. 11:22

5 Copy the three sets of nodal points in Figure 11:23, making them about twice as far apart. Draw each network and write its route matrix. The figures show how many arcs leave each node. No loops are allowed in this question.

(a) A 2•   B 3•

C 3•

(b) A 3•   B 3•

E 4•

C 3•   D 3•

(c) A 1•   B 3•

D 2•   C 2•

Fig. 11:23

---

6 Using your matrices for question 5, add up each column. Find the connection between your answers and the nodal points at the top.

7 Figure 11:24 shows two motorways. Design a road network to join them without adding any roundabouts or any more bridges.

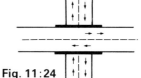

Fig. 11:24

E   One-way networks

A •———▶• B
This means 'from A to B only'.

Fig. 11:25

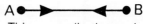

A •—▶ ◀—• B
This means 'both ways'.

1 Write route matrices for the networks in Figure 11:26. Note that in network (a) there is only *one* route from B to A.

(a)

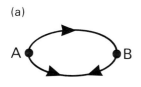

(b)

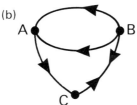

(c)

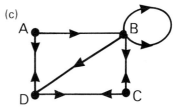

Fig. 11:26

2 Draw networks for the matrices given in Figure 11:27.

(a)
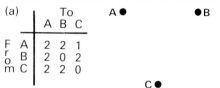

		To	
	A	B	C
F A	2	2	1
r B	2	0	2
o C	2	2	0
m			

A●   ●B

C●

Fig. 11:27

(b)

		To	
	A	B	C
F A	0	1	2
r B	0	2	0
o C	1	2	1
m			

A●

B●   C●

3 In Figure 11:28 the words 'From' and 'To' have been omitted, and the figures are enclosed in curved lines. This is the usual way we write matrices. Draw the networks described by these matrices.

(a) $\begin{pmatrix} 1 & 1 & 2 \\ 1 & 2 & 0 \\ 0 & 1 & 2 \end{pmatrix}$ A●   ●B

C●

(b) $\begin{pmatrix} 0 & 2 & 0 \\ 1 & 0 & 1 \\ 2 & 1 & 0 \end{pmatrix}$ ●A

●B

●C

(c) $\begin{pmatrix} 2 & 1 & 1 \\ 2 & 0 & 2 \\ 1 & 1 & 0 \end{pmatrix}$ A●   ●B

C●

Fig. 11:28

4 Write matrices like those in Figure 11:28 for the networks of Figure 11:29.

(a)
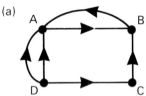

(b)
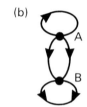

(c)
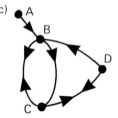

Fig. 11:29

5 (a) Copy the table given on the right.

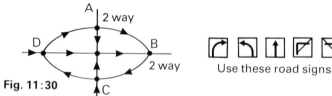

Fig. 11:30

Use these road signs

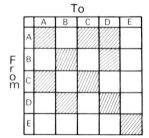

		To				
		A	B	C	D	E
F	A					
r	B					
o	C					
m	D					
	E					

(b) The network shows the one-way road system in a town. The table shows journeys. Some are impossible without passing through a third junction; these have been hatched (///). Some other journeys are not allowed. For example, you cannot go from A to D. Hatch seven more squares that represent journeys not allowed.

(c) In the remaining squares draw the road sign that a driver making that journey should see as he comes up to the junction. One square will be left blank. Why?

(d) You could make a model of this or a similar one-way road system.

12 Ratios; Proportional division

A Ratio, 1 : x

These gear wheels give a gear ratio of 1 : 2.

The large wheel has 24 teeth and the smaller wheel has 12 teeth, so the larger wheel turning once makes the smaller wheel turn twice.

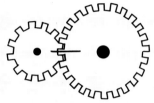

Fig. 12:1

Ratios can be written using the word 'to', using a colon (:), or as a fraction.

Example   12 to 24 = 1 to 2 = 1 : 2 = $\frac{1}{2}$

1   The ratio of John's money to Carol's money is 1 : 2. What is the ratio of Carol's money to John's?

2   Dad is 2 metres tall; Sam is 1 metre tall. What is the ratio of:
(a) Dad's height to Sam's height   (b) Sam's height to Dad's height?

3   Write the ratio 1 to 3 as a fraction.

4

Fig. 12:2

CD is twice as long as AB, so CD : AB = 2 : 1 and AB : CD = 1 : 2.

EF is three times as long as AB, so EF : AB = 3 : 1 and AB : EF = 1 : 3.

Copy Figure 12:2, then write a sentence like the ones above about GH and AB.

5   In this question the lines AB, CD, EF and GH are in the same ratio as they were in Figure 12:2, but they are not the lengths drawn there.

(a) If AB is 5 cm long, how long is: (i) CD   (ii) EF   (iii) GH?

(b) If CD is 8 cm long, how long is: (i) AB   (ii) EF   (iii) GH?

(c) If EF is 6 cm long, how long is: (i) AB   (ii) CD   (iii) GH?

6   The ratio of the distance Jane cycles to the distance Jill cycles is 3 : 1.

(a) How many times as far as Jill goes does Jane go?

(b) If Jill goes 3 km, how far does Jane go?

7 The ratio of the top speed of my moped to that of Franco's car is 1:3. My moped's top speed is 70 km/h. What is the top speed of Franco's car?

8 Mo's tail: Minnie's tail = 1:4. Minnie's tail is 8 cm long. How long is Mo's?

*9 Copy the lines in Figure 12:3, then write the following as a ratio of two numbers. **Example** MN:IJ = 5:1

(a) IJ:KL   (b) KL:IJ   (c) IJ:MN   (d) PQ:IJ   (e) IJ:PQ

```
I  J        K      L      M              N       P                        Q
└┘          └──┘          └──────┘              └──────────────┘
```
Fig. 12:3

*10 In this question the lines IJ, KL, MN and PQ are in the same ratio as they were in Figure 12:3, but they are not the lengths drawn there.

(a) If IJ is 6 cm long, how long is: (i) KL   (ii) MN   (iii) PQ?

(b) If KL is 9 cm long, how long is: (i) IJ   (ii) MN   (iii) PQ?

(c) If MN is 10 cm long, how long is: (i) IJ   (ii) KL   (iii) PQ?

(d) If PQ is 7 cm long, how long is: (i) IJ   (ii) KL   (iii) MN?

*11 The ratio of Jeff's weight to Abe's is 1:2. Abe weighs 50 kg. What does Jeff weigh?

12 If AB is twice as long as CD you can either write
AB:CD = 2:1 or CD:AB = 1:2.

Write two statements each if:
(a) EF is 3 times as long as GH   (b) IJ is 4 times as long as KL.

13 Copy Figure 12:4 exactly, then mark a point C on the line so that AB:BC = 1:3. Write on your line the length of BC.

```
A    2cm    B
└────────────┘────────────────────────────────
```
Fig. 12:4

14 In Figure 12:5, QR is twice as long as PQ, so QR:PQ = 2:1.

Write a similar statement about:
(a) RS and PQ (Start your answer 'RS is 3 times as long ...')
(b) ST and RS   (c) ST and QR   (d) ST and PQ.

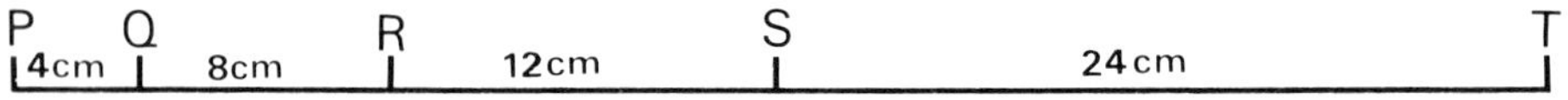

```
P   Q         R         S                    T
└4cm┘   8cm   └   12cm   ┘        24 cm        ┘
```
Fig. 12:5

15 In Figure 12:5, PQ is $\frac{1}{2}$ of QR, and PQ is $\frac{1}{3}$ of RS.

What fraction is: (a) QR of ST   (b) RS of ST   (c) PQ of ST?

16 Draw Figure 12:6 on squared paper. Then draw a larger rectangle, the same shape but with sides in the ratio 2 : 1 to the first.

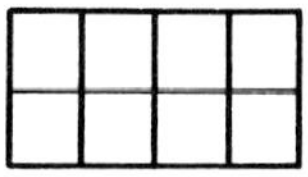

Fig. 12:6

17 The smaller rectangle you drew has 8 squares. How many squares has the larger? What is the ratio of the number of squares in the smaller to the number in the larger?

18 Copy Figure 12:7 on squared paper. Draw larger shapes with sides in the ratio 2 : 1 with the first. Each time find the ratio of the number of squares in the smaller to the number in the larger.

Fig. 12:7

19 Repeat question 18 with the larger shapes' sides in the ratio 3 : 1 to the smaller. What can you deduce about the ratio of the areas of similar shapes?

B   Simplifying ratios

A   3 cm   B   5 cm   C   7 cm   D

Fig. 12:8

AB = 3 cm and BC = 5 cm, so the ratio AB : BC = 3 : 5.

AB = 3 cm and BD = 12 cm, so the ratio AB : BD = 3 : 12.

The ratio 3 : 12 can be simplified by dividing both numbers by 3, giving AB : BD = 1 : 4.

1 Simplify to the smallest possible numbers:
(a) 20 : 30 (divide both by 10)   (b) 28:35 (divide both by 7)
(c) 15 : 20   (d) 16 : 24   (e) 30 : 12   (f) 40 : 24.

*2 Simplify:
(a) $8:20$ ($\div$ by 4)   (b) $12:28$ ($\div$ by 4)   (c) $18:27$ ($\div$ by 9)
(d) $48:40$ ($\div$ by 8)   (e) $49:56$ ($\div$ by 7)   (f) $63:49$ ($\div$ by 7)
(g) $64:56$ ($\div$ by 8)   (h) $36:63$ ($\div$ by 9)   (i) $40:56$ ($\div$ by 8).

*3 Simplify:
(a) $6:10$ (b) $6:9$ (c) $10:30$ (d) $15:25$.

4 Copy the following, replacing the stars by the correct numbers.
(a) $24:15=8:*$ (b) $15:*=5:3$ (c) $20:*=5:7$ (d) $*:18=11:9$
(e) $*:9=7:3$

5 Copy and complete:
(a) $8:12:16=2:3:*$ (b) $9:18:36=1:*:*$ (c) $12:15:27=4:*:*$

6 Fractions can be simplified like ratios. Simplify the following, making sure your final numbers are as small as possible. If necessary, divide more than once.

(a) $\dfrac{5}{15}$ (b) $\dfrac{9}{27}$ (c) $\dfrac{8}{24}$ (d) $\dfrac{10}{90}$ (e) $\dfrac{12}{16}$ (f) $\dfrac{10}{25}$ (g) $\dfrac{20}{36}$

(h) $\dfrac{22}{88}$ (i) $\dfrac{24}{84}$ (j) $\dfrac{45}{75}$ (k) $\dfrac{18}{48}$ (l) $\dfrac{33}{55}$ (m)$\dfrac{28}{98}$ (n) $\dfrac{30}{135}$

7 For the line shown in Figure 12:9 (which is not to scale): $BC:AB=3:1$; $CD:AB=2:1$; $DE:AB=4:1$.

What lengths should be written on:
(a) BC   (c) CD   (c) DE?

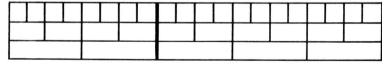

Fig. 12:9

8 Repeat question 7 if $BC:AB=2:1$; $AB:CD=1:3$; $DE:BC=1:2$.

9 Repeat question 7 if $DE:AB=4:1$; $CD:DE=2:1$; $BC:DE=1:2$.

10 Figure 12:10 illustrates that $8:12=4:6=2:3$.

Fig. 12:10

Draw a similar diagram to illustrate $6:9:12=4:6:8=2:3:4$.

C Using ratios

For Discussion

Example   Ann's pay to Tom's pay is in the ratio 4 : 5.
Ann earns £100. What does Tom earn?

Divide Ann's pay into the 4 parts of her ratio,
giving £25 a part. Tom receives 5 of these
parts, giving: *Answer* 5 × £25 = £125.

Fig. 12 : 11

Further questions

(a) Cement : sand = 2 : 7
    6 kg cement. How much sand?
    56 kg sand. How much cement?

(b) Girls to boys = 3 : 2
    24 boys. How many girls?
    30 girls. How many boys?

(c) Ratio kilometres : miles = 8 : 5
    15 miles. How many kilometres?
    40 kilometres. How many miles?

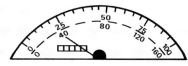

Fig. 12 : 12

1 Anne's height to Beryl's is in the ratio 3 : 4.
If Anne is 90 cm tall, how tall is Beryl?

2 AB : CD = 3 : 5. If AB is 12 cm long:
(a) how long is each part of AB
(b) how long is CD?

Fig. 12 : 14   **Fig. 12 : 13**

3 (a) How long is RS if PQ is: (i) 3 cm   (ii) 6 cm   (iii) 15 cm   (iv) 21 cm?

(b) How long is PQ if RS is: (i) 42 cm   (ii) 56 cm?

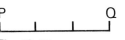

Fig. 12 : 15

4 Copy Figure 12:16 exactly, then draw a
line GH such that EF : GH = 2 : 3. Write the
length of GH on it.

Fig. 12 : 16

5 Copy Figure 12:17 exactly, then divide it into two equal parts. Finally, draw a line KL such that IJ : KL = 2 : 3 and write the length of KL on it.

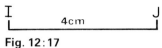

I ⌐————4cm————⌐ J

Fig. 12:17

6 Copy Figure 12:18 exactly, then draw a line OP such that MN : OP = 3 : 2. (Hint: Split MN into 3 parts.) Write the length of OP on it.

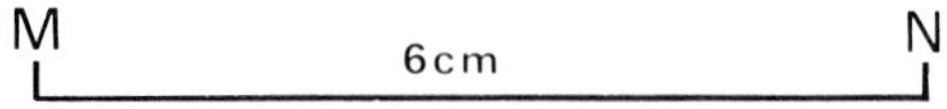

M ⌐——————6cm——————⌐ N

Fig. 12:18

7 Copy Figure 12:19 exactly, then draw a line ST such that QR : ST = 2 : 1, writing the length of ST on it.

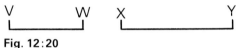

Q ⌐——————6cm——————⌐ R

Fig. 12:19

8 In Figure 12:20, calculate XY if VW = 10 cm and VW : XY = 2 : 3.

V   W X   Y

Fig. 12:20

*9 Figure 12:21 shows three sails neatly stowed away. Spar AB is divided into three equal parts by the sails.

  (a) If spar AB is 6 metres long, how long is each part of it?

  (b) How many parts on spar CD?

  (c) How long is CD? (Hint: Use the answers to (a) and (b).)

  (d) How long is EF?

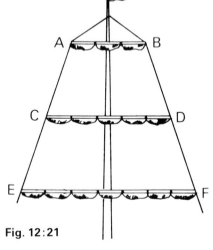

Fig. 12:21

Questions 10 to 14 all refer to Figure 12:21.

*10 If AB is 9 metres long, how long is: (a) each part of AB   (b) CD   (c) EF?

*11 If AB is 15 metres long, how long is: (a) CD   (b) EF?

*12 If CD is 5 metres long, how long is: (a) AB   (b) EF?

*13 If CD is 20 metres long, how long is: (a) AB   (b) EF?

*14 If EF is 49 feet long, how many feet long is: (a) AB   (b) CD?

*15 (a) In Figure 12:22, into how many parts has GH been divided?

(b) If GH = 9 cm, how long is each part? (c) If GH : IJ = 3 : 5, how long is IJ?

Fig. 12:22

*16 In Figure 12:22, find IJ if GH : IJ = 3 : 5 and:
(a) GH = 3 cm (b) GH = 12 cm (c) GH = 15 cm (d) GH = 6 cm.

17 Calculate the length of XY if:
(a) VW = 18 cm and VW : XY = 3 : 2 (b) VW = 15 cm and VW : XY = 5 : 6.

18 Calculate the length of VW if:
(a) XY = 8 cm and VW : XY = 3 : 4 (b) XY = 6 cm and VW : XY = 4 : 3.

Fig. 12:23   A   B

19 A circus transports its animals in wagons, each holding the same number. Say wagon-train A carries 6 ponies.

(a) How many ponies in each wagon?
(b) How many ponies could wagon-train B carry?

20 If A carries 9 bears, how many bears can B carry?

21 If B carries 20 monkeys, how many monkeys can A carry?

22 If B carries 100 performing fleas, how many fleas can A carry?

23 Wagons A cost £1500 altogether. What did wagons B cost altogether?

24 Wagons B weigh $2\frac{1}{2}$ tonnes altogether, when empty. What do wagons A weigh altogether, when empty?

25 A recipe for Orange Jelly:

500 ml water   150 g sugar   80 g gelatine
6 oranges   2 lemons   [Serves 6]

Write out the recipe in the same ratio, but to serve:
(a) 12 people   (b) 3 people   (c) 9 people.

Fig. 12:24

26 A bicycle has 3 gears. The ratios of the distance travelled for one turn of the pedals in different gears are:
1st gear : 2nd gear = 1 : 2
1st gear : 3rd gear = 2 : 5

In 1st gear, one turn of the pedals moves the cycle 50 cm.

(a) How far will one turn of the pedals move the bicycle in:
(i) 2nd gear   (ii) 3rd gear?

(b) How many turns of the pedals to go 1 km in:
(i) 1st gear   (ii) 2nd gear   (iii) 3rd gear?

Fig. 12:25

---

27 In Figure 12:26, BD is parallel to CE. The ratio AB : BC = 2 : 1. Measure AD and DE in mm. Write the ratio AD : DE as simply as possible. Draw your own triangle ACE, then try other ratios to see if AB : BC always equals AD : DE.

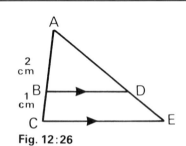

Fig. 12:26

28 A, B and C share some money. A has $\frac{1}{3}$ of it. B and C share the rest in the ratio 3 : 2 and C receives £30. How much money was there to start with?

D   Proportional division

For Discussion

Example   Divide £36 in the ratio 5 : 4.

         5 : 4 gives 9 parts.
         £36 divided into 9 parts gives £4 for each part.

      5 parts = £20   4 parts = £16
Fig. 12:27

Further question

Brass contains copper and zinc in the ratio 2 : 1.

How much copper and zinc is there in:
(a) 30 g of brass   (b) 45 g of brass   (c) 6 kg of brass?

1 In Figure 12:28, AX : XB = 2 : 5.

If AB is 14 cm long, how long is: (a) AX   (b) XB?

Fig. 12:28

2 Repeat question 1 if AB is 35 cm long.

3 Repeat question 1 if AB is 42 cm long.

4 In Figure 12:29, CY : YD = 3 : 5.

Fig. 12:29

(a) If CY is divided into 3 equal parts, how many of the same size parts could YD be divided into?

(b) Into how many parts altogether would CD now be divided?

(c) How long would each part be if CD = 8 cm?

(d) How long would this make CY and YD?

5 In Figure 12:29, find the lengths of CY and YD if CY : YD = 3 : 5 and CD is:
(a) 24 cm   (b) 40 cm   (c) 16 cm?

*6 Two robbers share the swag in the ratio 1 : 4, Bill having 1 part and Fagin 4 parts. If they steal £5, the five parts will each be £1, so Bill gets £1 and Fagin gets £4 (Figure 12:30a). If they steal £10, each part will be £2, so Bill gets £2 and Fagin gets £8 (Figure 12:30b).

Bill's   Fagin's

Fig. 12:30a

Bill's   Fagin's

Fig. 12:30b

Draw bags of money to show how much each gets if they steal:
(a) £15   (b) £20   (c) £25   (d) £50   (e) £500.

*7 Bill and Fagin are sent to prison. For how many years does each get sent down if their sentences are in the ratio 2 : 3 and total:
(a) 5 years   (b) 10 years
(c) 15 years   (d) 20 years?

Fig. 12:31   Bill's stretch   Fagin's stretch

77

8 Copy and complete the table for Figure 12:32.

Each time check that MX + XN = MN.

M　　　　X　　　　　N

Fig. 12:32

Length of MN	20 cm	10 cm	12 cm	12 cm	16 cm	28 cm	27 cm	22 cm
MX : XN	7 : 3	3 : 2	5 : 1	1 : 5	5 : 3	3 : 4	5 : 4	3 : 8
Total parts	10							
Each part	2 cm							
MX	14 cm							
XN	6 cm							

9 Jane and Kim both have records in the ratio L.P.s to singles = 4 : 3.

(a) Jane has 49 records. How many are L.P.s?

(b) Kim has 35 records. How many are singles?

10 Jock, Iain and Sandy all like the ratio of their whisky to water to be 4 : 5. One evening Jock has 45 ml to drink, Iain has 108 ml and Sandy has 270 ml. How many millilitres of whisky does each drink?

11 Frank feeds his seals according to their age. A two-year-old seal is fed six fish. How many fish should a three-year-old seal receive?

12 Angela takes six steps to cross a room 4 metres wide. How wide is a room if she takes:
(a) 3 steps to cross　　(b) 9 steps to cross?

13 Mr Mean pays all his workmen the same miserable bonus. He needs £100 to pay eight workmen. How much will he need to pay twelve workmen?

14 Draw the shapes in Figure 12:33 on squared paper, then draw larger shapes with the sides increased in the ratios given. Find the ratio of the areas for each pair of shapes.

　　　2 : 1　　　　　　3 : 2　　　　　3 : 2　　　　　　4 : 3　　　　4 : 3

Fig. 12:33

13 Graphs: co-ordinates

A Points on grids

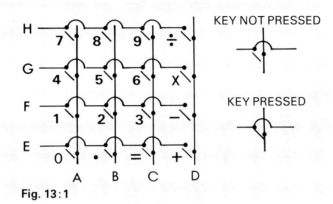

Fig. 13:1

Figure 13:1 shows the switching circuit for a simple calculator keyboard. To save having to use 16 'wires', each key connects a column wire to a row wire. For example, the 2 key connects column wire B to row wire F. We could write this as (B,F). What are the other key connections?

1 (a) Using squared paper, copy Figure 13:2, including the spider and the trapped fly. Be careful to write the numbers *on* the lines, as shown, *not* in the spaces.

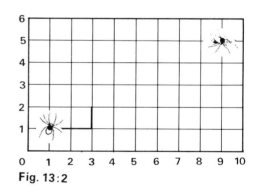

Fig. 13:2

(b) The squares are a web spun by a mathematical spider. Draw lines to show the spider's journey to the fly if it goes:

Forwards two, then up one (this much is done for you), then forwards three, then up two, then forwards one, then up one, then forwards two.

You can use colour for the journey line.

(c) On its journey the spider started at the point (1,1). It turned first at (3,1) then again at (3,2). Note that the first number is read along the bottom line and the second number is read up the side. List, in order, the other four turning points.

(d) On its way back the spider always goes to the left or down. Draw the path of this return journey on the same grid if the spider starts by going down to (9,3), then goes back to (8,3) where it turns again and goes to (8,2). It turns again at (8,2) and (7,2), then, after a final turn at (7,1), goes straight home.

2 The spider has just returned to base when another fly lands at exactly the same place as the first.

(a) Draw the web again, with the spider and the second fly.

(b) The spider sets out again: Forwards two, up one, forwards two, up one, forwards two, up one, forwards two and finally up one. Draw this new journey.

(c) Name every turning point. The first two are (3,1) and (3,2). Remember to read the bottom number before the side one.

(d) On its way back the spider turns when it reaches:
(6,5); (6,4); (3,4); (3,3); (1,3).

Draw the line of its return journey.

3 Find the longest possible journey from (1,1) to (9,5) on the web in Figure 13:2 without going over any line twice. Describe it by turning points.

B Co-ordinates and axes

For Discussion

Figure 13:3 shows a 5 by 7 **dot matrix display**. This is used by a computer to display letters and patterns. To make the letter Z the following dots are lit up: (0,0); (1,0); (2,0); (3,0); (4,0); (0,1); (1,2); (2,3); (3,4); (4,5); (0,6); (1,6); (2,6); (3,6); (4,6).

Check these points, then list the ones needed for other letters, e.g. an H.

Fig. 13:3

1 (a) Copy Figure 13:4 on squared paper (1 cm is best for this). Be careful to write the figures *on* the lines and remember to write 'x-axis' and 'y-axis' as shown. Make sure your crosses are in the same place as the ones in the book. Count along, then up, to decide where they should go.

(b) Write down the positions of all the points marked. Start your answer: a is (1,2), b is .... These are the **co-ordinates** of the points.

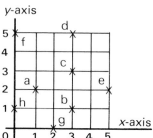

Fig. 13:4

2 What are the co-ordinates of the origin (the name of the point where the axes cross)?

3 (a) Draw x- and y-axes on squared paper, numbering them from 0 to 5.

(b) Plot (mark on the grid) the following points: (2,5); (3,4); (3,3); (2,2); (2,1); (2,0); (1,0); (1,1); (1,2); (0,3); (0,4); (1,5).

(c) Check all these points, then use your ruler to join them in the same order as you plotted them.

4 (a) Copy Figure 13:5 on squared paper.

(b) List the co-ordinates of every corner, starting at 'a' and going clockwise, like this: (2,3); (3,4); etc.

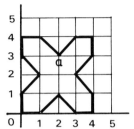
Fig. 13:5

5 (a) Draw x- and y-axes on squared paper, numbering them from 0 to 5.

(b) Plot the points (2,4); (3,3); (3,1); (2,0); (1,0); (0,1); (0,3); (1,4).

(c) Use your ruler to join these points in order.

6 Write down, for Figure 13:6:
(a) the name of the point where line AB crosses line CD
(b) the co-ordinates of this point
(c) the name of the line AB
(d) the name of the line CD.

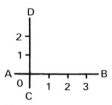
Fig. 13:6

7 (a) Draw three pairs of axes on squared paper, numbering them from 0 to 5.

(b) Write the name of each axis at its end.

(c) On one grid plot (1,0); (1,3); (3,3). Join (1,0) to (1,3). Join (1,3) to (3,3). Name the co-ordinates of a fourth point which, when joined to (3,3), completes a rectangle.

(d) On the second grid plot (1,1) and (3,1). Join them. Write the co-ordinates of two points that will make a square when joined to the first two. Draw the square.

(e) On the third grid join the origin to (1,2) with a ruler. Write the co-ordinates of a third point that will make an isosceles triangle when joined to the first two, like Figure 13:7.

Fig. 13:7

8 (a) Draw a pair of axes, numbered from 0 to 5. Write their names at their ends.

(b) Plot (1,1); (3,1); (3,3); (1,3). Join them to make a square. Then join (3,1) to (4,2); (3,3) to (4,4); (1,3) to (2,4); (2,4) to (4,4); (4,2) to (4,4).
What is the name of the solid whose picture you have drawn?

(c) Repeat step (a), then plot the following points, joining them as necessary to make a picture of a solid like a match-box.
(0,1); (3,1); (5,3); (5,4); (3,2); (0,2); (2,4)

(d) Repeat step (a). Join in order the points (0,0); (1,2); (2,0); (5,3); (4,5); (1,2). This solid is called an 'Equilateral Triangular Prism'.

9 (a) Draw and label a set of axes from 0 to 5 each.

(b) Plot and join: (1,0); (1,1); (1,2); (1,5).

(c) Write the co-ordinates of two more points that lie on this line.

(d) Plot the point $(1,2\frac{1}{2})$. (Yes, you can!)

(e) Plot the point $(1,3\frac{3}{4})$.

(f) Write the co-ordinates of another two points that lie on the same line.

(g) How many points are there on the line (not just the ones you have marked)?

(h) How many points lie between (1,1) and (1,2)?

10 (a) Draw and label a set of axes from 0 to 5 each.

(b) Plot the points (0,3); $(1\frac{1}{2},3)$; $(3\frac{1}{2},3)$. Join them.

(c) If this line was continued to the right for ever, would (5,3) be on it? Would (20,3)? Would (1000,3)? Name two other points, on the line but off the grid.

11 (a) On mm graph paper draw axes 10 cm long. (Figure 13:8 shows part of them.) Number them from 0 to 1 in tenths.

Each 1 cm represents 0.1 and each 1 mm represents 0.01, so (0.3,0) is 3 cm squares from the origin along the x axis and (0.3,0.26) is 3 cm squares along then 26 mm squares up. This point is marked with a cross.

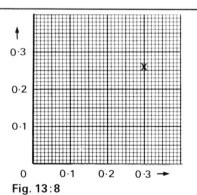
Fig. 13:8

(b) Plot the following points, then join them with a *curved* line.
(0,1); (0.1,0.99); (0.2,0.98); (0.3,0.95); (0.4,0.92); (0.5,0.87); (0.6,0.8); (0.7,0.71); (0.8,0.6); (0.85,0.53); (0.9,0.44); (0.95,0.31); (0.98,0.2); (0.99,0.14).

14 Algebra: notation; simplification

A Using letters

```
10 INPUT A
20 LET B = A + 2
30 PRINT B
```

Algebra is the use of letters to stand for numbers.

You may use a letter instead of a number for one of two reasons:

(i) The letter may stand for lots of numbers; the letter A in the computer program is like this.

(ii) The letter may be used because you do not know what number it stands for, like the letter B in the computer program. You cannot tell what B is until you know the value of A.

In written algebra we usually use *small* letters to stand for the numbers.

Algebra shorthand (or 'notation')

Instead of writing $2 \times a$ for 'Two lots of a' we can miss out the $\times$ sign and write just $2a$.

Note that you cannot do this in a computer program, when you must write $2 * a$, nor does it work for numbers multiplied together, for 2×7 is not 27!

$2f$ means '2 lots of the number f' or '$2 \times f$'

1 What number must the letter stand for if:

(a) $5 + m = 8$ (b) $7 + p = 15$ (c) $p - 7 = 9$ (d) $q - 13 = 8$?

2 If s stands for the number 9, find the value of:

(a) $s + 1$ (b) $27 - s$ (c) $2s$ (d) $9s$.

3 What number must each letter stand for if:

(a) $2f = 12$ (b) $3t = 15$ (c) $10x = 100$
(d) $7a = 42$ (e) $9x = 54$ (f) $8c = 64$?

*4 Find the value of the letter if:

(a) $4 + t = 10$ (b) $8 + u = 19$ (c) $8 + v = 13$
(d) $7 + w = 16$ (e) $9 + x = 17$ (f) $y + 3 = 14$
(g) $z + 7 = 18$ (h) $a + 11 = 23$.

*5 Find the value of the letter if:

(a) $8 - c = 7$ (b) $19 - d = 18$ (c) $23 - c = 20$
(d) $3 - c = 0$ (e) $25 - d = 15$ (f) $v - 9 = 0$
(g) $w - 13 = 8$ (h) $x - 7 = 7$ (i) $y - 39 = 1$.

*6 If $t = 6$ find the value of:

(a) $t + 7$ (b) $8 + t$ (c) $12 + t$
(d) $t + 5$ (e) $t - 1$ (f) $t - 4$.

*7 **Example** If $t = 6$ then $2t$ means 2 lots of 6, which is $2 \times 6 = 12$.

If $t = 6$ find:

(a) $3t$ (b) $4t$ (c) $5t$ (d) $6t$ (e) $7t$ (f) $10t$.

*8 Find the value of the letters if:

(a) $5x = 40$ (b) $7c = 56$ (c) $8e = 32$
(d) $10f = 100$ (e) $12f = 60$ (f) $11d = 99$.

9 **Examples** $\dfrac{c}{2}$ means 'half of c' or 'c divided by 2'

                $\dfrac{k}{3}$ means 'a third of k' or 'k divided by 3'

Write a sentence like the ones above about:

(a) $\dfrac{g}{2}$ (b) $\dfrac{h}{3}$ (c) $\dfrac{k}{4}$ (quarter)

(d) $\dfrac{m}{5}$ (fifth)   (e) $\dfrac{n}{6}$ (sixth)   (f) $\dfrac{p}{10}$ (tenth).

10 If $c = 24$ find the value of:

(a) $\dfrac{c}{3}$ (b) $3c$ (c) $c + 3$ (d) $c - 3$ (e) $\dfrac{c}{4}$

(f) $\dfrac{c}{6}$ (g) $c - 6$ (h) $6 + c$ (i) $6c$.

11 Find the value of the letter if:

(a) $x + 3 = 9$ (b) $3y = 9$ (c) $\dfrac{a}{3} = 9$ (d) $7b = 56$

(e) $\dfrac{c}{8} = 8$ (f) $\dfrac{d}{9} = 6$ (g) $7 + e = 56$.

12 **Example** If $n = 15$ then $\frac{2n}{3} = \frac{30}{3} = 10$. (Remember that $\frac{30}{3}$ means $30 \div 3$.)

Find the value of:

(a) $\frac{2n}{3}$ if $n = 6$

(b) $\frac{2n}{4}$ if $n = 6$

(c) $\frac{3n}{4}$ if $n = 8$

(d) $\frac{4n}{5}$ if $n = 5$

(e) $\frac{4n}{3}$ if $n = 9$

(f) $\frac{5n}{4}$ if $n = 8$

(g) $\frac{2n}{7}$ if $n = 21$

(h) $\frac{8n}{16}$ if $n = 4$.

13 Find:

(a) $\frac{4}{2n}$ if $n = 1$

(b) $\frac{6}{3n}$ if $n = 1$

(c) $\frac{8}{2n}$ if $n = 2$

(d) $\frac{16}{4a}$ if $a = 2$

(e) $\frac{15}{3x}$ if $x = 5$

(f) $\frac{15}{30c}$ if $c = 1$.

14 **Examples** If $\frac{x}{5} = 2$ then x must be 10, as $\frac{10}{5} = 10 \div 5 = 2$.

If $\frac{5x}{5} = 2$ then the $5x$ must be 10, giving $x = 2$.

If $\frac{3x}{4} = 6$ then $3x = 24$ (because $\frac{24}{4} = 6$), giving $x = 8$.

Find the value of the letter if:

(a) $\frac{2x}{5} = 4$

(b) $\frac{3d}{2} = 6$

(c) $\frac{4m}{3} = 8$

(d) $\frac{5n}{2} = 10$

(e) $\frac{3p}{4} = 6$

(f) $\frac{7x}{8} = 7$

(g) $\frac{30}{2x} = 5$

(h) $\frac{26}{2x} = 1$.

15 Make up some equations like the ones in question 14 and work out the answers.

B Addition and subtraction

3*a*, 4*x*, *h* and 9 are examples of **terms**.

Terms are usually connected to each other by + and − signs.

Terms can be added and subtracted, as long as the letter is the same in each.

Examples (a) $2e + 3e \rightarrow 5e$ (Read the arrow sign ($\rightarrow$) as 'becomes'.)

(b) $4k - 3k \rightarrow k$ (We write just *k*, not 1*k*)

(c) $x - x \rightarrow 0$ (We write just 0, not 0*x*)

1 Simplify:

(a) $3x + x$ (b) $5a - a$ (c) $14c - 3c$ (d) $9h - 8h$ (e) $7d - 7d$.

*2 All the following are wrong answers given by pupils. Copy the questions, but change the answers to the correct ones.

(a) $4f + 2f \rightarrow 8f$ (b) $7d + d \rightarrow 72d$ (c) $2x + x \rightarrow 2x$
(d) $8z + 4z \rightarrow 84z$ (e) $c + 2c \rightarrow c2c$ (f) $4f - f \rightarrow 4$
(g) $6y - y \rightarrow 6$ (h) $2g - g \rightarrow 20$ (i) $2x - x \rightarrow 2$
(j) $8y - 7y \rightarrow 1$ (k) $3x - x \rightarrow 0$ (l) $7x - 7x \rightarrow 1$

*3 Simplify:

(a) $2x + x$ (b) $7a + a$ (c) $19m + m$
(d) $17a + 3a$ (e) $23a + a$ (f) $16x + x$
(g) $14n + n$ (h) $23a + 12a$ (i) $14c + 23c$
(j) $69d + d$ (k) $48e + 2e$.

*4 Simplify:

(a) $7c - 6c$ (b) $19z - 18z$ (c) $8e - e$
(d) $4a - a$ (e) $5a - 2a$ (f) $12x - 3x$
(g) $8x - 8x$ (h) $4p - 3p$ (i) $7q - 7q$
(j) $11x - 10x$ (k) $9c - 9c$.

5 Copy each question, then simplify the expression.

(a) $2x + 3x + 4x$ (b) $7a + 3a + 5a$ (c) $8a + a + 2a$
(d) $4b + b + 2b$ (e) $17c + 23c + 18c$ (f) $12d + 10d + d$
(g) $a + a + a$ (h) $x + x + x + x + x$

6 Simplify the following expressions. Add or subtract the two terms at the beginning, then add or subtract the third term.

Examples $3x - 2x + 8x \rightarrow x + 8x \rightarrow 9x$

$7k + 8k - k \rightarrow 15k - k \rightarrow 14k$

(a) $4v + 3v - 2v$ (b) $7a + 9a - 3a$ (c) $8c + 4c - c$
(d) $5c + 2c - 6c$ (e) $9e - 3e + 3e$ (f) $16y - 2y + 5y$
(g) $y + y - 2y$ (h) $3y + 2y - 5y$ (i) $5f + f - 4f$
(j) $2h - h + h$ (k) $3z - z + 2z$ (l) $x - x + x$

7 Examples $4a - 2a - a \rightarrow 2a - a \rightarrow a$

$13n - 8n - 5n \rightarrow 5n - 5n \rightarrow 0$

Simplify:

(a) $7b - 2b - b$ (b) $8x - 5x - 2x$ (c) $7a - 2a - 4a$
(d) $9m - 8m - m$ (e) $4w - 2w - w$ (f) $2x - x - x$
(g) $7y - 3y - 4y$ (h) $8p - 2p - p$ (i) $69x - 28x - 17x$
(j) $53a - 26a - 17a.$

---

8 You can check that $3f - 2f \rightarrow f$ by substituting a number for f. If you choose $f = 2$, then $3f = 6$ and $2f \rightarrow 4$, so $3f - 2f \rightarrow f$ is correct, as $6 - 4$ is 2.

Check by substitution the answers to the questions you have done.

C   Like and unlike terms

Terms with the same letter, or no letter, are called **like terms**.

Examples $4x$ and $2x$; 7 and 9; a and $3a$.

1 In the following sets, which element is *unlike* the others?
(a) $\{2a, 3a, 2\}$ (b) $\{3x, 3, 5\}$ (c) $\{x, y, x\}$

2 **Remember that you can only add terms with the *same* letters.**

Remember that you can*not* add numbers to letters.

Example $3a + 4a \rightarrow 7a$ *but* $3a + 4$ cannot be added to make anything else.

Example $1 + 5x + x \rightarrow 1 + 6x$ *but* $1 + 6x$ cannot be added to make anything else.

Simplify:
(a) $3x + 2x + 7$ (b) $4c + 3c + 2$ (c) $8a + 2 + 3a$ (d) $4y + x + 3y.$

3 Remember that you can only subtract terms with the *same* letters.

Example $8x - 3x + 2y \rightarrow 5x + 2y$

Example $4 - 3 + 2a \rightarrow 1 + 2a$

Simplify:
(a) $9g - 8g - 10$ (b) $6d - 5d - 3$ (c) $4x - 3x - g$.

4 **Example** $5x + 1 + 4x \rightarrow 9x + 1$. Note that we can add the $5x$ to the $4x$ even though the $+ 1$ comes between them.

Example $3 + 2x + 8 \rightarrow 11 + 2x$.

Simplify:
(a) $7 + 2m + m$ (b) $16x + 16 + 6x$ (c) $8 + y + 2y$ (d) $5v + 2z + 4v$.

*5 Simplify:
(a) $4x + 3x + 2$ (b) $3 + 2b + 7b$ (c) $4x + 7 + 3$
(d) $5 + 2 + x$ (e) $4 + 1 + z$ (f) $7x + x + 7$.

*6 Simplify:
(a) $8a - 7a$ (b) $9c - 8c$ (c) $5c - 2c + 3$
(d) $9c - 6c + 7$ (e) $8m - 7m + 3$ (f) $4p + 6p - 10$
(g) $8a - 3a + 5$ (h) $4 + 4 - 4x$ (i) $3x - 2x - 1$
(j) $7 - 6 - x$ (k) $5 + 8x - 2x$.

*7 Simplify:
(a) $7a + 1 + 3a$ (b) $4a + 2 + a$ (c) $5 + 3a + 1$ (d) $4 + 2m + 3$.

8 **Examples** $3a - 4 - 2a \rightarrow a - 4$

$3a + 4 - 2a \rightarrow a + 4$

Note that both examples have $3a - 2a$. In the second example the $+$ belongs to the 4 and does not affect the 'a' terms.

Copy the following expressions, then simplify them.

(a) $4x - 3 - 2x$ (b) $4x + 3 - 2x$ (c) $7a + 1 - 3a$
(d) $7a - 1 - 3a$ (e) $6 + a - 2$ (f) $6 - a - 2$
(g) $4 - 2x - 2$ (h) $4 - 2x + 2$ (i) $a + 3 + a$
(j) $a - 3 + a$ (k) $3 - 3x + 3$ (l) $3 + 3x + 3$
(m)$7 + 2m - m$ (n) $16x + 16 - x$ (o) $5v + 2z - 4v$
(p) $2 - 3x + 7 - 4x$.

9 **Example** $4x + 3 - 4x \rightarrow 3$.

Note that we do not need to write $+3$.

Copy and simplify:
(a) $5x + 2 - 5x$ (b) $7a + 1 - 7a$ (c) $6 + 2x - 6$ (d) $8 + 3x - 8$ (e) $4x - 2 + 4x$
(f) $7x - 7 + 7x$ (g) $8 + 3x - 3x$ (h) $7x + 1 - 1$ (i) $4 + 2x - x$.

---

10 **Example** To simplify $5a + 3 + 8a + 7 + c$.

    (i)   Copy the question.

    (ii) Look for any terms *like* the first (the $5a$). You find $+8a$, and you know that $5a + 8a \rightarrow 13a$, so cross out the $5a$ and the $+8a$ and write $13a$ in your answer, like this:
        $\cancel{5a} + 3 + \cancel{8a} + 7 + c \rightarrow \mathbf{13a}$

   (iii) Take the next term $(+3)$ and look for like terms. You find $+7$, and know that $3 + 7 = 10$. Your answer now looks like this:
        $\cancel{5a} + \cancel{3} + \cancel{8a} + \cancel{7} + c \rightarrow \mathbf{13a + 10}$

   (iv) This only leaves c, so the final answer is $\mathbf{13a + 10 + c}$.

Simplify:
(a) $4x + 3 + 7x + 2b + 1$ (b) $3m + 2m + 1 + 7a + a$
(c) $4x + 1 + 3a + 7 + 2a + 5x$ (d) $4p + 3x + 2m + 2m + 3m + 1$
(e) $4b + 3c + 2a + 1 + 2b + 5$.

D   Powers

A number written before a letter means that number of letters **added** together.

A raised number (or **index**) written after a letter means that number of letters **multiplied** together.

It is very important that you do not mix these up.

Examples $c + c \rightarrow 2c$ **but** $c \times c \rightarrow c^2$ ('c squared')

                  $c + c + c \rightarrow 3c$ **but** $c \times c \times c \rightarrow c^3$ ('c cubed')

          $c + c + c + c \rightarrow 4c$ **but** $c \times c \times c \times c \rightarrow c^4$ ('c to the fourth')

1 Simplify:
(a) $e \times e$ (b) $e \times e \times e$ (c) $a \times a$ (d) $a \times a \times a$ (e) $c \times c \times c \times c \times c$.

2 Simplify:
(a) $e + e$ (b) $e + e + e$ (c) $a + a$ (d) $a + a + a$ (e) $c + c + c + c + c$.

3 Simplify:
(a) $f \times f$ (b) $f + f$ (c) $f \times f \times f$ (d) $f + f + f$.

4 If $k = 8$, find the value of:
(a) k^2 (b) $3k$ (c) $2k$ (d) $k - 1$ (e) $k - k$.

5 Find the value of k^2 if:
(a) $k = 5$ (b) $k = 6$ (c) $k = 7$.

6 Write in symbols, like x^2:
(a) d cubed (b) s to the fourth (c) t cubed (d) r squared
(e) x to the sixth (f) x to the fifth.

*7 Copy and complete the table.

Value of x	3	5	7	9	10	11	12
Value of $2x$							
Value of x^2							

8 **Example** $5^3 = 5 \times 5 \times 5 = 25 \times 5 = 125$.

Write out in a similar way: (a) 2^3 (b) 3^3 (c) 4^3.

9 **Examples** $3a + a \rightarrow 4a$; $3a^2 + a^2 \rightarrow 4a^2$; $3a^3 + 2a^3 \rightarrow 5a^3$.

Simplify:
(a) $4a + a$ (b) $2c + 3c$ (c) $4c^2 + 2c^2$ (d) $3a^2 + a^2$ (e) $5c^3 + 3c^3$.

10 $A = \{$terms in $x\}$; $B = \{$terms in $x^2\}$; $C = \{$terms in $x^3\}$

(a) List sets A, B and C from the terms:
$3x$, x^2, $2x^2$, $3x^3$, $2x^3$, $3x^2$, x, x^3, $2x$.

(b) State true or false:
(i) $x^2 \in B$ (ii) $2x^3 \notin B$ (iii) $n(C) = 2$ (iv) $n(A) \neq 3$.

11 Simplify:
(a) $3r^2 + r^2$ (b) $4r^3 + 2r^3$ (c) $3x^3 + x^3 + 8x^3$ (d) $4x^2 + 2x^2 + 3x^2$
(e) $3x^2 + 2x^2 + 7x^2$ (f) $3 + 2x^2 + 4$ (g) $7x^3 + 9x^3 + 3$
(h) $4x^2 + 3x^3 + x^2$ (i) $8x^2 + 7x + 2x^2$ (j) $6 + 2x^2 + 3$
(k) $2x + x + x^2$ (l) $3x - x + x^2$ (m) $7x^2 - 2x^2 + 3x^2$
(n) $4x + 5x^2 - x$ (o) $6 + 2x - 2x + 3$ (p) $x^2 + x^2 - 2x$
(q) $4x^3 + 3x^2 + 2x + 1$.

15 Area: rectangles

A Integral areas

The **perimeter** is the distance all round the edge of a shape.
The **area** is the amount of space inside a shape.

1 The rectangle in Figure 15:1 is made from six
squares, each measuring 1 cm along each
side. Figure 15:2 shows a square of area one
square centimetre, or 1 cm².

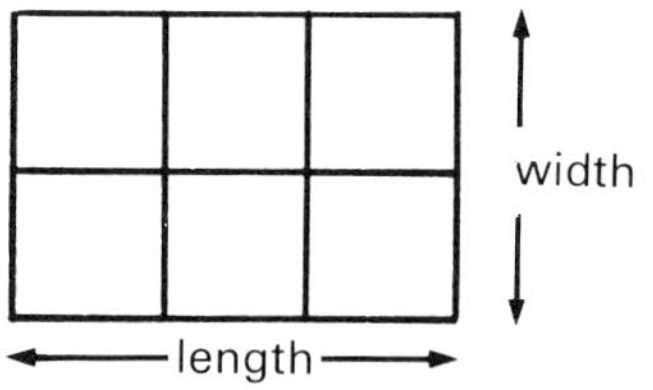

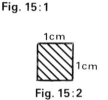

Fig. 15:1

(a) What is the length of the rectangle in cm?

(b) What is the width of the rectangle in cm?

(c) What is the area of the rectangle in cm²?

(d) What is the perimeter of the rectangle in cm?

Fig. 15:2

2 'Soothe' sore throat tablets are packed so
that each tablet is in a 1 cm square
compartment. Figure 15:3 shows a size 1
packet; 4 cm long and 2 cm wide.

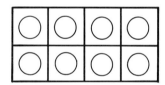

Size 2 packets are 4 cm long and 3 cm wide.
Size 3 packets are 5 cm long and 4 cm wide.

Fig. 15:3

Draw accurate true-size diagrams of all three packets, writing under each diagram
its area (in cm²) and its perimeter (in cm).

3 Write a rule for calculating the area of a rectangle.

4 Jill has drawn Figure 15:4 to show the floor
of her lounge. Calculate the length of:
(a) line PQ   (b) line RS
(c) the total perimeter.

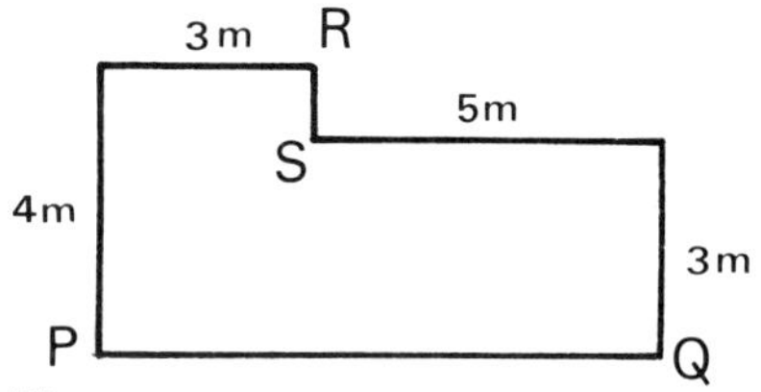

Fig. 15:4

5 Jill's floor (Figure 15:4) can be divided into
two rectangles in two different ways, as
shown in Figure 15:5.

Calculate the area in m² of:
(a) A   (b) B   (c) A + B
(d) C   (e) D   (f) C + D.

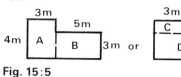 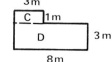

Fig. 15:5

6 Figure 15:6 shows the plans of two other rooms in Jill's house. Copy them (not exactly), then find the area of each floor by dividing it into two rectangles.

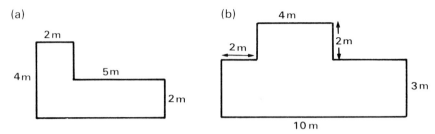

(a)

(b)

Fig. 15:6

*7 Remember that the area of a rectangle is its length multiplied by its width, and that the perimeter is the distance all the way round. Write down the missing numbers, (a) to (n), in the following table.

Length	8 cm	7 cm	5 cm	1J cm	13 cm	23 cm	26 cm
Width	2 cm	4 cm	3 cm	9 cm	8 cm	7 cm	14 cm
Area	(a) cm²	(c) cm²	(e) cm²	(g) cm²	(i) cm²	(k) cm²	(m) cm²
Perimeter	(b) cm	(d) cm	(f) cm	(h) cm	(j) cm	(l) cm	(n) cm

8 Kristy has crocheted 24 squares and she now wants to sew them together to make a bedspread. She knows that one way would be an 8 by 3 rectangle, that is, 8 squares long and 3 squares wide.

Fig. 15:7

(a) Find three other ways that Kristy could join her 24 squares.

(b) Each square has a side of 40 cm. How much tape would Kristy need to bind the edges of each possible bedspread?

(c) Which bedspread size would be the most sensible one for Kristy to make?

9 Copy the shapes in Figure 15:8 approximately, then calculate their perimeters and areas. Dimensions are in centimetres.

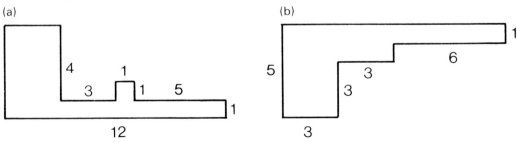

(a)

(b)

Fig. 15:8

10 A shepherd has 16 hurdles, each 1 metre long. Give the length, width and area of each of the rectangular pens he could make (including one square one). It would be sensible to give your answers in a table.

11 The sorcerer's apprentice has found a spell that makes rectangles grow. They double their length and width each day. On Sunday the sorcerer's room was a rectangle 2 metres by 1 metre. Copy and complete the table for a week's growth.

Day	Sunday	Monday	Tuesday	Wednesday	Thursday	Friday	Saturday
Length	2 m	4 m					
Width	1 m	2 m					
Area	2 m²	8 m²					
Perimeter	6 m	12 m					

12 The length and width of the sorcerer's room kept doubling. Did the perimeter keep doubling? Did the area keep doubling? If not, what did happen?

13 Compare the area of the room on Saturday with that of a football pitch (about 7330 m²). Which is bigger? How many times as big?

14 An artist's pictures consist of rectangles made by drawing lines parallel to the edges of his canvas. Investigate the number of rectangles made by different numbers of lines.

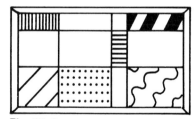

Fig. 15:9

B Fractional areas

Figure 15:10 is made up from four 1 cm squares and two small rectangles. Each rectangle is half a square, so together they make a whole square. The total area is 4cm² + 1cm² = 5 cm².

The same answer can be found by:
Area = length × width = 2.5 cm × 2 cm = 5.0 cm².

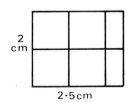

Fig. 15:10

1 Using a protractor to make accurate right-angled corners, draw a rectangle 4.5 cm long and 4 cm wide, then divide it into whole and half squares.

(a) How many whole squares are there in your diagram?

(b) How many half squares?

(c) How many cm^2 do these whole and half squares make altogether? (Not 20)

(d) Multiply 4.5 cm by 4 cm and check that your answer agrees with the answer to part (c).

2 Figure 15:11 has an area of four whole 1 cm squares, four half squares and one quarter square.

Its total area is $6\frac{1}{4}$ cm^2 or 6.25 cm^2.

This area can be calculated by 2.5 cm × 2.5 cm = 6.25 cm^2.

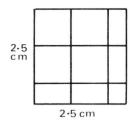

2·5 cm

2·5 cm

Fig. 15:11

Using a protractor to make accurate right-angled corners, draw a rectangle 3.5 cm long and 1.5 cm wide, then divide it into whole, half and quarter squares.

(a) How many whole squares are there in your diagram?

(b) How many half squares?

(c) How many quarter squares?

(d) How many cm^2 are there altogether?

(e) Check your answer to (d) by multiplying 3.5 cm by 1.5 cm.

3 Yasmin's passport photograph measures 3.5 cm by 5 cm. Calculate its area.

*4 State the areas of the shapes in Figure 15:12. Choose your answers from: 4 cm^2; 4.5 cm^2; 4.25 cm^2.

(a)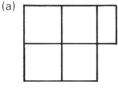

Fig. 15:12

(b)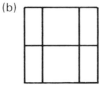

(c)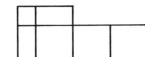

*5 Draw accurately a rectangle 4.5 cm long and 2.5 cm wide. Show by drawing that its area is 11.25 cm^2 (eight whole squares, six half squares and one quarter square).

6 In Figure 15:13, each shaded area can be found by subtracting the area of the small rectangle from the area of the big one. Calculate each shaded area using this method.

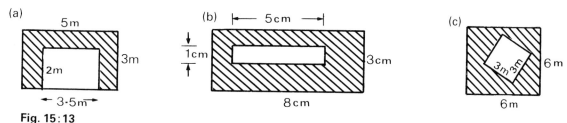

(a) 5m · 3m · 2m · 3·5m

(b) 5cm · 1cm · 3cm · 8cm

(c) 3m 3m · 6m · 6m

Fig. 15:13

7 Figure 15:14 shows one half of a tennis court. Copy it (not exactly), then calculate the areas of the parts marked A, B and C. Also calculate the area of the whole court.

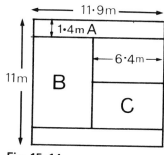

11·9m · 1·4m A · 6·4m · 11m · B · C

Fig. 15:14

8 Copy and complete this table for rectangles. If you find it hard to work out the answers, try sketching the rectangles.

Length	12 cm	10 cm	9 cm		2 cm	3 cm	3 cm
Width	8 cm			5 cm			
Area		50 cm^2	36 cm^2	45 cm^2			
Perimeter					6 cm	8 cm	10 cm

9 A brick has a rectangle for each face. If a brick is 21.5 cm long, 10 cm wide and 6.5 cm high, work out the area of each of the three different rectangular faces and the total surface area of the brick.

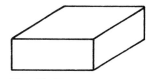

Fig. 15:15

10 Find some objects with faces that are rectangles (this book, your desk, etc.). Find the areas of the rectangles.

11 Make a square metre from 1 mm-squared paper. As each side of the sheet is 1000 mm long, the area of the whole square metre is 1 000 000 (one million) square millimetres. Use a calculator to find how long it would take you to colour in each mm square if you coloured one per second.

Using Your Calculator

Big Muskie

(*Arthur Shay*)

Big Muskie is one of the biggest machines ever built. It is used by an American coal-mining company at Musckingum mine in Ohio to remove up to 50 metres depth of soil. It works 24 hours a day, 364 days a year, except for three 30-minute breaks each day, and of course when it needs maintenance. If it breaks down the company reckons it loses £165 every 30 seconds. In 1982 the cost of replacing Muskie was reckoned to be about £35 000 000.

It can remove three million cubic metres of earth a month. Just how much this is can be seen by noting that when the Panama Canal was built it took 42 000 men 10 years to dig out 270 million cubic metres of earth.

Big Muskie is 150 metres long, 46 metres wide and 68 metres high. (A full-size football field is 120 metres long and 90 metres wide. An average two-storey house is 9 metres high.)

Big Muskie weighs more than 12 000 tonnes, or more than 128 Boeing 727 jumbo-jets. The bucket can scoop up 325 tonnes, the weight of ten railway goods wagons.

Three or four times a day it walks on two huge feet, each 42 metres long and 7 metres wide, at about $\frac{1}{4}$ km per hour, and at each 4.5 metre step it uses a barrel of oil for lubrication.

Use your calculator and the above information to answer the following questions.

1   There are 100 cm in a metre.

(a) How deep can Big Muskie dig, in cm?

(b) About how many times as tall as you is this?

2 (a) How many minutes a day does Big Muskie work?

(b) How many minutes does it work a year, if it does not break down?

(c) Change your answer to part (b) to hours.

3 If Big Muskie broke down for 15 minutes, what would it cost the company?

4 When digging the Panama Canal:

(a) How many million cubic metres of earth were removed each year on average?

(b) 1 million = 1 000 000. About how many cubic metres of earth did each man remove on average each year?

(c) If each man worked 350 days a year, how many cubic metres of earth did one man remove each day, on average?

5 Taking a month as 30 days, how many cubic metres of earth does Big Muskie remove: (a) each day   (b) each hour (working 22.5 hours a day)?

6 How many metres longer is Big Muskie than it is wide?

7 How many two-storey houses, stacked on top of each other, would be needed to equal Big Muskie's height?

8 What is the approximate weight of a Boeing 727?

9 How many bucket-fulls for Big Muskie to have dug up its own weight?

10 What would twelve railway wagons weigh?

11 An average-sized room in a house would be about 25 square metres. How many times as large as this is the area of one of Big Muskie's feet? (Area of a rectangle is length multiplied by width.)

12 1 km (one kilometre) is 1000 m (one thousand metres). How many metres does Big Muskie walk in an hour?

13 How many barrels of oil would Big Muskie use in travelling 30 metres?

14 (a) How many steps would Big Muskie have to take to walk 100 metres?

(b) How many steps would you have to take to cover the same distance?

16 Common fractions: conversion

A Kinds of fraction

A **fraction** is part of a whole one.

$\frac{1}{4}$ is a **common fraction**; 0.25 is a **decimal fraction**.

When we refer to 'fractions' we usually mean common fractions.
When we refer to 'decimals' we usually mean decimal fractions.

1

A   B   C   D   E   F

Fig. 16:1

In Figure 16:1, square A is divided into two equal parts. The shaded part is $\frac{1}{2}$ (half) of the square.

What fraction of each square is shaded in squares B to F?

2 In Figure 16:2, $\frac{3}{8}$ (three-eighths) of the rectangle is shaded. What fraction, in figures and words, is *not* shaded?

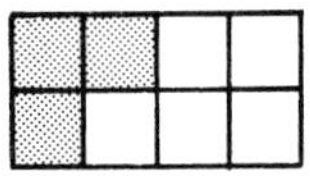

Fig. 16:2

3 (a) Copy Figure 16:3 exactly, then shade in $\frac{3}{10}$ (three-tenths) of it.

(b) What fraction of your rectangle, in figures and words, is not shaded?

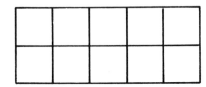

Fig. 16:3

4 In Figure 16:4:

(a) What fraction of the large triangle is one small triangle?

(b) What fraction is shaded? (Answer in figures.)

(c) What fraction is not shaded? (Answer in figures.)

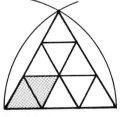

Fig. 16:4

5 What fraction of the rectangle in Figure 16:5 is made up from the following squares:
(a) A   (b) A and B   (c) B and D
(d) A and C and D?

Fig. 16:5

6 In Figure 16:6, $\frac{5}{12}$ of the dots are enclosed.

Draw five sets of twelve dots, then enclose one of the following fractions of the dots on each of your diagrams:
(a) $\frac{1}{2}$ (b) $\frac{1}{4}$ (c) $\frac{1}{3}$ (d) $\frac{3}{4}$ (e) $\frac{7}{12}$

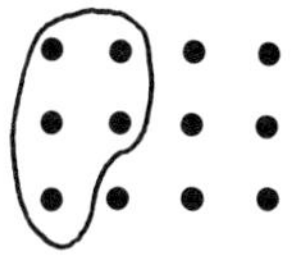

Fig. 16:6

7 In Figure 16:7, $2\frac{1}{2}$ (two and a half) squares have been shaded.

How many squares are shaded in each part of Figure 16:8?

Fig. 16:7

(a)   (b)

Fig. 16:8

8 Four quarters make one whole ($\frac{4}{4}=1$). Three whole ones will be three times as many quarters, twelve quarters, so $3=\frac{12}{4}$.

How many whole ones are: (a) $\frac{5}{5}$ (b) $\frac{7}{7}$ (c) $\frac{14}{7}$ (d) $\frac{24}{8}$?

9 **A fraction like $\frac{7}{4}$ is called a top-heavy fraction.**

A number like $1\frac{3}{4}$ is called a mixed number.

Example $\frac{17}{4}$ will make 4 whole ones (16 quarters) with one quarter left over, so $\frac{17}{4} = 4\frac{1}{4}$.

Change the following top-heavy fractions to mixed numbers.
(a) $\frac{5}{4}$ (b) $\frac{15}{4}$ (c) $\frac{9}{8}$ (d) $\frac{11}{8}$ (e) $\frac{7}{6}$ (f) $\frac{9}{5}$ (g) $\frac{11}{7}$ (h) $\frac{30}{7}$

*10 Renata is making sandwiches. Each slice of bread is a square. Draw four small pictures (about 2 cm sides) to show how the square of bread could be cut into:

(a) halves (two ways)   (b) quarters (three ways).

*11 What fraction of the cakes in Figure 16:9 is each slice? Answer both in figures and in words.

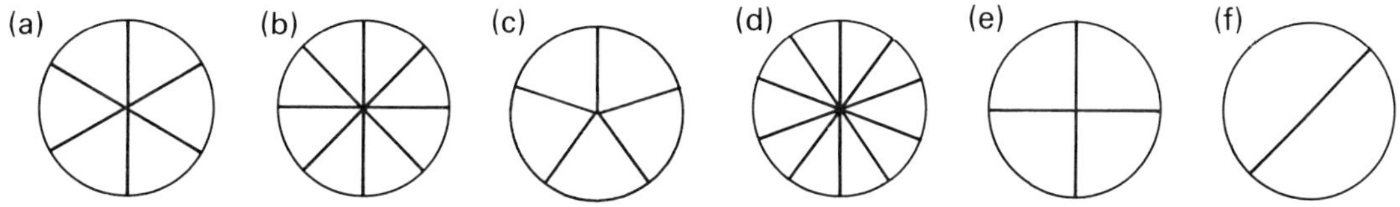

(a)   (b)   (c)   (d)   (e)   (f)

Fig. 16:9

*12 Figure 16:10 shows $1\frac{1}{2}$ cm^2.

How many cm^2 are (a), (b) and (c) in Figure 16:11?

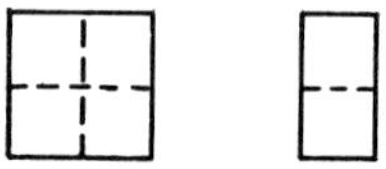

Fig. 16:10

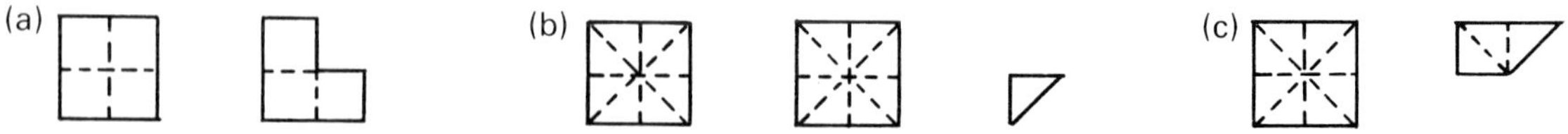

(a)

Fig. 16:11

(b)

(c)

*13 Into how many equal parts must a pie be cut to make each part:
(a) $\frac{1}{2}$ (b) $\frac{1}{4}$ (c) $\frac{1}{5}$ (d) $\frac{1}{8}$ (e) $\frac{1}{10}$ (f) $\frac{1}{20}$?

14 Construct an equilateral triangle like the one in Figure 16:4. Start with a line 3 cm long, then using your compasses set to a 3 cm radius, find the position of the top point. Divide the triangle into nine smaller triangles, then shade $\frac{5}{9}$ of it.

15 Change to fifths:
(a) $3\frac{1}{5}$ (b) $6\frac{1}{5}$ (c) $7\frac{2}{5}$ (d) $9\frac{3}{5}$.

16 Arrange in decreasing order of size, starting with $\frac{1}{2}$:
$\frac{1}{4}$; $\frac{1}{7}$; $\frac{1}{2}$; $\frac{1}{6}$; $\frac{1}{5}$; $\frac{1}{10}$; $\frac{1}{25}$; $\frac{1}{100}$; $\frac{1}{3}$.

17 Examples   3 thirds make 1 whole, so 15 thirds make 5 whole ones.

$4\frac{2}{3}$ is 4 wholes and 2 thirds, making $12 + 2 = 14$ thirds.

Change:
(a) 4 to quarters   (b) 2 to fifths   (c) 3 to eighths   (d) 4 to sevenths
(e) $6\frac{1}{2}$ to halves   (f) $7\frac{1}{4}$ to quarters   (g) $3\frac{3}{8}$ to eighths   (h) $1\frac{1}{15}$ to fifteenths
(i) $7\frac{2}{9}$ to ninths   (j) $8\frac{9}{17}$ to seventeenths.

18 Arrange each of the following sets in decreasing order of size (largest first).
(a) $\{\frac{1}{2}, \frac{1}{4}, \frac{1}{3}\}$ (b) $\{\frac{1}{5}, \frac{1}{7}, \frac{1}{6}\}$ (c) $\{\frac{1}{90}, \frac{1}{11}, \frac{1}{9}\}$ (d) $\{\frac{3}{5}, \frac{1}{5}, \frac{2}{5}\}$ (e) $\{\frac{4}{7}, \frac{2}{7}, \frac{3}{7}\}$ (f) $\{\frac{3}{7}, \frac{5}{7}, \frac{6}{7}\}$
(g) $\{\frac{2}{11}, \frac{8}{11}, \frac{1}{11}\}$ (h) $\{1, \frac{3}{4}, 1\frac{1}{4}\}$ (i) $\{2, \frac{5}{4}, 1\frac{1}{8}\}$ (j) $\{3\frac{1}{4}, \frac{16}{4}, \frac{11}{4}\}$ (k) $\{\frac{17}{8}, \frac{18}{8}, 1\frac{7}{8}\}$

19 Here is a quick method to find whether one fraction is bigger or smaller than another:

Multiply each top number by the bottom number of the other fraction.

Example   To find which is the bigger of $\frac{7}{8}$ and $\frac{9}{10}$.

$\frac{7}{8} \diagdown \frac{9}{10}$ gives   70   72

As $70 < 72$ then $\frac{7}{8} < \frac{9}{10}$ ($<$ says 'is less than')

Find which is the smaller of: (a) $\frac{4}{5}$; $\frac{3}{4}$ (b) $\frac{5}{6}$; $\frac{7}{8}$ (c) $\frac{4}{9}$; $\frac{3}{7}$ (d) $\frac{8}{11}$; $\frac{5}{7}$ (e) $\frac{13}{25}$; $\frac{4}{7}$.

20 Figure 16:12 shows a series of fractions called a **Farey Sequence**. Find the line labelled $\frac{1}{3}$. It goes through the co-ordinate (3,1), giving $\frac{1}{3}$. The line labelled 2 goes through (1,2), giving $\frac{2}{1} = 2$.

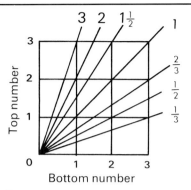

Fig. 16:12

(a) Copy the diagram. Check the fractions.

(b) The steeper the slope of a line, the bigger the fraction, so:
$$3 > 2 > 1\tfrac{1}{2} > 1 > \tfrac{2}{3} > \tfrac{1}{2} > \tfrac{1}{3}$$

(c) Draw a grid from 0 to 4 and draw labelled lines as in Figure 16:12 to show whole numbers and fractions from 4 to $\frac{1}{4}$. Then write them in order using the $>$ sign.

21 Try question 20 for bigger grids. Try to find out more about Farey Sequences.

22 Try to fold a piece of paper into:
(a) $\frac{1}{2}$ (b) $\frac{1}{4}$ (c) $\frac{1}{8}$ (d) $\frac{1}{16}$ (e) $\frac{1}{3}$.

What is the smallest fraction you can fold it into?

B   Equivalent fractions

For Discussion

A

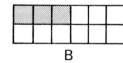
B

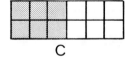
C

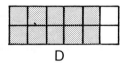
D

Fig. 16:13

(a) The shaded part of A shows $\frac{*}{12} = \frac{*}{6} = \frac{*}{3}$.

(b) The shaded part of B shows $\frac{*}{12} = \frac{*}{4}$.

(c) The shaded part of C shows $\frac{*}{12} = \frac{*}{6} = \frac{*}{4} = \frac{*}{2}$.

(d) The shaded part of D shows $\frac{*}{*} = \frac{*}{*}$.

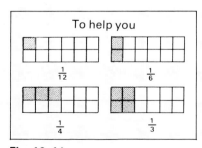

Fig. 16:14

To help you

$\frac{1}{12}$ $\frac{1}{6}$

$\frac{1}{4}$ $\frac{1}{3}$

101

1   $F = \{\frac{2}{4}, \frac{6}{18}, \frac{3}{6}, \frac{2}{20}, \frac{2}{8}, \frac{4}{12}, \frac{8}{16}, \frac{10}{20}, \frac{4}{16}\}$

$A = \{$fractions equal to $\frac{1}{2}\}$ $B = \{$fractions equal to $\frac{1}{3}\}$

$C = \{$fractions equal to $\frac{1}{4}\}$ $D = \{$fractions equal to $\frac{1}{10}\}$

List sets A to D, choosing your elements from set F.

2   **Example** $\frac{4}{6}$ can be simplified, (or cancelled) to $\frac{2}{3}$ by dividing both the 4 and the 6 by 2.

Simplify:
(a) $\frac{5}{10}$ (b) $\frac{6}{8}$ (c) $\frac{7}{21}$ (d) $\frac{9}{12}$ (e) $\frac{21}{27}$ (f) $\frac{22}{33}$.

*3   Figure 16:15 shows a wall made up from five different lengths of black and white bricks. How many bricks are there in:
(a) row A   (b) row B   (c) row C   (d) row D   (e) row E?

Fig. 16:15

*4   In Figure 16:15, what fraction of each row is one brick in that row?

*5   Simplify the following fractions by cancelling.
(a) $\frac{8}{10}$ ($\div$ by 2)   (b) $\frac{4}{6}$ ($\div$ by 2)   (c) $\frac{6}{20}$ ($\div$ by 2)   (d) $\frac{6}{9}$ ($\div$ by 3)
(e) $\frac{8}{12}$ ($\div$ by 4)   (f) $\frac{15}{20}$ ($\div$ by 5)   (g) $\frac{10}{15}$ (h) $\frac{9}{12}$ (i) $\frac{14}{21}$

*6   Copy and complete:
(a) $\frac{1}{2} = \frac{2}{4} = \frac{*}{6} = \frac{*}{8} = \frac{*}{10} = \frac{6}{*} = \frac{7}{*} = \frac{8}{*}$
(b) $\frac{1}{3} = \frac{2}{6} = \frac{3}{9} = \frac{*}{12} = \frac{*}{15} = \frac{6}{*} = \frac{7}{*} = \frac{8}{*}$
(c) $\frac{1}{4} = \frac{2}{8} = \frac{3}{12} = \frac{*}{20} = \frac{8}{*} = \frac{11}{*} = \frac{12}{*} = \frac{*}{100}$

*7 $\frac{1}{2}, \frac{1}{3}, \frac{1}{4}, \frac{4}{8}, \frac{6}{12}, \frac{3}{12}, \frac{4}{16}, \frac{8}{16}, \frac{5}{10}, \frac{3}{9}, \frac{5}{20}, \frac{4}{12}, \frac{5}{15}$

(a) Copy these fractions. Put a ring round each one that is the same as a half.

(b) Copy the fractions again. Put a ring round each one that is the same as a third.

(c) Copy the fractions again. Put a ring round the ones equal to a quarter.

8 In Figure 16:15:

Each brick in row A is $\frac{1}{12}$ of a row.

Each brick in row B is $\frac{1}{6}$ of the row.

Two bricks in row A equal one brick in row B, so $\frac{2}{12} = \frac{1}{6}$.

(a) Look at rows A and C and find how they show that $\frac{3}{12} = \frac{1}{4}$. There is no need to write anything.

(b) Using the wall to help you, copy and complete:
   (i) $\frac{6}{12} = \frac{*}{2}$ (ii) $\frac{4}{12} = \frac{*}{6} = \frac{*}{3}$ (iii) $\frac{6}{12} = \frac{*}{6} = \frac{*}{4} = \frac{*}{2}$ (iv) $\frac{8}{12} = \frac{*}{6} = \frac{*}{3}$ (v) $\frac{9}{12} = \frac{*}{4}$
   (vi) $\frac{10}{12} = \frac{*}{6}$ (vii) $\frac{12}{12} = \frac{*}{6} = \frac{*}{4} = \frac{*}{3} = \frac{*}{2}$

9 Example   Cancel $\frac{150}{200}$ to make it as simple as possible.

First divide both numbers by 10 to give $\frac{15}{20}$.

Then divide both 15 and 20 by 5.

We usually write it like this:

$$\frac{\overset{3}{\cancel{15\cancel{0}}}}{\underset{4}{\cancel{20\cancel{0}}}} = \frac{3}{4}$$

Cancel the following fractions to make them as simple as possible.
(a) $\frac{36}{42}$ (b) $\frac{50}{75}$ (c) $\frac{16}{64}$ (d) $\frac{120}{300}$ (e) $\frac{250}{400}$ (f) $\frac{36}{100}$ (g) $\frac{80}{100}$ (h) $\frac{125}{1000}$
(i) $\frac{140}{285}$ (j) $\frac{26}{91}$ (k) $\frac{66}{165}$ (l) $\frac{42}{504}$

10 Four seeds in five germinate (start to grow). What fraction do not germinate?

11 Eight friends share three apples equally. What fraction of an apple does each receive?

12 A bar of chocolate will break into 24 pieces of equal size. Twenty-four girls could have equal shares ($\frac{1}{24}$ each). What other number of girls could have equal shares and what fraction would each receive? (Give five possible answers.)

13 A farmer has 84 animals: 2 horses, 14 cows, 30 sheep, and some turkeys. What fraction of his animals is each kind, as simply as possible?

14 State the value of each letter if:
   (a) $\frac{5}{12} = \frac{a}{36} = \frac{20}{b}$ (b) $\frac{8}{9} = \frac{x}{18} = \frac{56}{y}$.

15 Draw a wall to show the connections between $\frac{1}{15}$, $\frac{1}{10}$, $\frac{1}{5}$, $\frac{1}{3}$ and $\frac{1}{2}$.

C Conversion: common to decimal

The sign ÷ represents one number over another, that is, a fraction.

A fraction can be thought of as the top number divided by the bottom number.

To change a fraction to a decimal, divide the top number by the bottom number.

Example Change $\frac{7}{8}$ to a decimal fraction.

Divide 7 by 8. To do this without a calculator you need to put a decimal point after the 7, then keep 'writing noughts' until it either works out exactly, or is as accurate as you require.

We write it like this: $8 \overline{)\ 7\ .\ 0^6 0^4 0}^{\ 0\ .\ 8\ 7\ 5}$ *Answer* $\frac{7}{8} = 0.875$

1 Write as a decimal:
(a) $\frac{1}{2}$ (b) $\frac{1}{4}$ (c) $\frac{3}{4}$ (d) $\frac{7}{10}$ (e) $\frac{7}{100}$ (f) $\frac{1}{8}$ (g) $\frac{1}{5}$ (h) $\frac{2}{5}$.

*2 Write as a decimal:
(a) $\frac{3}{5}$ (b) $\frac{4}{5}$ (c) $\frac{3}{8}$ (d) $\frac{5}{8}$ (e) $\frac{9}{10}$ (f) $\frac{9}{100}$ (g) $\frac{91}{100}$ (h) $\frac{19}{100}$.

3 Write as a decimal:
(a) $4\frac{1}{2}$ (b) $6\frac{1}{4}$ (c) $7\frac{2}{5}$ (d) $8\frac{1}{8}$ (e) $10\frac{64}{100}$ (f) $3\frac{13}{200}$.

4 $\frac{1}{2} = \mathbf{0.5}$; $\frac{1}{4} = \mathbf{0.25}$; $\frac{1}{8} = \mathbf{0.125}$

Learn the above equivalents, then, using the fact that $\frac{1}{8} = 0.125$, practise working out 'in your head': (a) $\frac{3}{8}$ (b) $\frac{5}{8}$ (c) $\frac{7}{8}$.

5 Many fractions do not convert to exact decimals; instead they **recur**.

Examples $\frac{1}{3} = 0.333333333 \ldots$ written as $0.\dot{3}$

$\frac{1}{7} = 0.142857\,142857\,142857 \ldots$ written as $0.\dot{1}4285\dot{7}$

Write as a recurring decimal, using dots:
(a) $\frac{2}{3}$ (b) $\frac{1}{6}$ (c) $\frac{2}{7}$ (d) $\frac{8}{11}$ (e) $\frac{5}{13}$ (f) $\frac{21}{23}$.

6 Write $\frac{1}{7}, \frac{2}{7}, \frac{3}{7}$ and $\frac{4}{7}$ as decimal fractions. Look for a pattern in your answers. Can you say what $\frac{5}{7}$ and $\frac{6}{7}$ will be without working them out? Do other recurring decimals follow a similar pattern ($\frac{1}{9}$'s; $\frac{1}{11}$'s; $\frac{1}{13}$'s; $\frac{1}{17}$'s; etc.)?

D Conversion: decimal to common

Examples   In 0.3, the last figure (3) is in the tenths column, so $0.3 = \frac{3}{10}$.

In 0.873 the last figure (3) is in the thousandths column, so $0.873 = \frac{873}{1000}$.

1   Write as a common fraction:
(a) 0.7   (b) 0.9   (c) 0.11   (d) 0.37   (e) 0.121   (f) 0.07   (g) 0.009
(h) 0.067   (i) 0.03   (j) 0.0001

*2   Write as a common fraction:
(a) 0.3   (b) 0.1   (c) 0.31   (d) 0.129   (e) 0.041   (f) 0.09   (g) 0.007
(h) 0.13   (i) 0.0003   (j) 0.0081

3   If possible we simplify the fractions by cancelling.

Note that all multiples of ten will only divide by multiples of 2 and 5, so only even numbers and numbers ending in 5 will cancel in these questions.

The cancelling is usually written as in exercise 16B question 9.

Write as a simplified common fraction:
(a) 0.5   (b) 0.8   (c) 0.25   (d) 0.04   (e) 0.15   (f) 0.35

4   Write as a simplified common fraction:
(a) 0.26   (b) 0.165   (c) 0.248   (d) 0.725   (e) 0.362   (f) 0.1265

5   Write as a mixed number, as simply as possible:
(a) 1.0625   (b) 8.1001   (c) 6.712   (d) 8.3014   (e) 12.036   (f) 25.008

---

6   How many fractions can you change to decimals in your head? Write them all down.

How many decimals can you change to fractions in your head? Write them all down.

Who in your class can do the most?

---

17 Relations

A Relation diagrams; domain; range

For Discussion

Figures 17:1, 17:2 and 17:3 show three different ways of representing the information that Ali has a pet dog, Brian has a pet dog and a pet cat, and Colin has a pet dog and a pet rat.

Figure 17:1 is called a **relation diagram**.

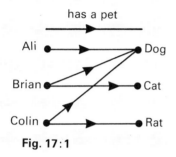

Fig. 17:1

Fig. 17:2

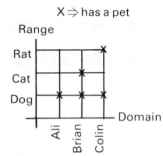

Fig. 17:3

1 Copy and complete the table and the grid for the relation diagram in Figure 17:4.

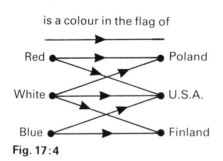

Fig. 17:4

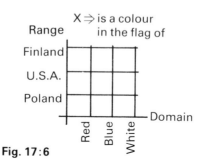

Fig. 17:5

Fig. 17:6

2 Copy and complete these tables, using 1 to show a truth and 0 to show a falsehood.

(a) 1 ⇒ Is a quarter of

	4	8	12	16
1	1	0		
2				
3				
4				

(b) 1 ⇒ Will divide exactly into

	2	6	12	20	30	60
2	1					
3	0					
4						
5						
6						

(c) 1 ⇒ Is smaller than

	1	2	3	4	5
1	0	1			
2	0				
3					
4					
5					

3 Draw the graphs for the tables in question 2. Figure 17:7 shows you how to start the axes. Remember to label your graphs clearly with what they represent.

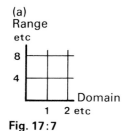

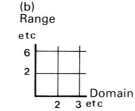

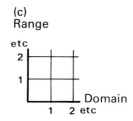

Fig. 17:7

4 A boy has two dice, one labelled A, B, C, D, E and F; the other labelled 1, 2, 3, 4, 5 and 6.

He throws both and records the results, (A,1), (B,6), and so on, always putting the letter first.

Write out all 36 possible different results.

Your answer is called the **Cartesian Product** of {A, B, C, D, E, F} and {1, 2, 3, 4, 5, 6}.

5 Set $A = \{a, b, c, d\}$. The Cartesian Product of set A with itself starts: (a,a), (a,b), (a,c) ... Copy and complete this.

How many pairs are there altogether?

Can you find a rule for how many there will be for any given set?

Can you find a rule for when there are two different sets, as in question 4?

B   Mappings and graphs

For Discussion

Mapping	Co-ordinates	Graph

Mapping
$x \rightarrow x - 2$
$2 \rightarrow \quad 0$
$3 \rightarrow \quad 1$
$4 \rightarrow \quad 2$
$5 \rightarrow \quad 3$
$6 \rightarrow \quad 4$

Co-ordinates
$(x, f(x))$
$(2, \quad 0)$
$(3, \quad 1)$
$(4, \quad 2)$
$(5, \quad 3)$
$(6, \quad 4)$

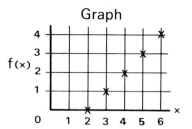

Fig. 17:8

1 (a) Copy and complete the table.

(b) Write the pairs of values as co-ordinates, (0,1), (1,2), etc.

(c) Plot the co-ordinates on a grid labelled 0 to 5 along the bottom and 0 to 6 up the side. Remember to go along first, then up. Label your graph: '$x \rightarrow x + 1$'.

$x \rightarrow x + 1$
$0 \rightarrow \quad 1$
$1 \rightarrow \quad 2$
$2 \rightarrow \quad 3$
$3 \rightarrow$
$4 \rightarrow$
$5 \rightarrow$

2 Repeat the steps of question 1 for:
(a) $x \rightarrow x + 2$ (b) $x \rightarrow x + 3$.

Note that the $f(x)$-axis must go up to the largest number in your table.

3 Repeat question 2 for $x \rightarrow x - 1$ with values of x from 1 to 6.

*4 (a) Copy and complete the table.

Note that $x \rightarrow 2x$ means that you multiply the number under x by 2 to find the number under $2x$.

$x \rightarrow 2x$
$1 \rightarrow 2$
$2 \rightarrow 4$
$3 \rightarrow$
$4 \rightarrow$

(b) Copy and complete these co-ordinates from part (a): (1,2); (2,4); (,); (,).

(c) Draw axes, x from 0 to 4, $f(x)$ from 0 to 8. Plot your co-ordinates.

5 (a) Draw a table for $x \rightarrow x^2$ for values of x from 0 to 4.
Remember that x^2 means x multiplied by x.

(b) Write the co-ordinates from your table, then plot them on a graph, x from 0 to 4 and $f(x)$ from 0 to 16.

6 Relations like $x \to x + 1$, $x \to x - 3$, and $x \to x^2$ are called **mappings**.

Example Under the mapping $x \to x + 1$, 16 becomes 17.

Say what 11 becomes under the mappings:
(a) $x \to x + 2$ (b) $x \to x - 5$ (c) $x \to 2x$ (d) $x \to 3x$ (e) $x \to x^2$ (f) $x \to 2x^2$.

7 Another way to write a mapping is with a letter f. The f stands for **function**.

Example $f(x) : x \to 2x$ reads 'A function of x such that x becomes twice x'.

If $x = 3$ then $f(x) = 6$.

List $\{f(x)\}$ if:
(a) $f(x) : x \to 2x$ with $x \in \{3, 6, 12\}$ (b) $f(x) : x \to x^2$ with $x \in \{6, 7, 8, 9\}$.

8 The mapping $x \to \frac{x}{2}$ cancels out the effect of $x \to 2x$, so that you end up with the number you started with (see Figure 17:9).

$x \to \frac{x}{2}$ is called the **inverse mapping** of $x \to 2x$.

Draw a diagram similar to Figure 17:9 for the mapping $x \to x + 2$ and its inverse.

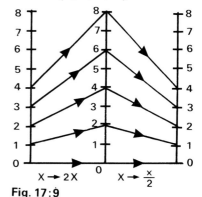

Fig. 17:9

9 Work out (without drawing a diagram if you can), the inverse mapping for:
(a) $x \to x + 3$ (b) $x \to x - 1$ (c) $x \to x - 5$ (d) $x \to 3x$ (e) $x \to 4x$.

10

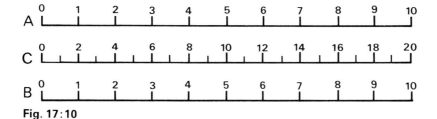

Fig. 17:10

Copy Figure 17:10 exactly. Place your ruler to join 8 on A to 6 on B. What number do you read on C? Try other pairs of numbers on A and B. What sum does C give you the answer to? This kind of diagram is called a **Nomogram**.

11 Try drawing some lines of your own.

Project

Reflection in a mirror

1 When you look into a mirror and hold up your right arm, does your reflection hold up its right arm too?

2 'Just look at yourself!' said Marmaduke's mum, holding up her mirror. Figure P2:1 shows what Marmaduke saw. Draw what his mother saw. Be very careful with the eyes, ears, hair, nose, mouth and tie. Check your answer with a mirror.

Fig. P2:1

3 Write the words shown in Figure P2:2 as they would appear when reflected in a mirror.

HAM SPAM EGGS BEANS
Fig. P2:2

4 Write a short sentence that can be read in a mirror, like the one in Figure P2:3.

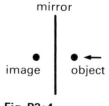

Fig. P2:3

5 In questions 1 to 4 you have been looking into the mirror. Now you are going to look down onto the mirror's edge and pretend you can see both the object (the real thing) and the image (the reflection in the mirror).

The mirror will be represented by a line.

Look at Figure P2:4. Turn your book and look in the direction of the arrow, then slowly slide a mirror along the mirror line. Check that the image is where it has been drawn.

Fig. P2:4

6 Jane is 1 metre from a mirror. How far from Jane is her image?

7 Copy Figure P2:5 exactly, leaving a 4 cm space to the right of the mirror line. Draw the images of the three objects. Check your answer with a mirror.

Fig. P2:5

Fig. P2:6

8 Copy Figure P2:6 exactly, leaving a 4 cm space below and to the right of the mirror lines. Draw the images in each mirror.

9 Copy and continue Figure P2:7 for all the capital letters of the alphabet.

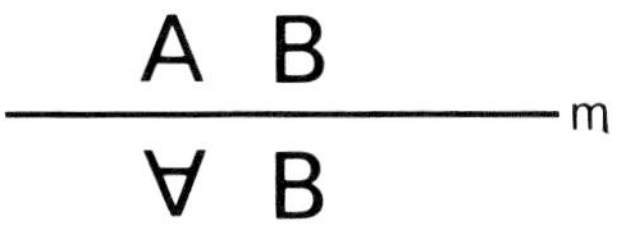

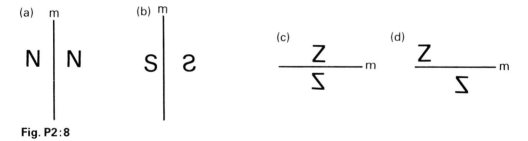

Fig. P2:7

10 Only one of the diagrams in Figure P2:8 is correct. What is wrong with the other three?

(a) m

N | N

(b) m

S | Ƨ

(c)

Z / Ƨ — m

(d)

Z / Ƨ — m

Fig. P2:8

11 Copy Figure P2:9 exactly. Reflect the ● and the **X**, measuring carefully, then join each object to its image with a straight line.

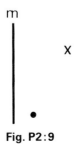

Fig. P2:9

111

12 Copy Figure P2:10 exactly. Reflect the flag in the mirror. (It is best to reflect each end first, then join the ends with a line.)

Fig. P2:10

13 (a) Copy Figure P2:11 exactly, then reflect the objects in the mirror.

(b) Join the objects together and the images together to make a triangle and its reflection.

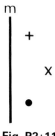

Fig. P2:11

14 Place a mirror in line with the arrows on Figure P2:12, then turn it through 360°, keeping it on the centre dot.

Repeat for Figure P2:13, then draw some of your own.

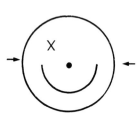

Fig. P2:12

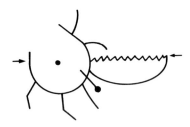

Fig. P2:13

15 In a kaleidoscope, mirrors give reflections to make a pattern, like the one in Figure P2:14. Draw and colour a kaleidoscope pattern.

Fig. P2:14

16 Stand two mirrors on edge as shown in Figure P2:15. They must be exactly at right-angles. Comment on your reflection in the mirrors. Repeat the experiment with one mirror horizontal and one vertical.

Fig. P2:15

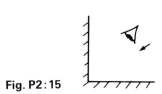

112

18 Reflection on a grid

In Figure 18:1 A′ is the **image** of A.

The image of a point is always the same distance behind the mirror as the object point is in front.

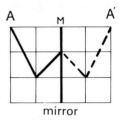

Fig. 18:1

Example In Figure 18:1, AM = A′M.

The line joining an object point to an image point always crosses the mirror line at 90°.

Example In Figure 18:1, the line joining A to A′ crosses the mirror line at 90°.

1 Copy Figure 18:2 on squared paper, then draw the images in the mirrors.

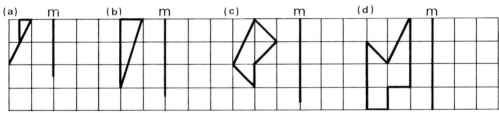

Fig. 18:2

2 Copy Figure 18:3, then draw in the positions of the mirrors.

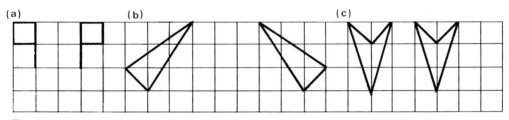

Fig. 18:3

3 Copy Figure 18:4 on squared paper, then draw the images in the mirrors.

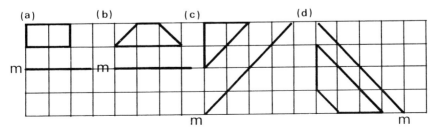

Fig. 18:4

113

4 Copy Figure 18:5 on squared paper, then draw the images in the mirrors.

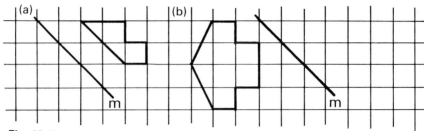

Fig. 18:5

5 Copy Figure 18:6 on squared paper, then draw in possible mirror lines. If you can see two possible lines, draw them both.

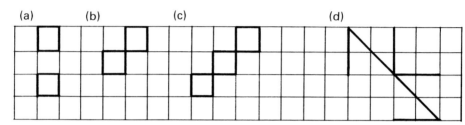

Fig. 18:6

6 (a) Copy Figure 18:7 and draw the images. (A′ is the image of A).

(b) Copy and complete the table.

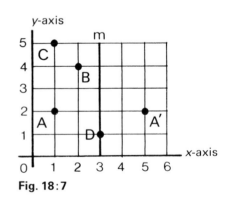

Fig. 18:7

Object letter	Co-ordinates	
	Object	Image
A	(1,2)	(5,2)
B		
C		
D		

7 (a) Figure 18:8 shows an object, A, reflected in two mirrors. The first image's position is marked A′ and the second is marked A″. Copy Figure 18:7 and mark the images B′, B″, C′ and C″.

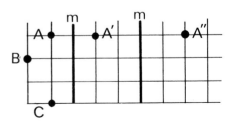

Fig. 18:8

(b) Join ABC and A′B′C′ and A″B″C″ to make three triangles.

(c) Comment on the second reflection of triangle ABC.

8 Copy Figure 18:9. Draw the first and second reflection of the pentagon.

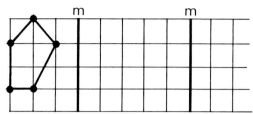

Fig. 18:9

9 (a) Copy Figure 18:10 and mark the images B′, C′ and D′.

(b) Join ABCD and A′B′C′D′.

(c) Draw up and complete a table like the one in question 6(b).

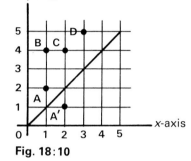

Fig. 18:10

10 (a) Copy the axes and the mirror line, but not the points, shown in Figure 18:10.

(b) Plot (3,3), (1,3), (2,4) and (2,5). Join them in order, making a four-sided figure (a concave quadrilateral).

(c) Reflect the figure in the mirror and state the co-ordinates of the image.

11 Copy Figure 18:11 and reflect the objects in all four mirror lines. Think very carefully about the hatched shading lines.

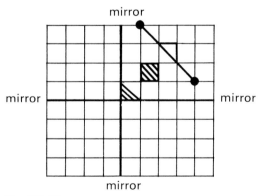

Fig. 18:11

12 Investigate the co-ordinates of object and image points for reflections in various mirror lines. Can you calculate the image position if you know the co-ordinates of the object and the equation of the mirror line?

Line symmetry is found in nearly all natural and man-made objects. Why not make a wall display of symmetrical objects?

1 Copy Figure 19:1. Mark each picture's lines of symmetry, or write 'it has none'.

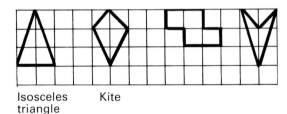

Isosceles triangle   Kite

Fig. 19:1

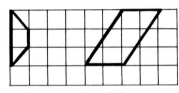

Isosceles trapezium   Parallelogram

2 The rectangle in Figure 19:2 has two lines of symmetry. Copy Figure 19:3 and mark in the lines of symmetry.

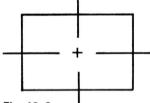

Fig. 19:2

Fig. 19:3

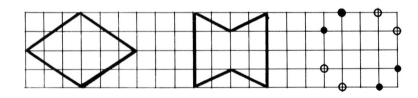

3 In your writing book, draw all the capital letters, making them three spaces high. Mark all the lines of symmetry (though you need not do *all* of them on the letter ◯).

4 Draw four circles, the same diameter as your protractor. Mark the points shown in Figure 19:4. Join the following sets of points, one set on each diagram.

116

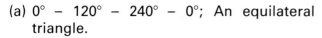

(a) 0° – 120° – 240° – 0°; An equilateral triangle.

(b) 0° – 90° – 180° – 270° – 0°; A square.

(c) 0° – 60° – 120° – 180° – 240° – 300° – 0°; A regular hexagon.

(d) 0° – 45° – 90° – 135° – 180° – 225° – 270° – 315° – 0°; A regular octagon.

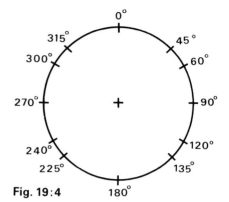

Fig. 19:4

5 Copy this table and complete it.

| Name | Sketch | Number of | | |
		Sides	Angles	Lines of symmetry
Equilateral triangle		3		
Square		4		
Regular pentagon		5		
Regular hexagon		6		
Regular octagon		8		
Regular decagon		10		

6 Use your protractor to make three copies of Figure 19:5.

Add as few lines as possible to give:

(a) on your first copy, line symmetry in the line AB

(b) on your second copy, line symmetry in the line CD

(c) on your third copy, line symmetry in both AB and CD.

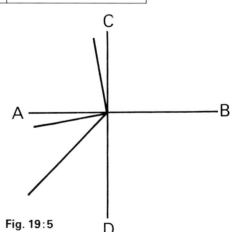

Fig. 19:5

7 Find how many ways you can slice a cube into two equal symmetrical pieces. Use plasticine, pastry, etc.

8 Experiment with folded paper to make symmetrical cut-out patterns.

A Kinds of triangle

Fig. 20:1

Scalene
No equal sides;
no equal angles

Fig. 20:2

Isosceles
2 equal sides;
2 equal angles

Fig. 20:3

Equilateral
3 equal sides;
3 equal angles

Fig. 20:4

Acute-angled

Fig. 20:5

Obtuse-angled

Fig. 20:6

Right-angled

1 In Figures 20:7, 20:8 and 20:9, equal sides and equal angles are marked with the same signs.

Copy sentences (a) to (g), completing them with capital letters to name the triangles.

Example △ HIJ is right-angled and scalene.

In Figure 20:7: (a) △ ... is equilateral.
                 (b) △ ... and △ ... and △ ... are isosceles.

In Figure 20:8: (c) △ ... is right-angled and isosceles.
                 (d) △ ... is right-angled and scalene.
                 (e) △ ... is acute-angled and scalene.

In Figure 20:9: (f) △ ... and △ ... are obtuse-angled.
                 (g) △ ... is right-angled and isosceles.

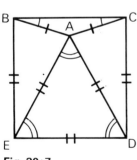

Fig. 20:7

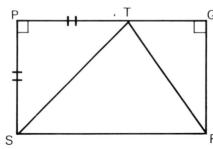

Fig. 20:8

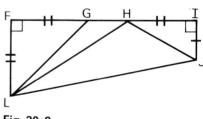

Fig. 20:9

*2 Which of the triangles in Figure 20:10 is:
(a) equilateral   (b) isosceles right-angled   (c) isosceles obtuse-angled
(d) scalene obtuse-angled   (e) isosceles acute-angled?

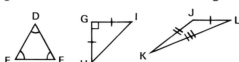

Fig. 20:10

3 Draw all possible lines of symmetry on:
(a) an isosceles triangle   (b) an equilateral triangle   (c) a scalene triangle.

4 Copy this table. Tick or cross to show whether the triangle is possible. If it is possible, draw an example and write its name underneath.

	Acute-angled	Obtuse-angled	Right-angled
Equilateral	✓	✗	
Isosceles			
Scalene			

5 Copy these sentences, completing them with 'All', 'Some', or 'No'.

(a) ... equilateral triangles are isosceles triangles.

(b) ... right-angled triangles are equilateral triangles.

(c) ... isosceles triangles are right-angled triangles.

(d) ... right-angled triangles are obtuse-angled.

(e) ... acute-angled triangles are isosceles triangles.

---

6 By drawing different kinds of triangle, find out if it is true that the largest angle is always opposite the largest side, and the smallest angle opposite the smallest side.

7 By drawing different triangles in circles, as in Figure 20:11, investigate the position of the centre of the circle for:

(a) acute-angled triangles

(b) obtuse-angled triangles

(c) right-angled triangles

(d) isosceles triangles

(e) equilateral triangles.

Fig. 20:11

8 Space five points equally round the circumference of a circle. How many different triangles can be made by joining three of the points? Repeat for different numbers of points. Is there a rule?

B Angle sum

The three angles of a triangle add up to 180 degrees.

Example In Figure 20:12, the third angle can be found by adding the two we are told, then taking the answer from 180°.

$$59° + 37° = 96°; \quad 180° - 96° = 84°.$$

The third angle is 84°.

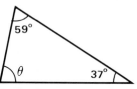

Fig. 20:12

1 Calculate the third angle in the three triangles of Figure 20:13.

(a) 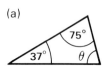 (b)  (c)

Fig. 20:13

2 How many degrees is each angle of an equilateral triangle?

*3 Calculate the angle marked θ in each triangle of Figure 20:14.

(a) (b) (c) (d)

 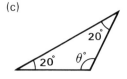 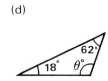

(e) (f) (g)

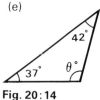 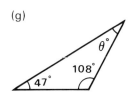

Fig. 20:14

4 An isosceles triangle has one line of symmetry (see Figure 20:15).

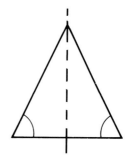

Fig. 20:15

(a) What must be true about the two angles marked with an arc?

(b) One angle of an isosceles triangle is 70°. Find two possible pairs of answers for the other two angles.

(c) What could the angles be in a right-angled isosceles triangle?

5 State all three angles of a triangle that is:

(a) right-angled with one angle 23°   (b) right-angled with two equal angles

(c) isosceles with one angle 100°   (d) isosceles with one angle 60°

(e) isosceles with one angle 72° (2 possible answers).

6 Can an obtuse-angled isosceles triangle have an angle of 46°? If so, state the sizes of the other two angles.

---

7 (a) In Figure 20:16, line AD is divided in the ratio 1:2:2. How long are AB, BC and CD?

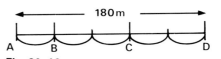

Fig. 20:16

(b) A triangle PQR has angles in the ratio 1:2:2. How many degrees is each?

8 Find the size of each angle if the angles of a triangle are in the ratio:
(a) 1:1:2   (b) 1:2:3   (c) 1:3:5   (d) 1:1:1

9 (a) In Figure 20:17, calculate *a* and *b*.

(b) How is the size of angle *b* connected with the 72° and the 58°?

(c) Is it always true that the exterior angle of a triangle (like *b*) is equal to the sum of the two opposite interior angles (like 72° and 58°)? Why?

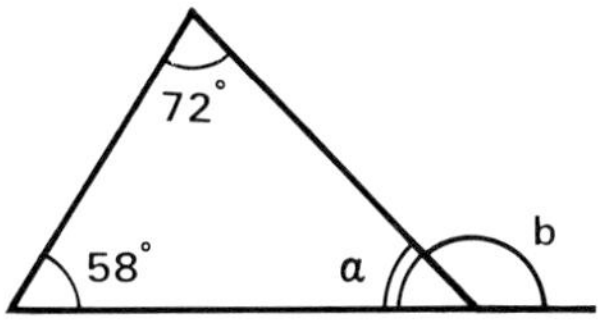

Fig. 20:17

10 Can you see how Figure 20:18 proves that the four angles of a quadrilateral total 360°? Go on to find the angle sum of other polygons.

Fig. 20:18

A Gram; kilogram; tonne

1 cubic centimetre of water weighs 1 gram (1 g).

1000 g = 1 kilogram (1 kg).

1000 kg = 1 tonne (tonne is *not* usually shortened).

Fig. 21:1

Fig. 21:2

1 (a) List the objects in Figure 21:2, one under the other in order of weight, heaviest first.

   (b) After each object in your list write its weight, chosen from:
   13 g;   10 tonnes; $\frac{1}{2}$ g;   1 kg;   80 000 tonnes;   100 g;   25 kg.

2 How many grams make:
   (a) 1 kg   (b) 5 kg   (c) $\frac{1}{2}$ kg   (d) $\frac{1}{4}$ kg?

3 **Examples**   500 g $= \frac{1}{2}$ kg $= 0.5$ kg

   750 g $= \frac{3}{4}$ kg $= 0.75$ kg

Copy these two examples, then write similar statements about 250 g and 100 g.

4 **Examples**   1.3 kg can be written as 1.300 kg $=$ 1300 g.

   26.12 kg can be written as 26.120 kg $=$ 26 120 g.

Note how 0's are written to make three figures after the point in the middle step. This is because 1000 g $=$ 1 kg.

How many grams is:
(a) 1.5 kg   (b) 1.7 kg   (c) 2.75 kg   (d) 3.16 kg   (e) 0.1 kg   (f) 0.01 kg
(g) 0.001 kg   (h) 0.06 kg   (i) 0.006 kg   (j) 0.0006 kg?

5 **Example** 675 g = 0.675 kg

Copy and complete:
(a) 3000 g = ... kg   (b) 2500 g = ... kg   (c) 2100 g = ... kg
(d) 2650 g = ... kg   (e) 1002 g = ... kg   (f) 1856 g = ... kg
(g) 856 g = ... kg   (h) 56 g = ... kg   (i) 6 g = ... kg.

6 How many 50 kg sacks can be loaded onto
the lorry in Figure 21:3?

Fig. 21:3

*7 Copy the following sentences, completing them with a weight chosen from:

7 g;   250 g;   1 kg;   45 kg;   0.5 tonne.

(a) Tina is 12 years old. She weighs ...
(b) A bag of sugar weighs ...
(c) A 2p coin weighs ...
(d) A packet of butter weighs ...
(e) Cy's car weighs ...

*8 Jane works in a grocer's shop. She weighs cheese on the scales in kilograms, but
has to write the weight on the label in grams. Figure 21:4 shows one example of
this.

Draw the scale reading and the label for:
(a) 0.268 kg of Mild Cheddar
(b) 0.682 kg of Stilton
(c) 0.100 kg of Cheshire
(d) 0.200 kg of Gruyère
(e) 0.250 kg of Wensleydale.

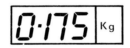

Fig. 21:4

Mild Cheddar
175g

*9 What would be the reading on the scales in Figure 21:4 when the weight is:
(a) 275 g   (b) 135 g   (c) 860 g   (d) 300 g   (e) 200 g   (f) 1000 g
(g) 2500 g?

*10 Write in grams:
(a) 1 kg   (b) 5 kg   (c) $\frac{1}{2}$ kg   (d) $\frac{1}{4}$ kg   (e) $\frac{3}{4}$ kg   (f) $1\frac{1}{2}$ kg   (g) $1\frac{1}{4}$ kg
(h) $1\frac{3}{4}$ kg.

*11 Change to grams:
(a) 6.5 kg   (b) 8.25 kg   (c) 0.168 kg   (d) 0.008 kg   (e) 1.006 kg
(f) 2.017 kg.

*12 How many kilograms make:
(a) 1 tonne   (b) 2 tonnes   (c) 5 tonnes   (d) 1.5 tonnes   (e) 2.5 tonnes?

| 9 g | 13.4 g | 5 g | 11.2 g | 5.6 g | 7 g | 3.5 g |

Fig. 21:5

13 (a) Find the weight of ten of each coin in Figure 21:5, giving your answer both in grams and in kilograms.

(b) Find the weight of £1's worth of 10p coins and the weight of £1's worth of 5p coins.

14 How much are the following worth?
(a) 35 g of 1p coins   (b) 70 g of 1p coins   (c) 70 g of 2p coins
(d) 70 g of mixed 1p and 2p coins   (e) 0.112 kg of 10p coins
(f) 0.112 kg of 5p coins

15 How many kilograms should the following weigh?
(a) £1's worth of 2p coins   (b) £1's worth of 1p coins
(c) £1's worth of mixed 2p and 1p coins
(d) £10's worth of mixed 10p and 5p coins

16 1 cm³ **(1 cubic centimetre) of water weighs 1 g.**

How many cm³ of water weigh:
(a) 1 kg   (b) 1 tonne   (c) 3.6 kg?

17 The tank in Figure 21:6 holds
$75 \times 50 \times 100$ cm³ of water.

(a) Where does the 100 come from?

(b) Work out how many cm³ of water there are in the tank.

(c) What would the water weigh in kg?

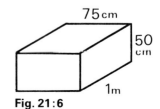

75 cm
50 cm
1 m
Fig. 21:6

18 How many kg of water could be held by:
   (a) a carton 15 cm by 12 cm by 7 cm
   (b) a match-box 5 cm by 4 cm by 1.5 cm
   (c) a cistern 0.5 m by 30 cm by 20 cm
   (d) a cube of side 100 mm?

19 People used to weigh themselves in stones and pounds (lb).

   1 lb $\triangleq$ 454 g ($\triangleq$ means 'is about equal to')

   14 lb = 1 stone

   You now need a sheet of 2 mm graph paper at least 200 mm by 150 mm.

   Draw axes, one for stones and one for kg, as in Figure 21:7.

   Mark 1 stone every 14 mm and 10 kg every 20 mm, going up to 11 stone and along to 70 kg.

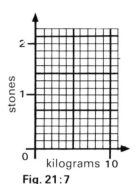

   Fig. 21:7

   (a) How many lb does one square represent?

   (b) How many kg does one square represent?

   (c) 0 kg = 0 st and 70 kg $\triangleq$ 11 st, giving the points (0,0) and (70,11). Plot these two points and join them accurately with a straight line.

20 Read off from your conversion graph how many kg are the same as:
   (a) 3 st   (b) 8 st   (c) 1 st 8 lb   (d) 2 st 10 lb   (e) 9 lb.

21 How many stones and pounds are equivalent to:
   (a) 20 kg   (b) 50 kg   (c) 31 kg?

22 Read off four more weights of your own. Find your own weight and your friends' and family's in:
   (a) kg   (b) st and lb.

23 Make card boxes to hold the following weights of water.
   (a) 1 g   (b) 10 g   (c) 100 g   (d) 1 kg

B Arithmetic in metric weight

For Discussion

Can I wash all this at the same time?

1 double sheet	1.1 kg	= 1 kg 100 g
1 single sheet	560 g	= 0 kg 560 g
3 pillowcases	339 g	= 0 kg 339 g
2 bath towels	1340 g	= 1 kg 340 g
2 hand towels	510 g	= 0 kg 510 g
3 pairs of pyjamas	1020 g	= 1 kg 020 g

Fig. 21:8

1 Figure 21:9 shows how Alan worked out
1 kg 162 g + 3 kg 18 g.

He got the wrong answer. Correct it for him.

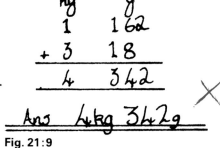

Fig. 21:9

2 (a) 2 kg 106 g + 1 kg 41 g   (b) 8 kg 316 g + 7 kg 29 g
(c) 7 kg 115 g + 1 kg 972 g   (d) 4 kg 273 g + 1 kg 888 g

3 Figure 21:10 shows how Anna worked out
3.6 g + 18 g.

She got the wrong answer. Correct it for her.

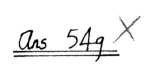

Fig. 21:10

4 (a) 5.4 g + 26 g   (b) 4.61 kg + 15.9 kg   (c) 5 kg + 4.6 kg + 0.39 kg
(d) 70 kg + 1.6 kg + 0.99 kg

5 Figure 21:11 shows how Irmar worked out
3 kg 57 g + 2 kg 98 g.

He got the wrong answer. Correct it for him.

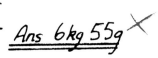

Fig. 21:11

6 (a) 8 kg 16 g + 5 kg 92 g   (b) 9 kg 27 g + 11 kg 81 g   (c) 8 kg 48 g + 4 kg 84 g
(d) 7 kg 6 g + 8 kg 7 g

7 **Example**   To find 18 kg − 4.62 kg

$$\begin{array}{r} 18.00 \text{ kg} \\ - 4.62 \text{ kg} \\ \hline 13.38 \text{ kg} \end{array}$$

(a) 17 kg − 1.28 kg   (b) 19 kg − 2.43 kg   (c) 15 kg − 4.66 kg
(d) 36 kg − 1.77 kg

8 (a) 212 × 6   (b) 0.212 kg × 6   (c) 3.8 kg ÷ 4   (d) 7.6 kg ÷ 5

9

Age in years	0	1	2	3	4	5	6	7	8	9
Weight in kg	3	9.5								

Neil's mum records his weight on his birthday each year. Copy and complete the table, using the chart shown in Figure 21:12 to read the weights.

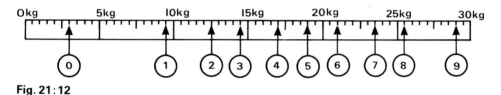

Fig. 21:12

10 From 0 to 1 years, Neil's weight *increased* by 6.5 kg.
The top rectangle in Figure 21:13 shows this, using the scale 5 mm to 0.5 kg.
Copy and complete the diagram, which is called a **bar-chart**.

WEIGHT INCREASE

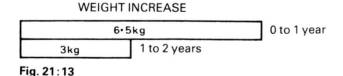

Fig. 21:13

11 **Example**   To add 1538 g to 7 kg.
          Write 1538 g as 1.538 kg.
          Then 1.538 kg + 7 kg = 8.538 kg.

Find in kg:
(a) 2316 g + 8 kg   (b) 4326 g − 3.75 kg   (c) 3016 g − 2.1 kg
(d) 126 g + 2 kg   (e) 8 kg + 417 g   (f) 15 kg − 15 g   (g) 46 g + 1.8 kg
(h) 134 g − 0.098 kg.

12 A recipe requires 250 g sugar and 50 g gelatine to provide 6 helpings. My scales read in kg. What should they read when I weigh the sugar and weigh the gelatine (two answers for each part) for:
(a) 6 helpings (b) 12 helpings (c) 3 helpings (d) 21 helpings?

13

Tess: 5.443 kg

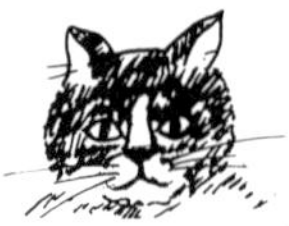

Nera: 2.381 kg

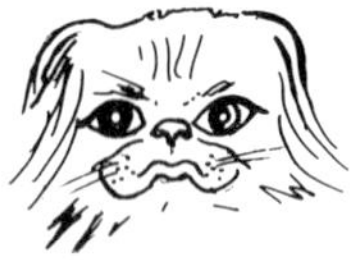

Chotapeg: 5 kg

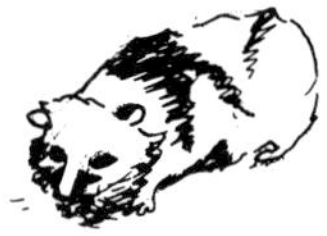

Pippa: 567 g

Fig. 21:14

(a) Write Pippa's weight in kg.
(b) What is the total weight of the four pets?
(c) How much heavier is Tess than Nera?
(d) How much heavier is Chotapeg than Pippa?

14 (a) If Chotapeg eats 200 g of food a day, how many grams of food per kg of body weight is he fed?

(b) If the others are fed at the same rate of 40 g food per 1 kg body weight, how many grams should each be fed per day, correct to the nearest gram?

(c) How many kg of food would each pet eat in a week?

15 Collect objects and pictures of objects whose weight you know or can find out. Make a display for your classroom, marking each weight in g, in kg, and in tonnes.

C Litre; centilitre; millilitre

1 cubic centimetre = 1 millilitre (1 ml)

1000 ml = 1 litre

Remember: centi means $\frac{1}{100}$ and milli means $\frac{1}{1000}$.

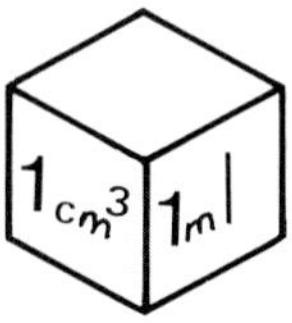

1cm³
1ml
Fig. 21:15

LUBE
LUBE
5
LITRES
J CURE
Contents 15cl
Take 1 5ml
spoonful three
times a day
Fig. 21:16

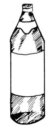

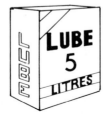

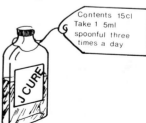

1 How many:
(a) cm in 1 m   (b) cg in 1 g   (c) cl in 1 litre   (d) mm in 1 m
(e) mg in 1 g   (f) ml in 1 litre   (g) cV in 1 V   (h) mV in 1 V
(i) V in 1 kV?

2 1 litre;   4 ml;   200 ml;   5 litres.

Which of the above capacities belongs to each object in Figure 21:17?

(a) 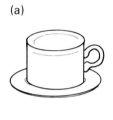   (b) 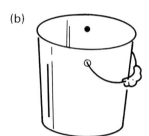   (c) 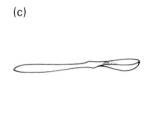   (d)

Fig. 21:17

3 How many ml in:
(a) 1 litre   (b) 5 litres   (c) $\frac{1}{2}$ litre   (d) $\frac{1}{4}$ litre   (e) 0.5 litre   (f) 0.4 litre
(g) 0.25 litre?

4 Write in litres:
(a) 6000 ml   (b) 600 ml   (c) 550 ml   (d) 555 ml.

*5 Copy and complete this table.

litres		2	3.5	4.5				0.01	0.001
ml	1000		3500		5500	6250	100		

6 How many 200 ml cupfuls would I require if a recipe requires:
(a) 1 litre   (b) 0.8 litre   (c) 0.6 litre   (d) $\frac{1}{2}$ litre?

7 Write in litres:
(a) 100 cl   (b) 1000 cl   (c) 500 cl   (d) 35 cl   (e) 8 cl 9 ml.

8 **1 ml = 1 cubic centimetre.**

(a) What is the weight of 1 cubic centimetre of water?

(b) What is the weight, in kg, of 1 litre of water?

9 State the weights of the following quantities of water, giving your answers both in kg and in g:
(a) 2 litres (b) 3.5 litres (c) 4.75 litres (d) 500 ml (e) 50 ml.

10 **1 litre = 1000 ml = 100 cl**

Copy the above statement, then write similar ones for:
(a) 1.5 litres (b) 1.45 litres (c) 1.555 litres (d) 0.15 litres
(e) 0.1 litres.

11 You may still find pints and gallons, the British or 'imperial' units of capacity, being used.

8 pints = 1 gallon; 1 gallon is about 4.5 litres (11 gallons is almost exactly 50 litres).

Copy accurately the scales given in Figures 21:18 and 21:19, which convert approximately between metric and imperial measures.

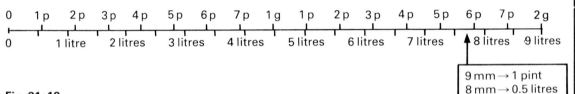

Fig. 21:18

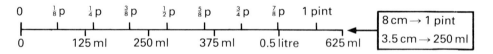

Fig. 21:19

12 Make a display of containers. Label each with its volume in ml and its volume in litres.

22 Common fractions: integer × fraction

For Discussion

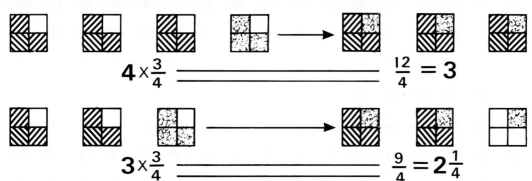

$$4 \times \frac{3}{4} \underline{} \frac{12}{4} = 3$$

$$3 \times \frac{3}{4} \underline{} \frac{9}{4} = 2\frac{1}{4}$$

Fig. 22:1

1 Draw a diagram like those in Figure 22:1 to show:

$$2 \times \frac{3}{4} = \frac{6}{4} = 1\frac{1}{2}.$$

2 Simplify to a single fraction:

(a) $3 \times \frac{1}{7}$ (b) $3 \times \frac{2}{7}$ (c) $\frac{3}{11} \times 3$ (d) $\frac{3}{7} \times 2.$

3 Example $4 \times \frac{8}{9} = \frac{32}{9} = 3\frac{5}{9}.$

Note: $3\frac{5}{9}$ from '9 into 32 goes 3 times with 5 left over'.

(a) $7 \times \frac{3}{4}$ (b) $\frac{3}{4} \times 7$ (c) $8 \times \frac{1}{5}$ (d) $9 \times \frac{2}{5}$ (e) $3 \times \frac{5}{8}$

4 Example $^{4}8 \times \frac{5}{\cancel{14}_7} = \frac{20}{7} = 2\frac{6}{7}.$

Note: 8 and 14 both divide by 2 (called '**cancelling**').

(a) $6 \times \frac{7}{16}$ (b) $5 \times \frac{9}{25}$ (c) $12 \times \frac{7}{16}$ (d) $35 \times \frac{1}{14}$ (e) $40 \times \frac{7}{25}$

*5   (a) $4 \times \frac{2}{9}$ (b) $7 \times \frac{1}{9}$ (c) $\frac{3}{25} \times 8$ (d) $2 \times \frac{14}{39}$ (e) $\frac{12}{41} \times 3$

*6 Simplify to a mixed number, as in the example in question 3:

(a) $2 \times \dfrac{3}{5}$ (b) $2 \times \dfrac{4}{5}$ (c) $3 \times \dfrac{4}{7}$ (d) $2 \times \dfrac{5}{7}$ (e) $4 \times \dfrac{5}{9}$ (f) $3 \times \dfrac{6}{11}$

*7 Cancel, as in the example for question 4:

(a) $8 \times \dfrac{3}{16}$ (b) $3 \times \dfrac{5}{6}$ (c) $8 \times \dfrac{1}{12}$ (d) $6 \times \dfrac{1}{9}$ (e) $12 \times \dfrac{3}{8}$ (f) $10 \times \dfrac{7}{15}$

(g) $\dfrac{6}{7} \times 14$ (h) $\dfrac{4}{5} \times 10$ (i) $20 \times \dfrac{7}{10}$ (j) $10 \times \dfrac{7}{20}$ (k) $10 \times \dfrac{4}{15}$

(l) $21 \times \dfrac{13}{28}$.

8 How many eighths make 7 whole ones?

The answer is 56 eighths, or $\dfrac{56}{8}$.

How many eighths make $7\frac{3}{8}$?

It must be $56 + 3 = 59$ eighths or $\dfrac{59}{8}$, so $7\dfrac{3}{8} = \dfrac{59}{8}$.

Note: An easy way to get the 59 is '$(8 \times 7) + 3$'.

Similarly: $5\dfrac{3}{7} = \dfrac{38}{7}$. (The 38 from '$(5 \times 7) + 3$'.)

Example $7\frac{3}{8} \times 12 \rightarrow \dfrac{59 \times \overset{3}{\cancel{12}}}{\underset{2}{\cancel{8}}} = \dfrac{177}{2} = 88\frac{1}{2}.$

Note: Set out your fractions as shown; it is very unwise to write $\dfrac{59}{8} \times 12$ and even worse to write $59/8 \times 12$.

(a) $4\frac{3}{8} \times 12$ (b) $3\frac{2}{5} \times 15$ (c) $4\frac{7}{12} \times 9$ (d) $3\frac{5}{9} \times 21$ (e) $16 \times 8\frac{7}{12}$

9 **Example** $\dfrac{\overset{2}{\cancel{8}}}{\underset{1}{\cancel{3}}\,\underset{3}{\cancel{12}}} \times \overset{3}{\cancel{9}} = 6$

Note: Either number, or both numbers, on the top line may be cancelled with the number on the bottom line.
8 and 12 are both divided by 4; 3 and 9 are both divided by 3.

(a) $\dfrac{4 \times 27}{18}$ (b) $\dfrac{3 \times 4}{21}$ (c) $9 \times 2\frac{1}{6}$ (Change $2\frac{1}{6}$ to $\frac{13}{6}$)

(d) $8 \times 3\frac{2}{5}$ (e) $\dfrac{12 \times 20}{15}$ (f) $\dfrac{100 \times 17}{20}$

10 Find $\dfrac{5}{8}$ of:

(a) £160   (b) £60.00   (c) £3.28   (d) £8.64   (e) £16.16   (f) £35.

11 A man leaves £186 000 in his will. His widow receives $\frac{7}{15}$ of this and his son receives $\frac{4}{15}$.

(a) His daughter receives the rest. What fraction is this?

(b) How much money does each person receive?

Fig. 22:2

12 A man is bailing out his punt with his boater. The boater hold $2\frac{3}{8}$ litres.

(a) How many litres can he bail out in 12 goes?

(b) How many litres can he bail in 5 min if he can bail every 2 seconds?

Fig. 22:3

13 Write the rules to find out whether a number divides by 2, 3, 5, 6 or 9. Look at exercise 10A if you need help. You could also learn that a number divides by 4 if the last two digits divide by 4, and by 8 if the last three digits divide by 8. Why must this be so?

14 Cancel to the simplest possible fraction:
(a) $\frac{30}{105}$ (b) $\frac{84}{70}$ (c) $\frac{294}{105}$ (d) $\frac{84}{126}$ (e) $\frac{198}{330}$ (f) $\frac{770}{231}$ (g) $\frac{78.}{26}$

15 Name the different shapes in the Tangram square shown in Figure 22:4. Say what fraction of the square each shape is. The pieces, cut out of card or gummed paper, can be used to make many pictures and shapes.

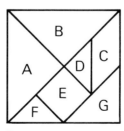

Fig. 22:4

23 Percentages: % ↔ fraction

A The idea of a percentage

In Figure 23:1, 23 out of the 100 squares have been shaded.

This could be written as a fraction:
$\frac{23}{100}$ of the diagram.

It could also be written as a percentage:
23% of the diagram.

The % sign is read as 'percent'.

$$\frac{23}{100} \rightarrow 23\%$$

Fig. 23:1

---

1 **100% is another way of saying 'all of them'.**

100% of the 500 pupils in Wheatley School are boys. How many boys are there in the school?

2 In his last exam, Bill scored 100%. The total possible mark was 200. How many marks did Bill get?

3 Write as a percentage:
(a) $\frac{24}{100}$ (b) $\frac{30}{100}$ (c) $\frac{80}{100}$ (d) 1 out of 100

(e) 56 out of a 100   (f) 84 out of a hundred.

4 (a) In a school, 40% of the pupils eat a school meal. What percentage do not?

(b) 75% of cats like Catto. What % do not?

(c) If 51% of the babies born in 1980 were girls, what % were boys?

(d) Mr Brown spends 87% of his wages. What percentage does he save?

5 In the U.S.A. the unit of money is the dollar. The sign for dollar is $.
$1 is split into 100 coins called cents. 1 cent is 1% of $1.

How many cents is:
(a) 16% of $1   (b) 34% of $1   (c) 19% of $1?

134

*6 (a) In Figure 23:2, what percentage of each diagram is shaded?

(b) Work out, without counting squares, what % of each diagram is *not* shaded.

   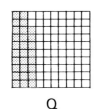   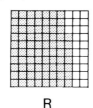   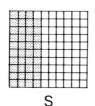   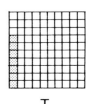

  P   Q   R   S   T

Fig. 23:2

*7

Test	Total Possible	Number Correct
A	100	68
B	100	72
C	100	45
D	100	80
E	100	70

(a) In five tests, Mary has the scores shown in the table. In Test A she scored 68 out of 100, or 68%. Write her percentage scores in the other tests.

(b) In Test A, Mary had 100 − 68 = 32 wrong. That is, she had 32% wrong. What % did she have wrong in the other tests?

(c) Add together your two answers for each test.
Example A→ 68% + 32% = 100% (Read→ as 'becomes'.)

*8 **100 pennies make £1, so 1p is 1% of £1.**

It follows that 6p is 6% of £1.

Write as a percentage of £1:
(a) 48p   (b) 16p   (c) 74p   (d) 100p.

*9 How many pence is:
(a) 1% of £1   (b) 16% of £1   (c) 35% of £1   (d) 100% of £1?

10 Example   To find 6% of £15.
6% of £1 = 6p
6% of £15 = 6p × 15 = 90p

Find:
(a) 6% of £2   (b) 6% of £12   (c) 1% of £2   (d) 5% of £3   (e) 15% of £4
(f) 70% of £2   (g) 80% of £20   (h) 65% of £25.

135

11 VAT (Value Added Tax) of 15% has to be added to each of the articles shown in Figure 23:3.

Example What VAT is payable on an article costing £9 before VAT is added?
15% of £9 = 15p × 9 = 135p = £1.35
Answer: The VAT to be paid is £1.35.

Find the VAT on the articles shown.

Fig. 23:3

12 What is the price of each article in Figure 23:3 when 15% VAT is included?

13 What is the missing percentage in each of the pie-charts shown in Figure 23:4?

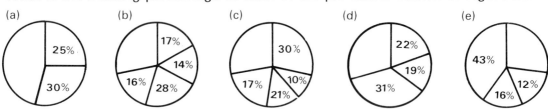

(a)   (b)   (c)   (d)   (e)

Fig. 23:4

14 Write sale tickets, like the one for a jumper in Figure 23:5, for: Blouse £10; Skirt £20; Coat £30; Shoes £15; Tights £1.50.

GRAND SALE
ALL PRICES REDUCED BY
20%
*   *

JUMPER was £6
NOW ONLY £4·80

Fig. 23:5

15 There are 360° at the centre of a circle.

(a) What is 1% of 360°?

(b) What is 24% of 360°?

(c) Write your answer to (b) to the nearest degree.

(d) Write each % of each circle in Figure 23:4 in degrees to the nearest degree. You may use a calculator.

(e) Draw accurate pie-charts for Figure 23:4.

B Percentage to fraction

% means 'out of 100'

Example $12\% = \dfrac{12}{100} = \dfrac{3}{25}$

Note: $\dfrac{12}{100}$ was cancelled to $\dfrac{3}{25}$ by dividing both 12 and 100 by 4.

1 Change the following percentages to fractions, cancelling each fraction to make it as simple as possible.
(a) 60%   (b) 20%   (c) 25%   (d) 75%   (e) 35%   (f) 24%   (g) 38%
(h) 57%   (i) 28%   (j) 62%

*2 Express the following percentages as simplified fractions.
(a) 10%   (b) 25%   (c) 5%   (d) 48%   (e) 80%   (f) 14%
(g) 60%   (h) 17%

*3 In an examination, 75% of the candidates passed. What fraction, as simply as possible, failed?

4 Example $57\% = \dfrac{57}{100} = 0.57$

Note: $\dfrac{57}{100}$ can be thought of as $57 \div 100$.

Moving the figures right two columns to divide by 100 gives 0.57

Change to a decimal fraction:
(a) 47%   (b) 68%   (c) 7%   (d) 9%   (e) 8%   (f) 1%.

5 Copy and complete the table. (Note: 0.3̇ is short for the recurring decimal 0.333333...)

Percentage	33⅓%	66⅔%	25%	50%	75%	10%
Fraction	$\frac{1}{3}$	$\frac{2}{3}$				
Decimal	0.3̇	0.6̇				

6 $10\% = \frac{1}{10}$; $25\% = \frac{1}{4}$; $50\% = \frac{1}{2}$; $75\% = \frac{3}{4}$; $33\frac{1}{3}\% = \frac{1}{3}$; $66\frac{2}{3}\% = \frac{2}{3}$

Learn the above facts. They will help you to answer the following questions.

Example   25% of 80 = $\frac{1}{4}$ of 80 = 20.

Find:
(a) 25% of 40   (b) 75% of 12   (c) 10% of 50   (d) 20% of 50
(e) 33⅓% of 90   (f) 50% of 240   (g) 66⅔% of 30   (h) 20% of 300
(i) 25% of £2   (j) 20% of £5   (k) 75% of 4 litres   (l) 50% of 1 kg.

7 A game is priced at £12. In a sale it is reduced by 25%. What is the new price?

8 In a class of 32 pupils, 75% passed an examination.

(a) How many pupils passed?

(b) How many pupils failed?

9 In a school, 20% of the pupils had measles. The school had 500 pupils.

(a) How many had measles?

(b) How many did not have measles?

10 At a football match, 40% of the spectators were men and 50% were children.

(a) What percentage of the spectators were women?

(b) If 10000 spectators watched the match, how many were men, how many were children, and how many were women?

11 The bar-chart in Figure 23:6 shows the hobbies of 1000 pupils at a school.

(a) How many pupils followed each hobby (or none)?

(b) How can you tell whether every pupil was asked?

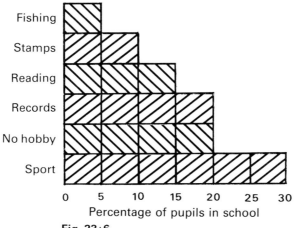

Fig. 23:6

12 A computer cost £5000 in 1980. What was its value in 1981 if it depreciated (dropped in value due to age) by 25%?

13 In a survey of the games pupils liked best, 25% said Rugby, 20% said Cross-country, 15% said Volley-ball, 30% said Soccer and 10% said they did not like any.
Change these percentages to fractions of 360° (see exercise 23A, question 15). Draw and label a pie-chart to show the results of the survey.

14 Design a survey of your own. Show the results on a pie-chart.

C   Fraction to percentage

To change a fraction to a percentage multiply it by 100%

A percentage is 'out of 100'. 50 is half of a hundred, so a half is 50%.

We could write: $\frac{1}{2} \rightarrow \frac{1}{2} \times 100\% = 50\%$.

Similarly: $\frac{3}{5} \rightarrow \frac{3}{5} \times 100\% \rightarrow \frac{3 \times \cancel{100}^{20}\%}{\cancel{5}_1} = 60\%$.

1 Change to a percentage:
(a) $\frac{17}{100}$ (b) $\frac{3}{4}$ (c) $\frac{7}{10}$ (d) $\frac{1}{5}$ (e) $\frac{3}{10}$ (f) $\frac{13}{20}$ (g) $\frac{1}{25}$ (h) $\frac{3}{20}$
(i) $\frac{17}{50}$ (j) $\frac{4}{5}$.

2 In Figure 23:7, three ways of showing the slope of the hill are illustrated.

Fig. 23:7   20 metres

Calculate the percentage slopes of the hills with the road signs shown in Figure 23:8.

(a)   (b) 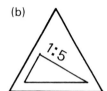   (c)   (d)

Fig. 23:8

3 Change to a percentage:
(a) $\frac{2}{10}$ (b) $\frac{9}{10}$ (c) $\frac{8}{10}$ (d) $\frac{2}{5}$ (e) $\frac{1}{4}$ (f) $\frac{7}{20}$ (g) $\frac{9}{20}$ (h) $\frac{4}{25}$.

4 To give one quantity as a fraction of another you must make the units the same. It is always best to change both quantities to the *smaller* unit.

Example   Express 7 m as a fraction of 1 km
$$\frac{7\,m}{1\,km} \rightarrow \frac{7\,m}{1000\,m} \rightarrow \frac{7}{1000}$$
Answer: 7 m is $\frac{7}{1000}$ of 1 km.

Example   Express 4p as a fraction of £1
$$\frac{4p}{£1} \rightarrow \frac{4p}{100p} \rightarrow \frac{4^1}{100_{25}} = \frac{1}{25}$$
Answer: 4p is $\frac{1}{25}$ of £1.

What fraction, as simply as possible, is:
(a) 1p of £1   (b) 6p of £1   (c) 1 cm of 1 m   (d) 20 m of 100 m
(e) 10 g of 1 kg   (f) 10 cm of 1 m   (g) 10 cm of 10 m   (h) 3 min of 1 h?

5 Change your answers to question 4 to percentages.

6 **Example** $0.35 = 0.35 \times 100\% = 35\%$

Write as a percentage:
(a) 0.50   (b) 0.36   (c) 0.67   (d) 0.9   (e) 0.09   (f) 0.08.

7 In an examination sat by 300 pupils, 240 passed.
(a) What fraction passed?   (b) What percentage passed?
(c) What percentage failed?

8 In a parish election, 420 out of 800 people voted. What % did *not* vote?

9 Change the following fractions to percentages, giving your answers as integers or mixed numbers. You may use a calculator.
(a) $\frac{1}{3}$ (b) $\frac{1}{4}$ (c) $\frac{4}{5}$ (d) $\frac{3}{8}$ (e) $\frac{9}{16}$ (f) $\frac{2}{7}$
(g) 0.385   (h) 0.025   (i) 0.235

10 In a series of tests out of 10, Michael scored 5, 7, 6, 4 and 8. He was absent twice. Find how this is recorded in the following table, then copy and complete it.

Name	Score out of 10							Total	Out of	Percentage
Michael	5	7	6	4	8	a	a	30	50	60%
David	4	8	7	3	a	a	9		50	
Stephen	6	5	a	7	9	5	10		60	
Eva	8	7	9	7	7	8	10			
Maria	7	3	8	5	7	6	6			
Nicola	9	9	5	7	9	3	7			
Alison	6	5	8	9	6	a	6			

11 The position of each pupil in question 10 can be found in two different ways, as shown in the following table.

Name	Position based on total	Position based on percentage
Michael	7th	6th
David		
etc.		

Copy and complete the table.
Which method of positioning do you think is fairer? Why?

12 How do you spend a normal day? Write down headings such as 'Sleep', 'School', 'Meals', 'Play', then list the time to the nearest half-hour which you spend on each. Change these times to fractions of a day, then to percentages of a day. Draw a bar-chart of the results.

A Further substitution

Reminders

$b + b + b = 3b = 3 \times b$

If $b = 9$ then $b + 3 = 9 + 3 = 12$ and $3b = 3 \times b = 3 \times 9 = 27$.

If $k = 3$ then $2k + 5 = 6 + 5 = 11$.

1 Simplify:
(a) $p + p$ (b) $p + p + p$ (c) $2 \times p$ (d) $3 \times p$.

2 In this question, $c = 7$. Find the value of:
(a) $c + 3$ (b) $2 + c$ (c) $c - 6$ (d) $c - 7$ (e) $10 - c$ (f) $7 - c$
(g) $c + c$ (h) $c - c$.

3 In this question, $d = 7$. Find the value of:
(a) $2d$ (b) $3d$ (c) $d + d + d$ (d) $4d$ (e) $d + d + d + d$.

4 In this question, $h = 8$. Find the value of:
(a) $2h$ (b) $2h + 1$ (c) $1 + 2h$ (d) $3h + 2$ (e) $2 + 3h$ (f) $2h - 1$
(g) $16 - 2h$ (h) $7h + 1$ (i) $4 + 6h$.

In questions 5 to 7, find the value of each expression if $a = 4$, $b = 7$, $c = 8$ and $d = 0$.

5 (a) $a + b$ (b) $b + c$ (c) $c + b$ (d) $a + c$ (e) $c + a$

6 (a) $c - a$ (b) $c - b$ (c) $a + b + c$ (d) $a + b + 1$ (e) $c - b + a$
(f) $a + c - b$ (g) $a + b - 2$

7 (a) ab (b) ac (c) bc (d) $2ab$ (e) $2ac$ (f) $2d$
(g) ad (h) $abcd$

*8 Copy and complete:
(a) $b + b = \ldots$ (b) $b + b + b + b = \ldots$ (c) $x + x = \ldots$ (d) $x + x + x = \ldots$
(e) $3f$ means $\ldots \times \ldots$ (f) $4a$ means $\ldots$

In questions 9 to 12, find the value of each expression if $w = 9$ and $k = 3$.

*9   (a) $w + 2$ (b) $w + 5$ (c) $4 + w$ (d) $2 + w$

*10   (a) $w - 2$ (b) $w - 6$ (c) $w - 7$ (d) $10 - w$ (e) $20 - w$

*11   (a) $2w$ (b) $w + w$ (c) $3w$ (d) $w + w + w$ (e) $5w$ (f) $6w$
      (g) $7w$ (h) $8w$

*12   (a) $2k + 4$ (b) $2k - 3$ (c) $5 + 2k$ (d) $7 - 2k$ (e) $3k + 1$ (f) $3k - 1$

*13   In this question, $r = 2$, $s = 5$ and $t = 7$. Find the value of:
     (a) $r + s$ (b) $s + r$ (c) $s - r$ (d) $t - s$ (e) $r + s + t$
     (f) $s + t + r$ (g) $t + s + r$.

*14   In this question, $r = 2$, $s = 5$ and $t = 7$. Copy and complete:
     (a) $rs = r \times s = 2 \times 5 = \ldots$
     (b) $st = s \times t = 5 \times \ldots = \ldots$
     (c) $rt = \ldots \times \ldots = \ldots \times \ldots = \ldots$
     (d) $2st = 2 \times s \times t = 2 \times 5 \times 7 = 10 \times 7 = \ldots$
     (e) $2rs = \ldots \times \ldots \times \ldots = \ldots \times \ldots \times \ldots = \ldots \times \ldots = \ldots$

15   If $a = 5$, $b = 8$ and $c = 18$, find the value of:
     (a) $2a + b$ (b) $2b + c$ (c) $a + 2b$ (d) $3a + b - c$ (e) $2a + 3b - c$
     (f) $\frac{b}{2}$ (g) $\frac{c}{3}$.

16   Arrange in order of size, biggest first:
     $n + 5$, $n + 7$, $n - 8$, $n - 3$, n.

17   **Example**   The perimeter of a regular hexagon of side s cm is $6s$ cm.

     State the perimeters of the following regular polygons, each of side s cm:
     (a) equilateral triangle   (b) square   (c) pentagon   (d) octagon.

18   Yasmin cannot count all the weeds in her garden! If there were x weeds to start
     with *each time*, how many would there be if:
     (a) Yasmin had pulled up 5 weeds
     (b) Yasmin had pulled up 3 weeds
     (c) 10 new weeds grew
     (d) the number of weeds doubled
     (e) the number of weeds increased ten times
     (f) the number of weeds halved?

Fig. 24:1

143

19 Bolts at Bill's Do-It-Yourself shop always cost twice as much as nuts.

Size A nuts cost x pence each; Size B nuts cost y pence each.

State the cost of:
(a) two size A nuts
(b) three size A nuts
(c) two size B nuts
(d) a size A bolt
(e) a size B bolt
(f) two size A bolts
(g) a size A nut and bolt
(h) a size B nut and bolt
(i) two size A nuts and bolts.

Fig. 24:2

20 The nuts in question 19 increase in price by 2p each.

State the new price of:
(a) a size A nut   (b) a size B nut   (c) two size A nuts   (d) a size A bolt
(e) a size B bolt.

21 Raj has x pence and Anna has y pence. How many pence have they altogether?

22 Ann has p rings and Jill has q rings. How many rings have they altogether?

23 For the increased prices in question 20, state the total cost of:
(a) one nut of each size   (b) one bolt of each size   (c) two nuts of each size
(d) two bolts of each size   (e) four nuts and two bolts of each size.

---

24 You may use a calculator in this question.

If $a = 2.5$, $b = 7.6$ and $c = 1.32$, find the value of:
(a) $3a$ (b) $5b$ (c) $9a$ (d) $3a + b - c$ (e) $2a + 3b - c$
(f) $\dfrac{b}{2}$ (g) $\dfrac{c}{3}$ (h) $\dfrac{b}{4}$ (i) $\dfrac{c}{6}$ (j) $\dfrac{c}{9}$.

25 Find the values of a, b, c, d and e when:
$$\frac{2}{3} = \frac{a}{6} = \frac{b}{15} = \frac{8}{c} = \frac{d}{21} = \frac{18}{e}.$$

26 If $a = 2$, $b = 3$ and $c = 4$, try to write expressions that equal 0, 1, 2, 3, 4, etc. using only a, b, c and suitable signs.

B   Further notation

> In algebra, multiplication signs may be omitted
> but plus or minus signs must be retained.

Example $2 \times a + 3 \times b \times c$ can be shortened to $2a + 3bc$.

1 Write in a shorter form:
(a) $3 \times a$ (b) $4 \times a \times b$ (c) $2 \times s + 3 \times t$
(d) $5 \times s + 7 \times t$ (e) $4 \times m - 3 \times n$ (f) $4 \times e - 3 \times f \times g$.

2 Write out in full, as in question 1:
(a) $6s$ (b) $3xy$ (c) $2abc$ (d) $5pqr$
(e) $7a + 3b$ (f) $4ab + 2c$.

*3 Write out in full, as in question 1:
(a) $3d$ (b) $4x$ (c) $7d$ (d) $7fg$ (e) $4ab$ (f) $2a + 3$
(g) $4d + 7$ (h) $4m - 3n$.

In questions 4 to 6, find the value of each expression if $a = 7$, $b = 4$, $c = 1$ and $d = 0$.

4 (a) $5b + 2$ (b) $4a - 9$ (c) $23 + 37c$ (d) $76 + 5d$ (e) $11a - 9$

5 (a) $2a + b$ (b) $3a + c$ (c) $4a - d$ (d) $5a - 2c$ (e) $7b + 5a$

6 (a) ab (b) $ab + c$ (c) $ab - c$ (d) $ab - 3b$ (e) $6a + 5ad$
(f) abc (g) $3bc$ (h) $2abc + b$ (i) $abc + bc$ (j) $49abcd$

---

7 You should be able to answer this question without a calculator!

If $a = 2.3$, $b = 7.6$ and $c = 0.18$, find the value of:

(a) ab (b) $b - a$ (c) $b - c$ (d) $a - c$ (e) $a - 2c$ (f) $2b - c$
(g) $4a - 2c$ (h) $5b - 3c$ (i) $5c + 3a$ (j) bc (k) abc (l) $10a$

(m) $10c$ (n) $100a$ (o) $100b$ (p) $100c$ (q) $\frac{b}{2}$ (r) $\frac{a}{4}$ (s) $\frac{c}{6}$

(t) $\frac{c}{3}$ (u) $\frac{c}{18}$ (v) $\frac{ab}{8}$ (w) $\frac{bc}{5}$ (x) $\frac{ac}{10}$.

A The 12-hour clock

Fig. 25:1

Stands the church clock at ten to three?
And is there honey still for tea?

From 'Granchester' by Rupert Brooke

1 How many seconds are there in:
(a) 1 min (b) $\frac{1}{2}$ min (c) $\frac{1}{4}$ min (d) $\frac{3}{4}$ min?

2 How many minutes make:
(a) 1 hour (b) $\frac{1}{2}$ hour (c) $\frac{1}{4}$ hour (d) $\frac{3}{4}$ hour (e) $\frac{1}{3}$ hour?

3 How many hours are there in:
(a) 1 day (b) $\frac{1}{2}$ day (c) $\frac{3}{4}$ day (d) $\frac{1}{3}$ day?

4 The time on the clock in Figure 25:2 is 'Quarter past six' or '6:15'.

Fig. 25:2

Write in both words and figures the times on the clocks in Figure 25:3.

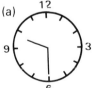 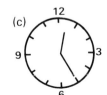 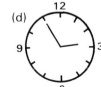 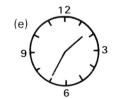

Fig. 25:3

146

*5 Write in words and figures the times on the clocks in Figure 25:4.

(a) 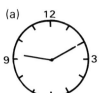 (b) 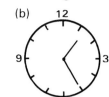 (c) 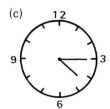 (d) 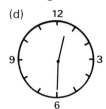 (e)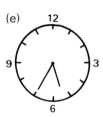

Fig. 25:4

6 If the clocks in Figure 25:4 are all 20 min fast, what is the correct time, in words?

7 Repeat question 6 if the same clocks are all 10 min slow.

8 Eight girls take part in a sponsored silence. Write, in figures, the time when each makes a noise if they start together at 7:40 a.m. and last out for the following times. Ann, 10 min; Babs, 20 min; Cath, 30 min; Di, 45 min; Eva, 50 min; Fay, 2 h 35 min; Gina, 5 h; Helga, 6 h 25 min.

9 A boy takes 45 minutes to cycle to his friend's house.

When should he set out (in figures) if he wants to arrive at:
(a) 5:50 p.m.   (b) 9:15 p.m.   (c) 6:25 p.m.   (d) half past twelve p.m.
(e) five to six p.m.   (f) ten past one p.m.?

10 Find the number of minutes to the next complete hour from:
(a) 9:36   (b) 11:41   (c) 1:16   (d) 9:18   (e) 3:43   (f) 5:11

11 Five pupils take the following times to do their homework. If they all finish at ten minutes to ten, at what time (in figures) did each start?
(a) 20 min   (b) 35 min   (c) 50 min   (d) 1 h 5 min   (e) 2 h 10 min

12 Through how many degrees does the hour hand rotate in:
(a) 1 h   (b) 4 h   (c) 6 h   (d) $8\frac{1}{2}$ h   (e) $11\frac{1}{2}$ h   (f) $3\frac{1}{4}$ h?

13 Through how many degrees does the minute hand rotate in:
(a) 1 min   (b) 10 min   (c) 25 min   (d) 35 min   (e) 1 h
(f) 1 h 15 min   (g) 1 h 35 min?

14 What is the angle between the minute hand and the hour hand at:
(a) half past two (*not* 120°!)   (b) twenty to five   (c) twenty past seven?

B The 24-hour clock

For Discussion

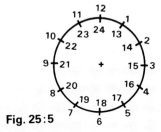

Midnight: 0000	4 a.m.: 0400
Midday: 1200	4 p.m.: 1600
4.21 p.m.: 1621	Five to eleven at night: 2255

Fig. 25:5

Yeovil (Eliott's Drive–Runnymede Road)   Western National 463

Eliott's Drive	0840	0925	1025	1125	1225	—	1325	1425	1525	1625	1725	1755	2055	2155
Westfield Grove	0843	0928	1028	1128	1228	—	1328	1428	1528	1628	1728	1758	2058	2158
Kingston *Bus Shelter*	0848	0933	1033	1133	1233	—	1333	1433	1533	1633	1733	1803	2103	2203
Middle Street *Co-op*	0853	0938	1038	1138	1238	1308	1338	1438	1538	1638	1738	1808	2108	2208
Allingham Road	—	0945	1045	1145	1245	1315	1345	1445	1545	1645	1745	—	2115	2215
Monmouth Hall	—	0947	1047	1147	1247	1317	1347	1447	1547	1647	1747	—	2117	2217
Runnymede Road	—	0950	1050	1150	1250	1320	1350	1450	1550	1650	1750	—	2120	2220

Fig. 25:6

1 Write in 24-hour clock time:
(a) 3 a.m.   (b) 7 a.m.   (c) 9 a.m.   (d) 11 a.m.   (e) 3 p.m.   (f) 7 p.m.
(g) 9:15 a.m.   (h) 7:45 p.m.   (i) twenty to eight p.m.

2 Write in a.m./p.m. time:
(a) 0800   (b) 0600   (c) 1400   (d) 2300   (e) 0516   (f) 1824.

3 Copy and complete these tables.

MORNING (a.m.)

12-hour time	4:20	5:35	6:42				11:15
24-hour time				0700	0920	1036	

AFTERNOON/EVENING (p.m.)

12-hour time	1:20		3:04		9:15	10:35	
24-hour time	1320	1404		1806			2321

4 Write in both 12-hour and 24-hour time:
(a) ten past eight in the morning   (b) five past two in the morning
(c) half past four in the morning   (d) half past four in the afternoon
(e) ten minutes to five in the afternoon   (f) twenty to eight in the evening.

5 Design a 24-hour clock face marked from 1 to 24 instead of 1 to 12. Through what angle does the hour hand travel in one hour? Show the times in question 3 on some sketches of the face. Why do you think this sort of design has not been adopted?

C Arithmetic in time

For Discussion

ROME by AIRBUS/B.727 of ALITALIA
Weekend arrangements   28/4 to 27/10
Out on Thursday home on Monday
12.10 dep	HEATHROW ↑	arr 18.05
15.30 arr ↓	ROME	dep 16.35
	FIUMICINO	
baggage allowance 20 kgs

VENICE* by B.757 of AIR EUROPE
Weekly on Saturday   30/3 to 24/9
| 08.15 dep | GATWICK ↑ | arr 13.35 |
| 11.15 arr ↓ | VENICE | dep 12.30 |
baggage allowance 20 kgs

PISA by DC9 of ALITALIA
Weekend arrangements   28/4 to 27/10
Out on Thursday home on Monday
| 09.00 dep | HEATHROW ↑ | arr 18.30 |
| 12.05 arr ↓ | PISA | dep 17.45 |
baggage allowance 20 kgs

RIMINI by B.737 of BRITANNIA AIRWAYS
Weekly on Sunday   22/5 to 11/9
| 09.45 dep | GATWICK ↑ | arr 14.45 |
| 12.55 arr ↓ | RIMINI | dep 13.40 |
baggage allowance 20 kgs

Fig. 25:7

Questions 1, 2 and 3 refer to the Radio 2 programme details shown in Figure 25:8.

1 How long does the afternoon sports programme last?

2 The Kenny Everett programme lasted 117 minutes. What time did the printer omit to show for 'Oh Mother!'?

3 How long do the following programmes last, in hours and minutes:
(a) David Jacobs   (b) Big Band Special?

4 Give the number of hours and minutes from:

(a) 1400 to 1800   (b) 0900 to 1200
(c) 0600 to 2300   (d) 0930 to 1200
(e) 0815 to 1630   (f) 1240 to 1345.

TWO	
5 00	Peter Marshall: S.
8 02	Racing Bulletin.
8 05	David Jacobs: S.
10 00	Gilbert O'Sullivan, with Star Choice: S.
11 02	Sports Desk.
11 03	Kenny Everett: S. Oh Mother! Rpt.
1 30	Sports, including Doncaster races at **2**, **2.30** and **3.05** (St Leger), plus Classified Results at **5.45**; Athletics; Cricket; Football – Half-time scores at **3.45**, Commentary from **4**, Classified Results at **5** & Pools at **5.50**.
6 00	Country Greats in Concert, rpt.
7 00	Three in a Row.
7 30	Sports Desk.
7 33	Big Band Special: S.
8 00	Robert Farnon's World of Music: S.
9 00	Last Night of the Proms (simultaneous broadcast with BBC 1 TV): S.
10 20	A Century of Music: S, rpt.
11 20	Sports Desk.
11 28	Pete Murray: S.
2 00-5	Richard Clegg: S.
VHF: 1 p.m.-7.30 As Radio 1.	

Fig. 25:8

*5 How long does each of the following buses take to travel from Rygate to Ford?

	(a)	(b)	(c)	(d)	(e)	(f)	(g)
Dep. Rygate	0900	1000	1030	1035	1040	1110	1125
Arr. Ford	1030	1130	1135	1245	1157	1205	1315

*6 Draw the watch faces in Figure 25:9 as they will appear in:
(a) 1 h   (b) 30 min   (c) 15 min.

 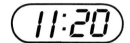  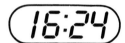

Fig. 25:9

*7 Draw the watch faces in Figure 25:9 as they were:
(a) 1 h ago   (b) 30 min ago   (c) 15 min ago.

8 Referring to Figure 25:8 (page 149):

(a) There are ten stereo (S) programmes. What is their total running time in hours and minutes? (Note: The Kenny Everett programme lasts 117 min.)

(b) The Pete Murray programme was on for the same time each Saturday for ten weeks. What was its total running time in hours and minutes?

9 Draw the watch faces in Figure 25:10 as they will appear in:
(a) 1 h 30 min   (b) 2 h 45 min   (c) 4 h 35 min   (d) 20 h 34 min.

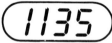  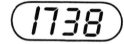

Fig. 25:10

10 What time would have been shown on each watch in Figure 25:10:
(a) 9 h earlier   (b) 2 h 15 min earlier   (c) 2 h 30 min earlier
(d) 4 h 50 min earlier?

11 Twelve people are to run in a sponsored relay. Each person is to run for 40 min. (a) For how long will they run altogether (in minutes)? (b) Change your answer to (a) to hours. (c) If the runners average 12 km/h, how far will they go altogether? (d) If they collect £2 for every kilometre run, how much will they receive? (e) How long must the fifth runner wait before she starts?

D   The calendar

30 days hath September, April, June and November. All the rest have 31, excepting February alone which has but 28 days clear, or 29 in each leap year.

Note: Every fourth year is a leap year, when February has 29 days. In a leap year the number made up of the last two figures divides exactly by 4. A normal year has 365 days, but a leap year has 366 days.

1   How many days are there in:
   (a) May   (b) December   (c) April   (d) October   (e) June?

2   (a) How many days are there in a week?

   (b) How many weeks are there in a year?

   (c) Is your answer to part (b) exact? If not, how many days are left over in a normal year?

3   Which of the following were leap years?
   1944, 1973, 1978, 1980, 1958, 1952.

4   **Example**   21st June 1972 can be written 21.6.72.

   Write in full:
   (a) 18.10.43   (b) 25.6.69   (c) 25.7.66.

5   Write in figures:
   (a) 21st Jan. 1964   (b) 10th May 1968   (c) 21st Nov. 1969.

6   If Feb. 1st is a Friday, what day is:
   (a) 5th Feb.   (b) 8th Feb.   (c) 15th Feb.   (d) 27th Feb.?

*7   Write the months of the year in order, saying how many days there are in each.

*8   Write in figures:
   (a) 4th May 1976   (b) 21st March 1970   (c) 31st December 1974
   (d) 16 June 1978   (e) 14 February 1974   (f) July 2nd, 1941.

*9   Write in full:
   (a) 6.4.75   (b) 9.8.71   (c) 8.11.51   (d) 18.11.81   (e) 11.11.11

*10 Which of the following were leap years?
1904, 1937, 1948, 1950, 1960, 1982.

*11 If May 3rd is a Sunday, what day that year is:
(a) May 10th   (b) May 19th   (c) June 1st?

12 January 1st 1981 was a Thursday. What day was January 1st in 1982?

13 Write the next leap year after each of the years in question 10.

14 Christmas Day 1979 was a Tuesday. On what day was Christmas Day in:
(a) 1980   (b) 1981?

15 The pirate Captain Kidd was born on 10th June 1645. He was hanged on 23rd May 1701. How many years old was he when he died?

16 How many days are there *inclusively* (that is, including the ones given) from:
(a) 3rd June to 6th June (*not* 3 days)
(b) 1st March to 21st May
(c) 1st July to 10th September
(d) 8th August to 9th December
(e) 10th December to 11th January
(f) 9.7.91 to 2.9.92?

17 At Jan's school, Assembly takes 30 minutes. Morning lessons are each 40 min, morning break is 20 min, afternoon registration is 10 min, and afternoon lessons are each 35 min. Copy Jan's timetable and write in the starred times.

0850   *   *   *   *   *   *

Assembly time	Lesson 1	Lesson 2	Break	Lesson 3	Lesson 4

1330   *   *   *   *

Registration	Lesson 5	Lesson 6	Lesson 7

18 In question 17: (a) How long is lunch-break? (b) How long is spent in lessons each day? (c) How long is spent in school in a five-day week (including lunch-breaks)?

19 Make a similar timetable for your school day.

A Rounding numbers

For Discussion

Which amounts in Figure 26:1 are **exact** and which are **approximate**? How approximate do you think they are, e.g. the nearest 1; the nearest 100?

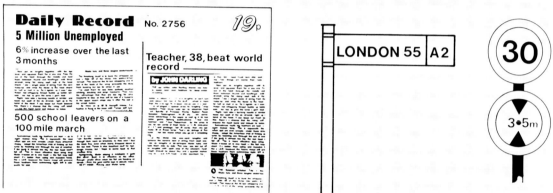

Fig. 26:1

The following examples show you how to round numbers.

If the 'key-figure' is 5 or more, increase the figure in front of it by 1.

Example Round 624 to the nearest ten.

H T U
6 2 4 → 620.

tens figure   key figure

Round 746 to the nearest ten.

H T U
7 4 6 → 750.

tens figure   key figure

Round 8248 to the nearest hundred.

Th H T U
8 2 4 8 → 8200.

hundreds figure   key figure

1 $A = \{27, 43, 57, 92, 161\}$ $B = \{248, 326, 758, 8264\}$
$C = \{1264, 9040, 9456, 17848\}$

(a) Write the elements of sets A, B and C rounded to the nearest ten.

(b) Write the elements of sets B and C rounded to the nearest 100.

(c) Write the elements of set C rounded to the nearest 1000.

*2 Copy and complete this table.

Number	26	42	78	126	141	258	924	2436
to nearest 10								

*3 Copy and complete this table.

Number	726	4841	7264	946	881	1160	5243	150
to nearest 100								

*4 Copy and complete this table.

Number	8264	9401	18 206	99 449	3526	4710
to nearest 1000						

5 $L = \{£3.72, £4.86, £5.21, £8.96\}$

$C = \{3 \text{ cm } 2 \text{ mm}, 3 \text{ cm } 8 \text{ mm}, 3.6 \text{ cm}, 3.1 \text{ cm}\}$

$M = \{3 \text{ m } 45 \text{ cm}, 10 \text{ m } 94 \text{ cm}, 6 \text{ m } 3 \text{ cm}, 9 \text{ m } 51 \text{ cm}\}$

Write set L to the nearest pound, set C to the nearest centimetre, and set M to the nearest metre.

6 **Example** 97 to the nearest ten becomes 100, because the key figure (7) tells you to increase the 9 by 1.

Example 397 to the nearest ten becomes 400.

$A = \{96, 4897, 7299, 1395, 97, 298\}$
$B = \{6974, 974, 724965, 12961, 2975, 9971\}$

Write the elements of set A to the nearest ten and the elements of set B to the nearest hundred.

7 Measure some objects around you, draw them and write their measurements rounded to: (a) the nearest cm (b) the nearest 10 cm.

B Using approximations

When shopping, approximation helps you make sure that you have enough money to pay for your goods. Round to the nearest 10p and add 'as you go'.

If goods cost: 48p + 96p + £1.15 + £3.97 + 16p + 32p + 41p + 63p + 49p = £8.57
Then add up: 50 + 100 + 120 + 400 + 20 + 30 + 40 + 60 + 50 = 870

1 Find to the nearest ten pence:
(a) 46p   (b) 38p   (c) 24p   (d) 93p   (e) 37p   (f) 71p.

2 **Example**   46p × 37 → 50p × 40 = 2000p = £20 approximately.

Using your answers to question 1, find an approximate value for the following.
(a) 46p × 38   (b) 24p × 93   (c) 37p × 71
(d) 46p + 38p + 24p + 93p + 37p + 71p.

3 Calculate the exact values of questions 2 (a) to (d).

4 **Example**   46p × 37 is £17.02 exactly. The approximation of £20 in the example for question 2 is £2.98 out.

How much out is each of your approximate answers in question 2?

5 Write to the nearest whole number:
(a) 7.406   (b) 294.83   (c) 46.27   (d) 958.724   (e) 13.008

*6 Find to the nearest £:
(a) 680p   (b) 510p   (c) 694p   (d) 224p   (e) 930p   (f) 641p
(g) 392p   (h) 489p.

*7 Using your answers to question 6, find an approximate value for:
(a) £6.80 + £5.10 + £2.24   (b) £2.24 + £9.30 + £6.41   (c) £6.41 + £3.92 + £4.89

*8 Find the exact values of question 7 (a) to (c).

*9 By rounding each number to the nearest ten, find an approximate answer to:
(a) 47 + 36 + 81 + 92   (b) 21 + 46 + 87 + 93   (c) 87 − 46   (d) 93 − 47.

*10 Find the exact values of question 9 (a) to (d).

11 Copy and complete this table. Be careful to round to the nearest *thousand*.

Ground	Spurs	Forest	Stoke	Luton	Villa	Total crowd
Crowd exactly	28746	48231	32421	41646	24349	exactly
Crowd to the nearest 1000						roughly

12 A litre of paint covers about 9 m². How many litres should be bought to give two coats of paint to a wall:
(a) 15 m by 3 m (b) 13 m by 4 m?

13 'I am 184 cm 8.26 mm tall' is a silly thing to say. Why? What would be more sensible?

14 An approximation for the area of an irregular shape can be found by counting squares inside it. A square is counted only if more than half of it is inside the shape. Find approximations for the areas of the leaves in Figure 26:2, first by counting using the centimetre squares, then more accurately by using the small squares. Each small square is $\frac{1}{25}$ cm² or 0.04 cm². Put a piece of tracing paper over the diagrams to avoid marking the book.

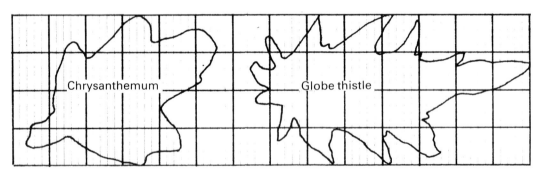

Fig. 26:2

15 Suggest something that it would be sensible to measure to:
(a) the nearest 100 (b) the nearest cm (c) the nearest km
(d) the nearest kg (e) the nearest £1.

16 Write six things that can be found:
(a) exactly (b) to within 1 mm.

17 Write six things that could never be found exactly.

27 Equations

A One-stage equations

Reminders   **7k is shorthand for 7 × k**

$\dfrac{k}{7}$ **is shorthand for k ÷ 7**

One important use of algebra is to 'solve equations'.

An **equation** will always have an equals sign and at least one letter, like the ones in the questions that follow.

An equation is **solved** by finding the value of the letter.

For Discussion

In Figure 27:1, seven KAT-KITS cost 84p. If one KAT-KIT costs k pence we could write the equation $7k = 84$. But $7 \times 12 = 84$, so the solution of this equation is $k = 12$.

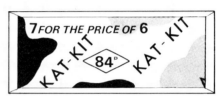

Fig. 27:1

In each of questions 1 to 11, find the values of the letters.

1   (a) $2d = 4$ (b) $7f = 14$ (c) $8d = 24$ (d) $9h = 63$ (e) $3w = 153$

2   (a) $n + 8 = 10$ (b) $n + 3 = 15$ (c) $n + 7 = 11$ (d) $13 - f = 10$

3   (a) $7 - a = 0$ (b) $16 - a = 9$ (c) $14 + a = 21$ (d) $a - 6 = 0$

4   (a) $\dfrac{s}{2} = 4$ (b) $\dfrac{d}{2} = 2$ (c) $\dfrac{e}{2} = 1$ (d) $\dfrac{x}{3} = 3$ (e) $\dfrac{e}{3} = 9$ (f) $\dfrac{h}{4} = 10$

*5   (a) $3x = 6$ (b) $4r = 8$ (c) $2w = 10$ (d) $3n = 12$ (e) $4x = 16$

*6   (a) $7g = 28$ (b) $10p = 80$ (c) $10p = 100$ (d) $16q = 32$ (e) $6x = 0$

*7   (a) $n + 4 = 6$ (b) $n + 1 = 8$ (c) $a + 3 = 5$ (d) $a + 11 = 15$ (e) $3 - y = 1$

*8   (a) $4 - a = 2$ (b) $6 - b = 2$ (c) $6 - b = 3$ (d) $14 - x = 1$ (e) $15 - y = 0$

*9   (a) $\dfrac{x}{2} = 3$ (b) $\dfrac{a}{2} = 4$ (c) $\dfrac{a}{3} = 2$ (d) $\dfrac{x}{2} = 5$ (e) $\dfrac{a}{4} = 4$

10 (a) $3 + x = 4.5$ (b) $23 + x = 27.6$ (c) $8.3 + x = 9.2$ (d) $5.1 - a = 4.2$

11 (a) $\dfrac{a}{5} = 15$ (b) $19x = 513$ (c) $\dfrac{30}{x} = 5$ (d) $\dfrac{100}{x} = 25$ (e) $\dfrac{10}{x} = \tfrac{1}{2}$

12 The equation $3h = 12$ can be thought of as 'When h is multiplied by 3 the answer is 12.'

This can be written as a flow-diagram: $h \rightarrow \times 3 \rightarrow 12$

Write a flow-diagram for: (a) $4x = 8$ (b) $5x = 15$ (c) $7x = 21$.

13 **Example** $3v = 12$ can be written: $v \rightarrow \times 3 \rightarrow 12$

Reversing the flow: $v \leftarrow \div 3 \leftarrow 12$

Note that we change the $\times 3$ to $\div 3$.

The second flow-diagram tells us that $12 \div 3 = v$, so that $v = 4$ is the solution to $3v = 12$.

Reverse your flow-diagrams for question 12 and find the values of a. Check that your answers are correct.

14 **Example**   Write a flow-diagram solution for $g + 7 = 10$.

$g \rightarrow + 7 \rightarrow 10$
$g \leftarrow - 7 \leftarrow 10$ (Note that $+7$ has become -7.)

The reversed flow-diagram tells us that $10 - 7$ equals g, so g must be 3.

Write a flow-diagram solution for:
(a) $g + 9 = 15$ (b) $h + 6 = 13$ (c) $p - 2 = 6$
(d) $k - 3 = 15$ (e) $x - 16 = 94$ (f) $q - 1.5 = 3.2$

---

15 The flow-diagram for $12 - n = 8$ is $n \rightarrow -$ from $12 \rightarrow 8$.

This reverses to: $n \leftarrow -$ from $12 \leftarrow 8$.

Note that '$-$ from 12' has not changed. To see why, try the following:
(a) Start with 1. Add 3. Take 3 from the answer.
(b) Start with 1. Multiply by 3. Divide the answer by 3.
(c) Start with 1. Take it away from 12. Take the answer away from 12.

In each case you arrive back at 1 again, but in (c) you performed the same operation twice.

Write flow-diagram solutions for questions 7, 8 and 9.

B   Two-stage equations

Example   Solve $3a + 5 = 20$.

Step One: $3a$ must be 15, because $15 + 5 = 20$.
Step Two: If $3a = 15$ then a must be 5, because $3 \times 5 = 15$.
Answer: $a = 5$.

In each of questions 1 to 11, find the values of the letters.

1 (a) $2a + 9 = 11$ (b) $3a + 2 = 14$ (c) $5x + 4 = 29$ (d) $7a - 3 = 11$

2 (a) $3a - 9 = 6$ (b) $4 + 3n = 13$ (c) $11 + 3s = 20$ (d) $4 - 2x = 0$

3 (a) $7 - 3x = 1$ (b) $14 - 2x = 0$ (c) $17 - 4d = 9$ (d) $2s - 1.5 = 6.5$

*4 (a) $d + 5 = 11$ (b) $2e + 5 = 11$ (c) $3x + 5 = 11$ (d) $4s + 1 = 9$

*5 (a) $c - 3 = 15$ (b) $2n - 3 = 15$ (c) $3p - 3 = 15$ (d) $6t - 3 = 15$

*6 (a) $7x - 1 = 20$ (b) $f - 6 = 0$ (c) $6g - 6 = 0$ (d) $12x - 1 = 23$

*7 (a) $7 - q = 1$ (b) $19 - a = 10$ (c) $14 - x = 9$ (d) $7 - 2x = 1$

8 (a) $\dfrac{m}{4} = 2$ (b) $\dfrac{2m}{4} = 2$ (c) $\dfrac{6x}{3} = 4$ (d) $\dfrac{5x}{2} = 10$

9 (a) $\dfrac{30}{x} = 3$ (b) $\dfrac{30}{2x} = 3$ (c) $\dfrac{14}{2x} = 1$ (d) $\dfrac{24}{3x} = 8$

10 (a) $\dfrac{d}{2} + 3 = 5$ (b) $\dfrac{c}{4} + 7 = 8$ (c) $\dfrac{v}{6} - 3 = 1$ (d) $\dfrac{x}{8} - 7 = 0$

11 (a) $3 - \dfrac{x}{2} = 2$ (b) $4 - \dfrac{x}{5} = 2$ (c) $16 - \dfrac{b}{3} = 12$ (d) $12 - \dfrac{2d}{3} = 10$

12 If you did not complete exercise 27A, do so now.

13 Example Solve $30 - \dfrac{3v}{4} = 24$ using the flow-diagram method.

$v \rightarrow \times 3 \rightarrow \div 4 \rightarrow -$ from $30 \rightarrow 24$

$v \leftarrow \div 3 \leftarrow \times 4 \leftarrow -$ from $30 \leftarrow 24$

The reverse flow gives $6 \times 4 \div 3$ which is 8.

The solution is $v = 8$.

Note that '$-$ from 30' does not change (see exercise 27A question 15).

Example Solve $\dfrac{18}{3v} = 2$ using the flow-diagram method.

$v \rightarrow \times 3 \rightarrow \div$ into $18 \rightarrow 2$

$v \leftarrow \div 3 \leftarrow \div$ into $18 \leftarrow 2$

The reverse flow gives 2 divided into 18, which is 9, divided by 3, which is 3.

The solution is $v = 3$.

Note that '$\div$ into 18' does not change. Check that this is correct as in exercise 27A question 15.

Write flow-diagram solutions for questions 7 to 11.

---

14 For each of the following problems, make up an equation and solve it. (You may find it easy to do these problems in your head, but they do show you the method to use when the questions are a lot harder.)

(a) A boy doubles a number, then adds on 3, making 15. Find the number. (Start: $2x + 3 = \ldots$)

(b) A girl thinks of a number, multiplies it by 4, then adds 1, making 29. Find the number. (Start: $4x \ldots$)

(c) A 27 cm length of string fits round a square of side x cm with 3 cm left over. Find the value of x. (Start: $4x + \ldots$)

(d) Tony's tie is 150 cm long. It goes round his wrist seven times with 10 cm left over. What is the circumference of his wrist (call it x cm)?

15 If Sasha is x years old now, she will be $x + 5$ years old in five years' time. (a) How old will Sasha be in ten years' time? (b) How old was Sasha three years ago? (c) Sasha's father is twice her age. How old is he? (d) In three years' time Sasha's father will be 83. How old is Sasha now? (Start: $2x + \ldots$)

28 Decimal fractions: division

A Division by powers of ten

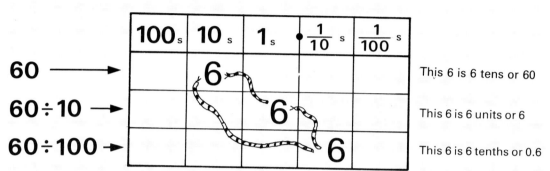

Fig. 28:1

To divide by 10, move one place to make the answer smaller.

To divide by 100, move two places to make the answer smaller.

Remember that every whole number is followed by a decimal point, although we do not usually write it; e.g. 364 could be written as 364. or 364.0

Examples $7 \div 10 = 0.7$ $364 \div 10 = 36.4$
                $3.4 \div 100 = 0.034$ $120.4 \div 100 = 1.204$
                $7 \div 1000 = 0.007$ $3.64 \div 1000 = 0.00364$

1 $A = \{246.8, 726, 7.3, 0.8, 9, 20, 3.03\}$
     $B = \{341.8, 212, 300.004, 9.02, 0.6, 11, 0.18, 0.05\}$
     $C = \{31, 300, 12.12, 6.3, 8, 0.01\}$

Rewrite these sets with each element of:
(a) A divided by 10   (b) B divided by 100   (c) C divided by 1000.

*2 $D = \{548.7, 72.6, 2364, 9, 555, 1000, 10, 0.5, 8.75, 0.015\}$

Rewrite set D with each element divided by:
(a) 10   (b) 100   (c) 1000.

3   State the value of each letter in the following:
(a) $32.8 \div a = 3.28$ (b) $624.6 \div b = 6.246$ (c) $4.23 \div c = 0.0423$
(d) $7.3 \times d = 73$ (e) $5248.5 \div e = 524.85$ (f) $0.3 \times f = 3000$
(g) $924 \div g = 9.24$ (h) $4 \div h = 0.0004$ (i) $0.0047 \times i = 4.7$

4   If ten stamps cost £1.20 how much does one cost, in pence?

5 If 100 m² of turf cost a man £96.50, how much did he pay per 1 m², in pence?

6 A man saved £680 in 100 weeks. How much did he save per week on average?

7 A farmer buys a hectare of land for £12 000. How much does he pay for each 1 m²? (A hectare is an area of 10 000 m².)

8 A school hires a 32-seater coach for £85.50. Two teachers travel free and the coach is full. How much should each pupil pay?

---

9 **Examples** $42.6 \div 30 = (42.6 \div 10) \div 3 = 4.26 \div 3 = 1.42$
$6780 \div 600 = (6780 \div 100) \div 6 = 67.8 \div 6 = 11.3$

Work out in a similar way:
(a) $743.4 \div 20$ (b) $32\,600 \div 50$ (c) $7140 \div 700$ (d) $632 \div 40$
(e) $425.6 \div 80$

10 Work like the examples in question 9, but without writing down the second step:
(a) $252 \div 60$ (b) $743.4 \div 70$ (c) $74.34 \div 700$ (d) $46 \div 200$
(e) $2.326 \div 200$

B   Division by integers

Examples   (a) $25.2 \div 7$

$$\begin{array}{r} 3 \, . \, 6 \\ 7 \,\overline{)\, 2\ 5 \, . \, {}^4 2} \end{array}$$

The division is exactly as for whole numbers.

(b) $125 \div 8$

$$\begin{array}{r} 1\ 5 \, . \, 6\ 2\ 5 \\ 8 \,\overline{)\, 1\ 2\ {}^4 5 \, . \, {}^5 0\, {}^2 0\, {}^4 0} \end{array}$$

$125 \div 8 = 15$ r5. The division is continued by writing 0's after the decimal point.

1 (a) 19.6 ÷ 7   (b) 16.38 ÷ 7   (c) 77.4 km ÷ 9   (d) £57.28 ÷ 8

2 (a) 26 ÷ 4   (b) 27 ÷ 6   (c) 431 ÷ 5   (d) 244 ÷ 8   (e) 333 ÷ 9
      (f) 423 ÷ 4   (g) 246 ÷ 8   (h) 326.7 ÷ 8

*3 (a) 46.8 ÷ 4   (b) 60.9 ÷ 3   (c) 84.24 ÷ 8   (d) 27.954 ÷ 9

*4 (a) 23 ÷ 5   (b) 45 ÷ 6   (c) 126 ÷ 4   (d) 260 ÷ 8   (e) 121 ÷ 5
      (f) 12 435 ÷ 6

5 Copy and complete this table for 13, 17 and 19 times.

1	2	3	4	5	6	7	8	9
13	26							117
17							136	
19					114			

6 (a) £457.14 ÷ 19   (b) 1367.82 ÷ 17   (c) 894.03 ÷ 17   (d) 13 018.2 ÷ 13

7 £13.52 has to be divided equally between 13 pupils. How much should each receive?

8 £1570.16 was collected by 19 teams during a sponsored relay. If each collected the same, how much was this?

---

9 Share £253.89 between two people in the ratio 13 : 8.

10 My winter and summer electricity bills are in the ratio 23 : 13. If the summer bill is £65.52, what is my winter bill?

11 A rectangle of perimeter 9.86 m has sides in the ratio 8 : 9. Find its area.

12 A number can be divided exactly by 4 if the last two digits divide exactly by 4. Find similar rules to show if a number divides exactly by 8 and 16.

The mean average is found by dividing the sum of the items by the number of items.

Example The mean of 2, 5 and 11 is $\dfrac{2+5+11}{3} = \dfrac{18}{3} = 6.$

```
5  REM "Mean"
10  LET A = 0
20  LET T = 0
30  PRINT "Type in numbers."
40  PRINT "Type −1 after typing in your
    last number."
50  INPUT N
60  IF N = −1 THEN GOTO 110
70  PRINT N;",";  (Delete if not needed)
80  LET A = A + 1
90  LET T = T + N
100  GOTO 50
110  PRINT "Mean average is ∧ ";T/A
```

Note
This program calculates the mean average for a list of numbers.

Variables
N is used to input each number, with −1 to tell the computer you have reached the end.
T is the total of all the numbers typed in.
A is how many numbers you have typed in.

1 Find the mean of:
(a) 9, 8, 6, 5   (b) 7, 24, 11, 13, 15   (c) 24, 13, 19, 14, 19, 67
(d) 27, 49, 31, 33, 30   (e) 124, 113, 119, 167, 114, 119.

2 (a) Work out each team's mean number of goals scored per match, called the 'goal average'. Give your answer as a decimal fraction, like 3.4.

   (b) Position the teams 1st to 4th based on goal average.

Team	Goals scored in ten matches
Atoms	1, 4, 1, 2, 3, 5, 2, 1, 0, 1
Breakers	2, 2, 3, 1, 4, 0, 0, 2, 1, 2
Cheats	3, 0, 1, 2, 0, 4, 2, 9, 3, 1
Dragons	0, 4, 1, 4, 2, 1, 3, 1, 4, 2

*3 Find the mean of:
(a) 2, 5, 9, 4, 10   (b) 7, 12, 8, 6, 9, 12   (c) 13, 17, 15, 14, 16
(d) 7, 2, 6, 5, 9, 8, 12, 3, 4, 2   (e) 1, 9, 8, 2, 7, 5, 9, 6, 9, 12.

*4 The table shows the marks scored by seven pupils on ten tests.

Example Liz scored a total of 62 marks, so her average was $62 \div 10 = 6.2$

(a) Work out the mean marks for the other pupils.

(b) Position the pupils in order from 1st to 7th, based on their average score.

	TEST									
	1	2	3	4	5	6	7	8	9	10
Liz	6	5	7	8	6	6	5	4	7	8
Ann	5	8	7	7	8	5	7	6	4	7
Jill	8	10	10	8	7	6	5	8	4	9
Dick	7	8	10	10	8	9	9	8	2	6
Tony	6	7	5	7	4	3	7	6	5	4
Alan	4	8	7	7	6	5	8	9	8	10
Jim	7	3	6	7	6	4	5	5	8	4

5 Figure 29:2 shows the noon temperature at Sunsea from the 7th to the 16th of August last year. Read each day's temperature, then calculate the mean temperature to the nearest whole number.

Fig. 29:1

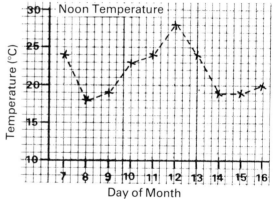

Fig. 29:2

6 **Example** In the TEST table for question 4 the mean mark for Test 1 is $(6 + 5 + 8 + 7 + 6 + 4 + 7) \div 7 = 43 \div 7 = 6\frac{1}{7}$.

Find the mean mark for the other tests.

7 Find the mean of the following ages:
11 y 6 m, 11 y 5 m, 11 y 8 m, 11 y 10 m, 11 y 4 m, 11 y 6 m, 12 y 1 m, 12 y.

8 After six tests a boy had a mean average of 8 marks. What was his total mark?

9 Some men have £68 altogether, averaging £4 each. How many men are there?

10 In eight cricket matches a bowler had the following statistics:

Number of wickets	6	7	2	3	3	4	0	5
Number of runs	42	84	46	32	27	31	20	41

(a) Find the total number of: (i) wickets   (ii) runs.

(b) Find the mean number of runs per match (total number of runs divided by total number of matches).

(c) Find the mean number of wickets per match.

(d) Find the bowling average (runs per wicket) over the whole eight matches.

11 A girl hopes to have a mean average of 8 marks in five tests.

(a) What must her total mark be?

(b) If she scores 9, 8, 6 and 7 in the first four tests, what must her fifth mark be?

12 Figure 29:3 shows the attendance of a class, with the Friday attendance missing. The mean attendance for the five days is 25, as shown by the dotted line. What was Friday's attendance?

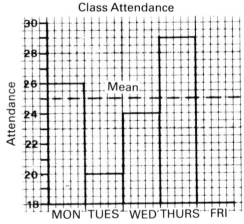

13 In a class the mean average pocket-money for the 14 boys was 60p, and for the 16 girls was 58p.

(a) What was the total amount paid to:
(i) the boys   (ii) the girls?

(b) What was the mean pocket-money for the whole class, to the nearest 1p?

Fig. 29:3

14 In a 100-mile race, a driver averaged 0.1 litres per mile.

(a) How many litres did he use altogether?

(b) If he had used 6 litres in the first 50 miles, what was his mean fuel consumption (litres per mile) for the first 50 miles and for the last 50 miles?

15 Find the mean age of the pupils in your class. How many pupils are within one month of the mean? Design a graph to show who is above the mean and who is below it.

30 Integers: kinds of integers

A Prime, rectangular and square numbers

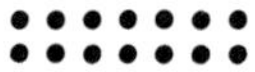

Fig. 30:1

A **rectangular number** makes at least one rectangle of dots.

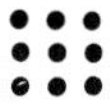

Fig. 30:2

A **square number** makes a square of dots.

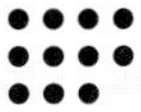

Fig. 30:3

A **prime number** will *not* make a rectangle of dots.

All square numbers, except 1, are also rectangular numbers.

All numbers, except 1, are either rectangular or prime.

1 is not prime, nor is it rectangular, but it is a square number.

1 Make, if possible, rectangle patterns for the following. (The numbers in brackets tell you how many patterns to make if there is more than one.)
(a) 10 (b) 17 (c) 25 (d) 21 (e) 37 (f) 15 (g) 16 (2)
(h) 20 (2) (i) 24 (3) (j) 42 (3)

2 $P = \{\text{prime numbers}\}$; $R = \{\text{rectangular numbers}\}$;
$S = \{\text{square numbers}\}$.

List sets *P*, *R* and *S*, choosing the elements from question 1.

***3** Repeat question 1 for:
(a) 14 (b) 19 (c) 18 (2) (d) 12 (2) (e) 36 (4).

4 Repeat question 2, but use the numbers in question 3.

5 List set S if $S = \{$squares from 1 to 100$\}$.

6 Copy and complete the following pattern.

Squares

First differences

Second differences

7

Fig. 30:4

Fig. 30:5

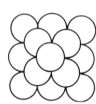

Fig. 30:6

A castle stacks its cannon-balls in square-based pyramids. Figure 30:4 shows the bottom layer. Figures 30:5 and 30:6 show bird's-eye views of the pyramid as it is built up.

Find the number patterns for the number of balls in the base layer, the number of layers and the total number of balls. Hence find the next five pyramid totals.

B Triangular numbers

Triangular numbers can be arranged as an equilateral triangle or a right-angled isosceles triangle of dots.

Figure 30:7 illustrates the triangular number 6.

$$6 = \overset{\bullet}{\underset{\bullet\ \bullet\ \bullet}{\bullet\ \bullet}} \quad \text{or} \quad \overset{\bullet\ \ \ \bullet}{\underset{\bullet\ \bullet\ \bullet}{\bullet\ \bullet}}$$

Fig. 30:7

```
5 REM "TRINUMS"
10 LET A = 1
20 LET T = 1
30 FOR N = 1 TO A
40 PRINT "*";
50 NEXT N
60 PRINT TAB(29); T
70 LET A = A + 1
80 LET T = T + A
90 GOTO 30
```

Notes

This program prints the triangular number sequence, illustrated with right-angled triangles of stars. You may need to alter the number in line 60 so that the numbers print in a column at the right of the screen.

On a BBC computer switch on the paging with

6 PRINT CHR$(14)

1 List, without drawing dots, the first twelve triangular numbers, starting with 1 and 3.

2 Write the first seven triangular numbers in a column, then draw equally spaced dots to illustrate them as shown in Figure 30:8.

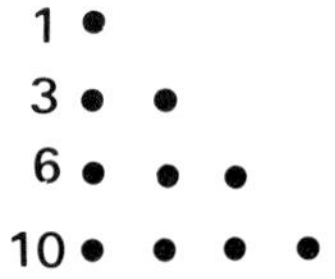

1 •
3 • •
6 • • •
10 • • • •

Fig. 30:8

3 All square numbers can be made by adding two consecutive triangular numbers. For example, 16 can be made from 6 and 10 as shown in Figure 30:9.

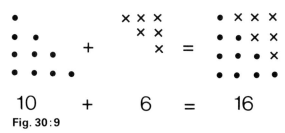

10 + 6 = 16

Fig. 30:9

Draw five squares of dots and crosses to show how the square numbers from 9 to 49 can be made by adding two triangular numbers.

4 Copy the table and continue it for squares up to 100.

Squares		Triangles
1	=	1
4	=	1 + 3
9	=	3 + 6
16	=	6 + 10

5 Work out the four products given, and then continue the sequence for the next six terms.

1×2; 2×3; 3×4; 4×5;   ...

Write down the connection between your answers and the triangular numbers.

6 The nth triangular number is $\dfrac{n(n+1)}{2}$. Check this, then find the following triangular numbers:
(a) the 20th   (b) the 30th   (c) the 100th   (d) the 25th
(e) the 36th   (f) the 49th.

7 Investigate other patterns of dots, e.g. the diamond of Figure 30:10.

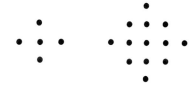

Fig. 30:10

C Factors

{1, 2, 3, 4, 6, 12} is the set {factors of 12}.

Each element of the set divides exactly into 12.

Pairs of numbers multiply to make the number:
$12 = 1 \times 12 = 2 \times 6 = 3 \times 4$.

```
5  REM "Factors"
10 PRINT "Type number."
20 INPUT N
30 PRINT "Factors of ∧ ";N
40 FOR B = 1 to N/2
50 IF N/B = INT(N/B) AND N<>0 THEN
   PRINT; B;",";
60 NEXT B
70 PRINT; N
```

Notes

This program will print the factors of any number.
Line 40 counts through until the halfway point is reached, then line 70 prints the number itself.
Line 50 finds if the value of B is a factor of the number N.

1 List the sets of factors of the following. The numbers in brackets show you how many factors there are.
   (a) 13 (2)   (b) 18 (6)   (c) 32 (6)   (d) 24 (8)   (e) 47 (2)   (f) 46 (4)
   (g) 50 (6)   (h) 60 (12)   (i) 64 (7)   (j) 100 (9)

2 Write each of the numbers in question 1 as the product of two factors in as many ways as possible.

   Example $16 = 1 \times 16 = 2 \times 8 = 4 \times 4$.

---

3 Investigate the result of multiplying odd and even numbers.

4 A number is **perfect** if its factors, excluding the number itself, sum to give the number.
   Check that 6 is a perfect number, then find the next largest, which is between 20 and 30.

5 At the time of writing the only other known perfect numbers are 496, 8128 and 33 550 336. Try to check they are perfect. Perhaps you could use a computer to find the factors.

D Primes

A prime number has only two factors.

1 is *not* a prime number.

```
5 REM "Prime 1"
10 PRINT "Type in your number."
20 INPUT N
30 CLS (Clear screen)
40 PRINT N
50 IF N < 2 THEN GOTO 120
60 IF N = 2 THEN GOTO 100
70 FOR A = 2 TO SQR(N)
80 IF N/A = INT(N/A) THEN GOTO 120
90 NEXT A
100 PRINT "Prime"
110 RUN
120 PRINT "Not prime."
130 IF N > 2 THEN PRINT "Divides by ∧";A
140 RUN
```

Notes

The loop in lines 70 to 90 checks for a factor of the number. If it finds one then the number is not prime.

These changes will speed up the program. Why?
65 IF N/2 = INT (N/2) THEN GOTO 120
70 FOR A = 3 TO SQR(N) STEP 2

Alternative version, to print all prime numbers up to a selected limit.

Use the above program with the following line changes:
```
5 REM "Prime 2"
10 PRINT "Type the largest number you wish checked."
20 INPUT B
40 PRINT "PRIMES"
50 FOR N = 2 TO B
100 PRINT N;";";
120 NEXT N
```
Delete lines 110, 130 and 140.

Notes

This method of checking becomes very slow for large numbers.

Can you think of a better method, and write a fast program?
(*Hint:* All numbers not prime must divide by another prime number.)

1 List the square numbers from 1 to 100.

2 Twelve prime numbers below 100 can be written as the sum of two square numbers. Write out the twelve sums. Start your answer: $2 = 1 + 1$; $5 = \ldots$

3 Write as the sum of three square numbers:
3, 11, 19, 43, 59 (two ways), 67, 83 (two ways).

4 Write the remaining six primes below 100 (i.e. those not used in questions 1, 2 and 3) as the sum of four squares. There are at least three ways for 79 and at least two ways for all the others except 7 and 23.

---

5 Make a set of cards like those in Figure 30:11. Ask a friend to think of a number between 1 and 31 and point to the cards containing it. How will the top left-hand numbers on the cards tell you what number your friend thought of? Find out why the cards work. If you want to make it less obvious, put the left-hand top number in a different position on each card and learn where you have put it.

1	3	5	7
9	11	13	15
17	19	21	23
25	27	29	31

2	3	6	7
10	11	14	15
18	19	22	23
26	27	30	31

4	5	6	7
12	13	14	15
20	21	22	23
28	29	30	31

8	9	10	11
12	13	14	15
24	25	26	27
28	29	30	31

16	17	18	19
20	21	22	23
24	25	26	27
28	29	30	31

Fig. 30:11

E Pascal's triangle

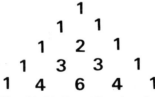

Fig. 30:12 Pascal's triangle

1 Copy Pascal's triangle and continue it for another five rows.

2 Copy and complete this table for each row of Pascal's triangle.

Row	1	2	3	4	5	6	7	8	9	10
Sum of row	1	2	4				64			

3 Use your answers to question 2 to write the sums of the next five rows.

4 Rewrite the first ten rows of Pascal's triangle in columns as shown.

What kind of numbers are those in:
(a) the second column (starting 1, 2, 3)
(b) the third column (starting 1, 3, 6)?

```
1
1  1
1  2  1
1  3  3  1
```

5 Using 5 or 6 mm squared paper, write faintly in pencil the first ten rows of Pascal's triangle as shown in Figure 30:13. Then shade in every odd-numbered square.

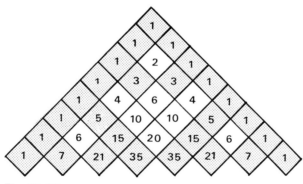

Fig. 30:13

6 Extend the pattern of question 5. As only the sum of an odd and even number gives an odd number there is no need to work out any more rows of the triangle. Use this rule: Shade a square only if the two squares above it have one shaded and one not shaded. (In Figure 30:14, S will be shaded and N will not be shaded.)

Fig. 30:14

F   The Fibonacci sequence

The **Fibonacci sequence**: 1, 1, 2, 3, 5, 8, 13, . . .

Here is Fibonacci hiding in Pascal's triangle!

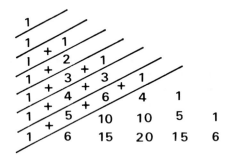

1 (a) What is true about every third number in the Fibonacci sequence?

(b) Where do you find multiples of 3 in the sequence?

(c) Where do you find multiples of 5?

2 Take any four numbers in order from the sequence. Multiply the two inside numbers and the two outside numbers, then find the difference between your answers.

Example   3, 5, 8, 13

$$5 \times 8 = 40; \qquad 3 \times 13 = 39; \qquad 40 - 39 = 1.$$

Repeat this three times for different sets of numbers.

3 Take any three numbers in order from the sequence. Multiply the outer two; square the middle one; find the difference. Repeat twice.

4 Write the first four Fibonacci numbers. Square the first three and total them; multiply the last two; both answers should be 6. Repeat for the first five, the first six and the first seven numbers. (With a calculator you could do more.)

5 Divide each number in Fibonacci's sequence by the number before it, at least up to $21 \div 13$; further if you have a calculator. The further you extend this division the nearer you come to a value called **The Golden Section**.

6 You also find the Golden Section in the Pentagram shown in Figure 30:15.

Measure carefully in mm, then use a calculator, to find $\dfrac{AG}{GH}$, $\dfrac{AH}{AG}$ and $\dfrac{AC}{AH}$.

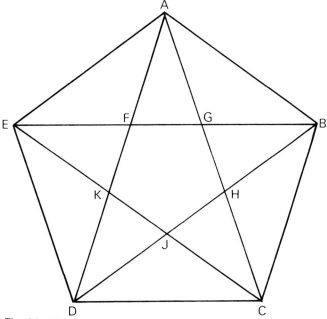

Fig. 30:15

7 Display 1 on your calculator. Then repeat the following sequence.
[M +] [+] [MR] [=]

8 Find out more about Fibonacci and the Golden Section. Find how it relates to a bee's ancestors, the number of petals on a flower, a fir cone, and famous pictures.

9 What will this computer program print?

```
5 REM "Mystery"
10 LET X = 1
20 LET Y = 1
30 PRINT X
40 LET Z = X + Y
50 LET X = Y
60 LET Y = Z
70 GOTO 30
```

Note
Switch on paging on a BBC computer with
6 PRINT CHR$ (14)

For Discussion

Average speed km/h	50	50	50	100	(e)	(f)	(g)	(h)	50	50	50	40
Time h	1	2	$\frac{1}{2}$	2	1	2	3	2	(i)	(j)	(k)	(l)
Distance km	(a)	(b)	(c)	(d)	60	60	60	80	50	100	150	20

1 Find (a) to (l) for this table:

Average speed km/h	40	40	55	60	75	70	20	30	(i)	(j)	(k)	(l)
Time h	1	3	1	2	(e)	(f)	(g)	(h)	1	2	3	10
Distance km	(a)	(b)	(c)	(d)	75	70	40	90	20	20	30	20

2 If you travelled at a constant speed of 30 m.p.h., how many miles would you go in:
(a) 1 hour   (b) 6 hours   (c) half an hour   (d) quarter of an hour?

3 What is my average speed in m.p.h. if I go:
(a) 150 km in 2 h   (b) 195 miles in 3 h?

4 **Example**   In the table shown in Figure 31:1 the distance from Sheffield to York is given as 52 miles.

How many miles is it from:
(a) Salisbury to York
(b) Stoke to Taunton
(c) Shrewsbury to Stranraer
(d) Stoke to Shrewsbury?

*5 Use the table in Figure 31:1 to find how far it is from:
(a) York to Stranraer
(b) Stranraer to Stoke.

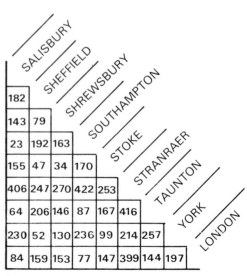

Fig. 31:1

*6 Find (a) to (l) in this table:

Average speed km/h	30	30	45	30	20	30	20	15	(i)	(j)	(k)	(l)
Time h	1	2	1	3	(e)	(f)	(g)	(h)	1	1	2	10
Distance km	(a)	(b)	(c)	(d)	20	30	40	30	25	40	40	50

*7 What is my average speed if I go:
(a) 200 km in 4 h
(b) 175 miles in 7 h?

8 A train travels 25 miles. What is its average speed if it takes:
(a) 1 h   (b) 2 h   (c) $\frac{1}{2}$ h   (d) $\frac{1}{4}$ h   (e) 20 min?

9 Find the average speed of a car which travels:
(a) 315 miles in 7 hours
(b)   504 km in 9 h
(c) 364 miles in 8 hours.

10 Find (a) to (l) in this table:

Average speed km/h	40	60	100	60	40	80	60	60	(i)	(j)	(k)	(l)
Time h	$\frac{1}{2}$	$2\frac{1}{2}$	$\frac{3}{4}$	$1\frac{1}{4}$	(e)	(f)	(g)	(h)	$\frac{1}{2}$	$1\frac{1}{2}$	$1\frac{1}{2}$	$1\frac{1}{2}$
Distance km	(a)	(b)	(c)	(d)	20	20	30	15	30	90	60	75

11 At 600 km/h how far does an aircraft travel in:
(a) $\frac{1}{2}$ h   (b) $\frac{1}{4}$ h   (c) 1 min   (d) 1 s (in metres to the nearest metre)?

12 Pierre runs 100 m in 10 s. What is his speed in:
(a) m/s   (b) m/min   (c) m/h   (d) km/h?

13 How many metres does a car travelling at 72 km/h (about 45 m.p.h.) cover in:
(a) 1 h   (b) 1 min   (c) 1 s?

14 (a) Walking at 90 m/min (a fast walking pace), how far do you go in 1 s?

(b) Allowing 4 s extra for safety, how long would it take you to cross a road 18 m wide?

(c) How many metres will a car travelling at 72 km/h cover in this time?

15 Copy and complete this table for the crossing of a 16 m wide road:

Speed of car km/h	36	72	108	144
Speed of car m/s	10			
Time to cross s	13	13	13	13
Distance covered by car m	130			

16 Figure 31:2 shows a graph drawn from the data in the table of question 15. Draw the graph on 2 mm graph paper, using scales of 1 cm to 10 km/h and 1 cm to 50 m. Read from the graph the minimum safe distance away that a car should be if you are to cross a 16 m wide road when the vehicle is travelling at:
(a) 50 km/h   (b) 100 km/h
(c) 120 km/h.

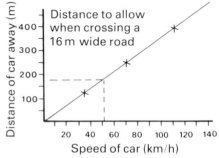

Fig. 31:2

17 Illustrate the information of questions 15 and 16 on a full-size model marked out on your school field.

18 Draw a chart to show the comparative average speeds of either different animals or different machines.

Using Your Calculator

A Very Odd Bird

The ostrich must rank first in the list of odd-looking birds, but there is more to it than meets the eye. For instance, it takes 3-metre strides and can reach 60 m.p.h. It can keep up a speed of 20 m.p.h. for up to ten hours.

Half of the 2-metre height of an ostrich is head and neck. It weighs 120 kg, of which its valued feathers weigh only about 1 kg. It eats about 7 kg of food a day, plus pebbles to grind it and anything that sparkles, including diamonds!

On 350 farms in South Africa, 100 000 ostriches are farmed for their feathers, a £13 million-a-year business. A good ostrich will be plucked twice a year for 15 years. Its feathers fetch between £40 and £75 at each plucking.

Ostriches have other uses besides dressing chorus girls. One ostrich egg replaces two dozen hens' eggs for an omelette; they can be boiled too (40 min for soft-boiled!). Ostrich steaks are very tasty, and each year 40 000 skins are made into leather; an ostrich evening jacket might cost well over £2000.

Using your calculator and the given information, answer the following questions.

1 Taking 5 miles as equivalent to 8 kilometres, how many strides would an ostrich make in 10 hours at 20 m.p.h.?

2 What fraction of your height is your head and neck?

3 How many times as heavy as you is an ostrich?

4 On average, how many ostriches per farm in South Africa?

5 On average, how much per year does each farm make from its ostriches?

6 How much will a top pedigree ostrich's feathers bring the farmer over its useful life?

7 On average, how many ostrich skins are processed per week?

32 Scales: scale drawing

For Discussion

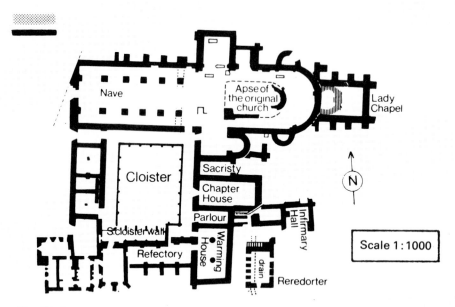

Fig. 32:1

1 How many centimetres long would the line in Figure 32:2 be if it was drawn:
(a) 10 times as big (b) 4 times as big (c) $\frac{1}{2}$ as big (d) $\frac{1}{10}$ as big?

Fig. 32:2

2 The lines in Figure 32:3 are drawn to a scale of 1 cm represents 10 cm. What true lengths do they represent?

(a)

(b)

(c)

(d)

Fig. 32:3

3 If the lines in Figure 32:3 had been drawn to a scale of 1 cm represents 5 cm (or 1:5) what lengths would they represent?

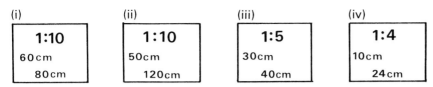

(i)
1:10
60cm
80cm
(ii)
1:10
50cm
120cm
(iii)
1:5
30cm
40cm
(iv)
1:4
10cm
24cm

Fig. 32:4

4 (a) Draw scale diagrams of the rectangles in Figure 32:4, using the scales given.

(b) Draw a diagonal (from corner to corner) on each of your rectangles and write on it both its scaled length and its true length.

***5** Copy and complete this table for the lines in Figure 32:5.

Scale	True length			
	(a)	(b)	(c)	(d)
1 : 10				
1 : 4				
1 : 8				
1 : 20				

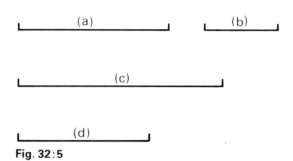

(a)
(b)
(c)
(d)

Fig. 32:5

a
PATIO
d
LAWN
c
e
f
PATH
g
FRUIT
VEGETABLES
b

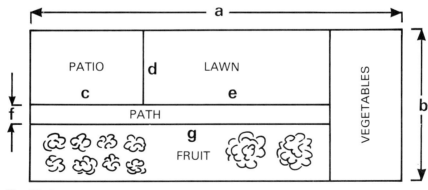

Fig. 32:6

***6** (a) Copy the garden plan shown in Figure 32:6. Measure the lengths accurately.

(b) The plan you have drawn is to a scale of 1 : 200. What real lengths, in metres, are represented by the lengths *a* to *g*?

7 Atique wishes to make a model of the supersonic airliner Concorde, using a scale of 1 : 100. He has the information given in Figure 32:7.

(a) What size to the nearest cm should he make its:
   (i) length   (ii) wing-span   (iii) height?

(b) How many passenger seats should he make?

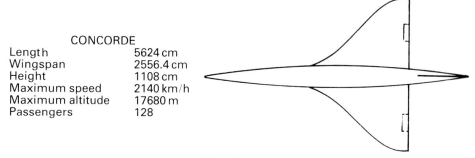

CONCORDE
Length	5624 cm
Wingspan	2556.4 cm
Height	1108 cm
Maximum speed	2140 km/h
Maximum altitude	17680 m
Passengers	128

Fig. 32:7

8 **Example**   1 cm rep. 1 m → 1 cm rep. 100 cm → 1 : 100

Write in ratio form (like 1 : 100):
(a) 1 mm rep. 1 cm   (b) 1 m rep. 1 km   (c) 1 mm rep. 10 cm
(d) 1 cm rep. 10 m   (e) 1 cm rep. 1 km   (f) 1 mm rep. 1 km
(g) 1 mm rep. 10 m.

9 Measure the four lines shown in Figure 32:8, then calculate the distances they represent.

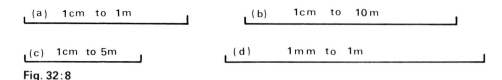

(a)   1 cm to 1 m   (b)   1 cm   to   10 m

(c)   1 cm to 5 m   (d)   1 mm to   1 m

Fig. 32:8

10 Draw four sets of three lines to the scales given. Write on each its scaled length in cm.
(a) 1 mm to 1 cm; {60 cm, 35 cm, 76 cm}   (b) 1 mm to 1 m; {50 m, 36 m, 108 m}
(c) 1 : 100; {1 m, 2.5 m, 90 cm}   (d) 1 : 200; {4 m, 3 m, 3.5 m}

11 Scales on a map are usually written as a Representative Fraction (R.F.).

Example   1 cm rep. 50 km → 1 cm rep. 5 000 000 cm giving R.F. $= \dfrac{1}{5\,000\,000}$.

Write as a representative fraction:
(a) 1 cm rep. 1 m   (b) 1 mm rep. 1 m   (c) 1 mm rep. 1 km
(d) 1 cm rep. 25 km.

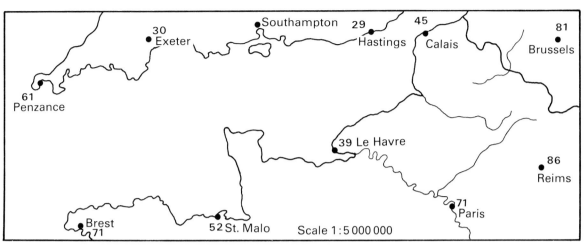

Fig. 32:9

12 Figure 32:9 shows part of Britain, France and Belgium, drawn using a representative fraction of $\dfrac{1}{5\,000\,000}$.

(a) How many km is 5 000 000 mm? (b) What does 1 mm represent in km?

(c) How far is each of the towns from Southampton, correct to the nearest 10 km?

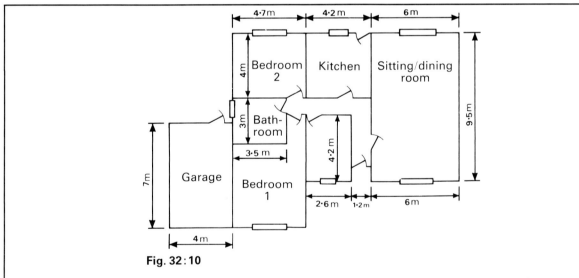

Fig. 32:10

13 (a) Figure 32:10 shows a plan of a bungalow, not to scale. Re-draw it using a scale of 1:200. Estimate any lengths not shown.

(b) Draw an imaginary view of the front of this bungalow.

14 Draw a scale plan of your classroom, your home or your garden.

A Pictograms

For Discussion

Figure 33:1 is called a **pictogram**. Each picture represents one pupil.

How Form 1MB come to school

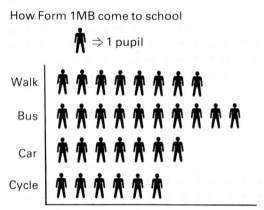

Fig. 33:1

1 Copy and complete the pictogram shown in Figure 33:2, using the data (or information) in this table:

Car colour	Red	Blue	Green	White	Yellow
Number of cars	50	20	14	18	11

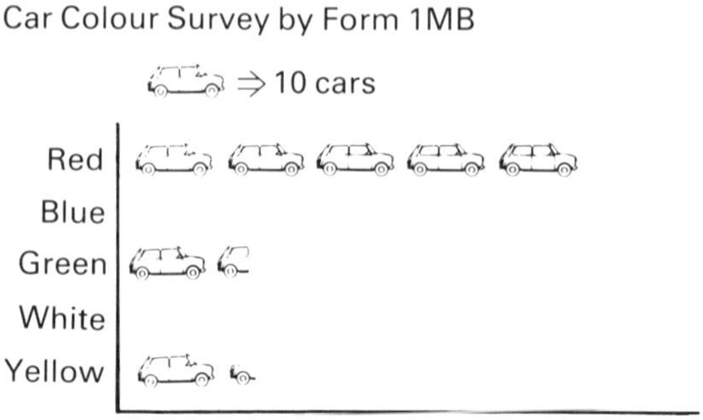

Car Colour Survey by Form 1MB

Fig. 33:2

2 Jeanne conducts a survey of her class, class 1MB, to find their favourite type of book. Draw a pictogram to illustrate her data:

Type of book	Western	Adventure	Animal	Science Fiction	Travel
Number of votes	4	7	8	8	3

3 Draw a pictogram, using one bottle to represent 1000 bottles, to illustrate the following data about milk production by Bull Dairies.

January 10 000, February 10 000, March 9500, April 9000, May 9500, June 11 000.

4 Using one pair of spectacles to represent 10 customers, draw a pictogram to show how many customers visit Hugh Seymore, Optician, given the data:

Mon 40, Tues 65, Wed 15, Thurs 58, Fri 37, Sat 81.

---

5 Gather data from your class and illustrate it with pictograms.

6 Make a collection of pictograms from newspapers and magazines. Discuss what they show and how clearly they represent it.

A Bar-charts

For Discussion

Figure 33:3 is called a **bar-chart**. The bars can be horizontal or vertical.

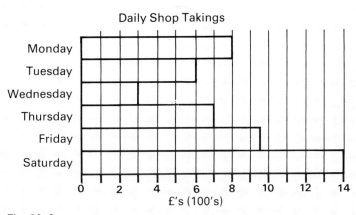

Fig. 33:3

Notes

This program should work on any BASIC computer, but you may need to CLEAR space for the array M( ) before line 10 and adjust the spacings in the lines that label and print the chart.

```
5  REM "Barchart"
10  DIM M(11)
20  PRINT "Type mark out of 10"
30  PRINT "Type −1 after last mark"
40  INPUT K
50  IF K = −1 THEN GOTO 130
60  LET T = M(K + 1) + 1
70  IF T < 11 THEN GOTO 110
80  PRINT "Overload. Sorry."
90  PAUSE 200 (2 sec pause)
100  GOTO 130
110  LET M(K + 1) = T
120  GOTO 40
130  CLS (Clear screen)
140  PRINT "BAR CHART OF MARKS OUT OF 10"
150  PRINT "Marks"
160  FOR A = 11 TO 1 STEP −1
170  IF A < 11 THEN PRINT "∧"; (or omit)
180  PRINT; A − 1;
190  IF M(A) > 0 THEN GOTO 210
200  GOTO 240
210  FOR B = 1 TO M(A)
220  PRINT "■■"; (Two or more squares or stars to align with numbers)
230  NEXT B
240  PRINT
250  NEXT A
260  PRINT
270  PRINT " ∧  ∧ "; (Spaces as necessary to align with bars)
280  FOR C = 1 TO 10
290  PRINT; C;" ∧ "; (This space may not be needed)
300  NEXT C
```

1 Copy and complete the bar-chart shown in Figure 33:4 for the following data:

<u>Rainfall in centimetres in Rio de Janeiro</u>

Rainfall (cm)	11	11	12	10	$7\frac{1}{2}$	5	4	$4\frac{1}{2}$	6	$7\frac{1}{2}$	10	13
Month	J	F	M	A	M	J	J	A	S	O	N	D

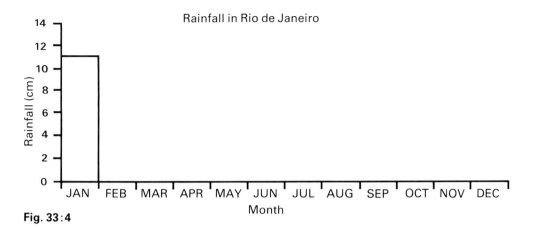

Fig. 33:4

2 Copy the tally-chart and complete the totals column. Then draw a bar-chart, numbered from 0 to 10, to illustrate the data.

	Tally	Totals
Walk	//// ///	8
Bus	//// ////	
Car	//// //	
Cycle	////	
	Grand total	30

3 Shelley asks her classmates for their shoe sizes. She collects the data:
4, 6, 6, 4, 7, 6, 5, 5, 4, 6, 7, 8, 4, 6, 5, 6, 5, 5, 6, 7, 4, 7, 5, 6, 4, 7, 5, 5, 7, 5.

Draw up a tally-chart, then draw a bar-chart to illustrate the data.

4 Draw up a tally-chart, then draw a bar-chart, for the following data, which gives the amounts (in pence) spent by pupils at a school tuck-shop.

8, 7, 5, 6, 10, 12, 6, 7, 10, 5, 9, 4, 3, 8, 11, 7, 7, 5, 8, 7, 4, 7, 4, 7, 6, 9, 8, 12, 11, 7, 7, 5, 8, 8, 4, 9, 10, 3, 5, 5.

---

5 Write in a column the 26 letters of the alphabet, then using a page from a book (not a text-book) make a tally-chart and a bar-chart to show the frequency of the letters, with the most common letter having a tally of 100.

6 Repeat question 5 using a foreign-language book. Compare the two charts and comment on what you find.

C   Line graphs

For Discussion

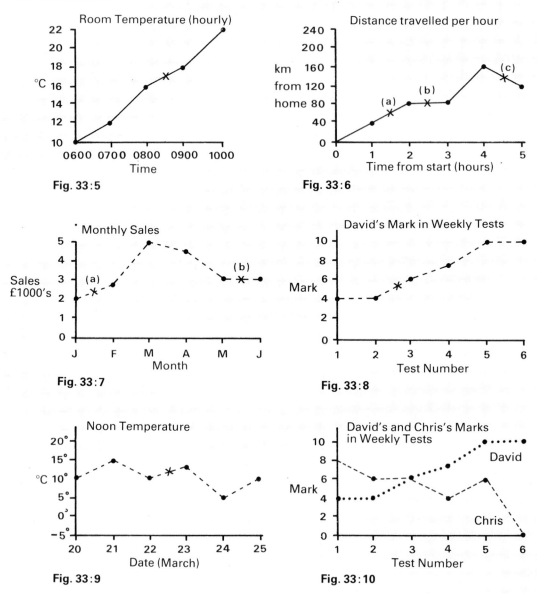

Fig. 33:5

Fig. 33:6

Fig. 33:7

Fig. 33:8

Fig. 33:9

Fig. 33:10

1 In Figure 33:5, at what time was the room temperature 18°C?

2 In Figure 33:6, at what two times was the distance from home the same?

3 In Figure 33:8, the point marked X has no meaning. Why?

4   in Figure 33:8, would David's teacher be pleased with him? Why?

5   In Figure 33:9, is the temperature on 26 March likely to be:
below 5°C; between 5°C and 15°C; above 15°C?

6   In Figure 33:10, who is making better progress, David or Chris?

7   Draw a line graph to show the following weights of a child.

Use a vertical scale of 1 cm to 5 kg from 0 to 40 kg.

Age (years)	1	2	3	4	5	6	7	8	9	10	11	12
Weight (kg)	10	13	17	19	23	26	28	30	33	35	37	40

8   It is not always necessary to start the vertical scale from zero. Beginning at 35°C, draw a graph to show Eva's temperature during an illness. Use a vertical scale of 1 cm to 1°C.

Day of illness	1	2	3	4	5	6	7	8	9	10
Temperature (°C)	37	37.2	37.8	38	39.6	40	40	39	37.2	36.9

---

9   Describe and illustrate five correctly used line graphs and five incorrectly used ones. Explain why each is correct or incorrect.

D   Pie-charts

For Discussion

Figure 33:11 shows a **pie-chart**.

(a) How many small divisions are there?

(b) How much money does each small division represent?

(c) How much did Ian spend on each item?

(d) How many degrees wide is each small division?

(e) How many degrees are there for each item?

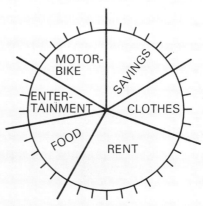

Fig. 33:11   How Ian spent £36.

1 A survey of 36 housewives asked them to state their favourite cake mix. The result was:

Riso 10; Quickbake 3; Mrs Bod's 12; Yuk 3; Egad 8.

Draw a pie-chart to illustrate this information.

*2 Of 36 thousand voters, 10 thousand voted Labour, 15 thousand voted Conservative, 6 thousand voted Liberal/S.D.P. and 5 thousand voted for 'Others'. Draw a pie-chart to illustrate this voting pattern.

*3 In a pet show there were 20 dogs, 24 cats, 12 birds, 10 mice and 6 'others'.

(a) In a pie-chart to show this, how many degrees would represent each animal?

(b) How many degrees would represent each kind of pet?

(c) Draw the pie-chart.

4 A survey of where 30 first-formers lived showed:
Langport 10; Somerton 10; Kingsbury 6; Curry Rivel 3; Aller 1.

(a) In a pie-chart, how many degrees would represent one first-former?

(b) How many degrees would represent each town?

(c) Draw the pie-chart.

5 Five children collect stamps. Ricardo has 2400, Kassin has 840, Marco has 600, Heptha has 360 and Andena has 120.

(a) How many stamps will one degree on a pie-chart represent?

(b) How many degrees will there be for each person?

---

6 A boy records the colours of cars passing his house.

He sees:
Red 67; Yellow 43; White 89; Green 21; Blue 20.

On a pie-chart how many degrees would represent each colour?

7 Collect statistical charts from newspapers and magazines. Write about them, saying what kinds of graphs they are and how clearly and honestly they represent the data.

Project

Number Patterns

1 Copy this division and check it.

$$0.1\,4\,2\,8\,5\,7\,1\,4\,2\,8\,5\,7\,1$$
$$7\,\overline{)\,1\,.\,0\,0\,0\,0\,0\,0\,0\,0\,0\,0\,0\,0\,0\,0}$$

Note that 142857 will keep on recurring (repeating). We show this with dots over the repeating set of figures.

Examples $1 \div 7 = 0.142\,857\,142\,857\,1 \ldots \rightarrow 0.\dot{1}42\,85\dot{7}$
$1 \div 3 = 0.333\,333\,333\,3333 \ldots \rightarrow 0.\dot{3}$
$11 \div 6 = 1.833\,333\,333\,3333 \ldots \rightarrow 1.8\dot{3}$

Write the first ten figures of:
(a) $0.\dot{6}$ (b) $0.\dot{3}\dot{7}$ (c) $0.\dot{4}8\dot{6}$ (d) $0.857\,14\dot{2}$ (e) $1.\dot{2}$ (f) $2.8\dot{3}\dot{7}$ (g) $2.7\dot{8}4\dot{2}$

2 Work out: (a) $2 \div 7$ (b) $3 \div 7$.

Compare your answers with the first example in question 1.

3 The recurring figures for division by 7 are, in numerical order, 1, 2, 4, 5, 7, 8.

$1 \div 7$ starts recurring with the highest figure, $0.1 \ldots$

$2 \div 7$ starts recurring with the second highest figure, $0.2 \ldots$

$3 \div 7$ starts recurring with the third highest figure, $0.4 \ldots$

What is the first recurring figure in:
(a) $4 \div 7$ (b) $5 \div 7$ (c) $6 \div 7$?

4 Figure P3:1 shows the figures that recur when dividing by 7, in the order that they appear in question 1. We know from question 3 that $3 \div 7$ starts 0.4, so from the clock we can read the answer: $3 \div 7 = 0.\dot{4}285\dot{7}1$.

Fig. P3:1

Use the clock and your answers to question 3 to write the answer to each number from 1 to 6 divided by 7.

5 Copy Figure P3:2. Use a 3 cm-radius circle and space the points equally. Join the points in the order that they are given in Figure P3:1, that is: 1 to 4, 4 to 2, and so on to 7 to 1.

Draw the line of symmetry for your diagram.

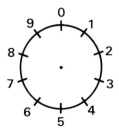

Fig. P3:2

191

6 Dividing by 17 gives sixteen figures in the recurring cycle. Find $1 \div 17$.

7 The recurring figures for $1 \div 17$, in numerical order, are:
0 1 1 2 2 3 4 4 5 5 6 7 7 8 8 9

Start at the 1st figure (0) for $1 \div 17$, the 2nd for $2 \div 17$, etc. The rest of the answer is read from the cyclic order given by the answer to question 6:

Note that there are two 1's, 2's, 4's, 5's, 7's and 8's.

To decide at which one you should start look at the figure following it in the cyclic order. The one with the lower figure after it is used first.

Example   For the 2's (4th and 5th for $4 \div 17$ and $5 \div 17$) the answer starting 23 is used first and the other 2 is used for $5 \div 17$.

Write out all the answers for 1 to 16 divided by 17.

8 Draw the recurrence pattern for 17, as in question 5.

9 Dividing by 13 gives two different recurrence patterns.

Find them and draw a circle pattern for each.

10 Cut out thirteen 2 cm squares and arrange them as shown in Figure P3:3.

Fig. P3:3

Now swap over the black and white cards according to the following rules:

(a) Black can only move to the right; white can only move to the left.

(b) A card can move onto an empty space, onto the blue card, or jump over a different colour card into an empty space.

Hint   Try reducing the number of black and white cards and build up a pattern of moves. When you find the pattern, write it down and develop it for more than thirteen cards.

You can also use pegs and pegboard, when the blue card becomes an empty hole.

Papers

Paper One

1 Add together: (a) £200 and £50   (b) £350 and £25   (c) £165 and £220
(d) £465 and £266   (e) £293 and £117   (f) £16.40 and £8.36

*2 (a) Using the flow-chart in Figure P1, copy and complete this stores table:

A	1	2	3			
Y	1	4	9			
Z	2	8				

(b) Write the numbers that the flow-chart tells you to print.

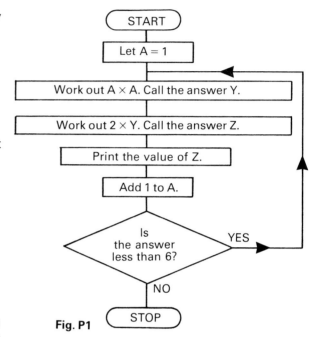

Fig. P1

3 What would be the result of giving a computer the flow-chart program in Figure P2?

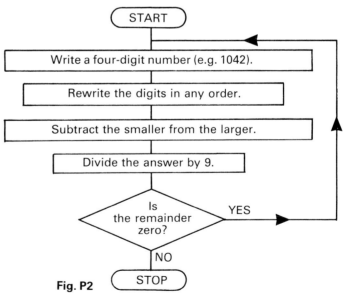

Fig. P2

4 What is the greatest number of times that four straight lines can cross? Can you find a rule that will tell you the greatest number of times *any* given number of straight lines can cross?

193

Paper Two

1 Write in figures:
(a) five hundred   (b) sixty-four   (c) one hundred and three
(d) two thousand and seventy-seven.

*2 List the set of multiples of:
(a) 7 from 7 to 70   (b) 8 from 8 to 80   (c) 9 from 9 to 90.

*3 (a)   163   (b)   3016
       + 289   + 259

*4 Write the following addition sums with the stars replaced by the correct figures.

(a)   3*8   (b)   *2*   (c)   6*6
    + 16*   + 307   + *5*
     *99   5*0   900

5 $A = \{4106, 1406, 1046, 6104\}$

(a) State the value of the figure 4 in each number.

(b) Write in words each number in A.

(c) Add the four numbers in A.

(d) Write each number in A backwards, e.g. 6014, then add up your answers. Is your total the same as your answer to part (c) backwards?

(e) Find two four-figure numbers that give the same answer when added as when reversed and added.

(f) Arrange the four numbers in A in order of size from biggest to smallest.

6 How many days, hours and minutes from 1:25 p.m. on May 1st to 3:05 a.m. on May 4th?

Paper Three

1 How many:
(a) pennies in a pound   (b) minutes in an hour   (c) days in July
(d) days in a leap year   (e) whole numbers that divide exactly into 12?

*2 (a)   467   (b)   316   (c)   156   (d)   406
      − 148   − 277   − 93   − 125

    (e)   616   (f)   640   (g)   300   (h)   203
      − 130   − 128   − 127   − 144

*3 What time, in words, is the clock in Figure P3 showing?

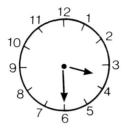

Fig. P3

*4 Starting each part from the position shown in Figure P3, what will be the time, in figures, when the minute hand (the longer one) has turned:

(a) 1 whole turn   (b) $\frac{1}{2}$ a turn   (c) $\frac{1}{4}$ of a turn   (d) $\frac{3}{4}$ of a turn

(e) 2 whole turns   (f) 12 whole turns   (g) $4\frac{1}{2}$ turns   (h) $3\frac{3}{4}$ turns?

5 Copy the table and write the times after the minute hand (the longer one) has made the numbers of turns stated.

Starting time	Number of turns						
	$\frac{1}{4}$	$\frac{1}{2}$	$\frac{3}{4}$	1	$1\frac{1}{4}$	$1\frac{3}{4}$	$2\frac{1}{4}$
9:00							
1:30							
8:20							
6:35							

6 A photocopier has a meter which tells the operator how many copies have been made. This table shows the reading at the end of each day during one week:

Friday	Monday	Tuesday	Wednesday	Thursday	Friday
11 267	13 467	15 897	16 029	17 003	20 000

Note that the counter does not return to zero each morning, and that no copies are made on Saturday or Sunday.

How many copies were made on each day (Monday to Friday) and altogether that week?

7 In question 6, the charges are 5p each for the first 100 copies each day, then 3p each for the rest. Work out the charge for each day and the total charge for the whole week.

8 Find five odd digits that add up to 14 (repetitions are allowed).

Paper Four

1 (a) $512 - 68$ (b) $406 - 99$ (c) $3012 - 1985$

*2 Measure each angle in Figure P4.

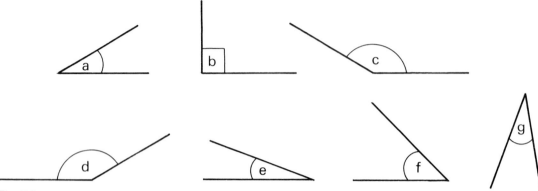

Fig. P4

*3 Draw and mark, as in Figure P4:
(a) any acute angle, x (b) any obtuse angle, y (c) any reflex angle, z.

4 (a) Use a protractor to help you draw a circle as in Figure P5. Mark the points A to I every 40°.

(b) How many degrees is obtuse angle AOD?

(c) How many degrees is reflex angle AOD?

(d) Measure angle AGD (marked g).

(e) What kind of an angle is g?

(f) Measure angles AED, AFD, AHD and AID.

(g) What is the connection between the size of obtuse angle AOD and the angles in parts (d) and (f)?

(h) Without drawing or measuring, state the size of the angle marked a in Figure P6.

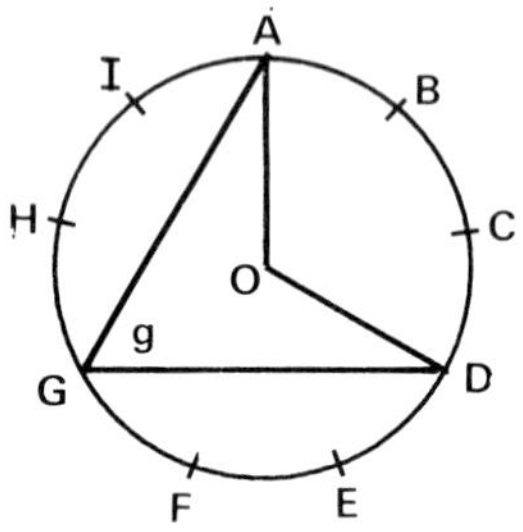

Fig. P5

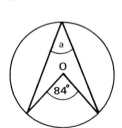

Fig. P6

5 $A = \{\text{acute } \angle\text{'s}\};$ $B = \{\text{obtuse } \angle\text{'s}\};$
$C = \{\text{reflex } \angle\text{'s}\};$ $D = \{\text{right } \angle\text{'s}\}.$

Referring to Figure P4:

(a) Write $\in$ or $\notin$ to make the following true:
$a \ A;$ $b \ A;$ $d \ B;$ $f \ B.$

(b) If the elements are chosen from the angles drawn, what is:
(i) $n(A)$ (ii) $n(B)$ (iii) $n(C)$ (iv) $n(D)$?

6 List all the factors of: (a) 12   (b) 60.

7 In a shop a certain article, made of plastic, costs 10p. There is no reduction for quantity, but I get 10 for 20p. What is the article?

Paper Five

1 Draw an accurate angle of: (a) 45°   (b) 105°.

*2 In the number 123.96, which figure is in the column of:
(a) hundreds   (b) tens   (c) units   (d) tenths   (e) hundredths?

*3 Write the number:
(a) 3 more than 5   (b) 3 tenths more than 5   (c) 3 hundredths more than 5
(d) 1 tenth more than 5.6

*4 Add 1 tenth to:
(a) 6.2   (b) 6.23   (c) 6.03

*5
(a) 1.625	(b) 5.621	(c) 4.209	(d) 13.108
– 0.837	– 1.301	– 1.928	– 7.889
(e) 66.35	(f) 30.05		
– 18.49	– 12.77		

Check your answers by adding each answer to the bottom line of each question.

6 $w = 19.08$ $x = 93.61$ $y = 3.95$ $z = 40.29$

(a) State the value of the figure 9 in the above numbers.

(b) Add the four numbers.

(c) Arrange the numbers in order of size, biggest first.

(d) With the numbers in the order you wrote for part (c), find the difference between the first and second, the second and third, and the third and fourth.

7 Rewrite your answer to question 6(c) with each number:
(a) increased by one tenth   (b) increased by one hundredth
(c) decreased by one tenth   (d) decreased by one hundredth.

8 (a) 4.7 – 2.83   (b) 6.5 – 0.97   (c) 4.06 – 1.33   (d) 5 – 1.74

9 Why was gladiator number O/50/500 drawing his pension?

Fig. P7

Paper Six

1 Find the change from £5 if the goods bought cost:
  (a) £3.50 (b) £4.75 (c) £3.20 (d) £4.19 (e) £1.16 (f) £2.07
  (g) £2.89 (h) 38p.

*2 Add £16, £8.62 and £10.49

*3 List the multiples of 12 from 12 to 60.

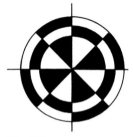

Fig. P8

*4 Draw an enlarged copy of Figure P8, making the circles of radii 3 cm, 4 cm and 5 cm. The angles between the 'spokes' will all be 45°.

5 $p = 6$ $q = 3.42$ $r = 5.9$ $s = 10.03$

Find:
  (a) $p + q$ (b) $p + q + r + s$ (c) $s - q$ (d) $p - r$ (e) $r - q$ (f) $s - r$
  (g) $p - q$ (h) $s + p - r$ (i) $s - p + r$.

6 Copy Figure P9, but make it twice as large. Centres are marked with dots. Start with the biggest circle. You could colour the rings.

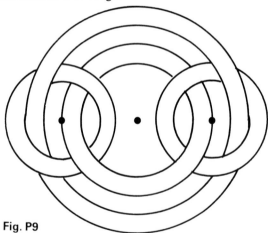

Fig. P9

7 (a) Draw nine touching circles, diameters 3 cm, to fit inside a square.

  (b) Draw seven touching circles, diameters 3 cm, to fit into a regular hexagon. Start with the middle circle.

8 Copy Figure 5:11 on page 35, making it twice as large. Colour in the small circle. Go round the circumferences of the two middle-size circles with a black felt-pen. Cut out the big circle, make a hole in the middle, and put it on a record player.

Paper Seven

1 In Figure P10, how many cm is it from:
(a) A to B   (b) A to C   (c) B to C?

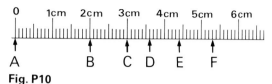

Fig. P10

*2 In Figure P10 it is 3.6 cm from A to D.

How many cm is it from:
(a) A to E   (b) A to F   (c) B to D   (d) B to E   (e) B to F   (f) C to D
(g) C to E   (h) C to F?

*3 Measure each line in Figure P11 to the nearest millimetre, giving the answer in cm.

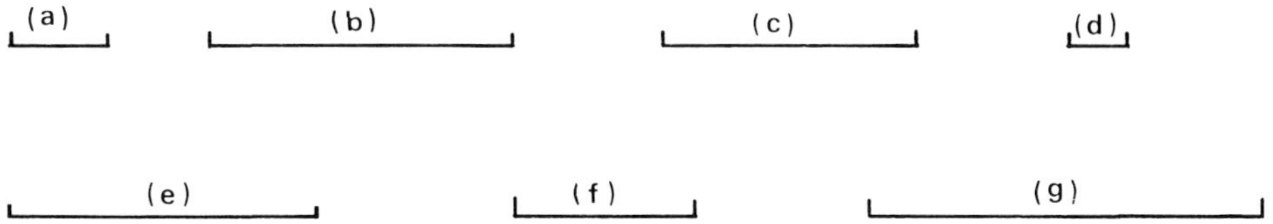

    (a)   (b)   (c)   (d)

    (e)   (f)   (g)

Fig. P11

*4 Find the change from £10 if the bill is:
(a) £7.60   (b) £8.15   (c) £9.95   (d) £3   (e) £1.55   (f) £2.08   (g) £3.17   (h) 96p.

*5 Take 36.29 away from 70.53

6 How many mm is: (a) 5 cm   (b) 5.3 cm   (c) 6 cm 2 mm   (d) 53.5 cm?

7 (a) Draw accurately, using your protractor, a rectangle 4.8 cm by 36 mm.

    (b) Draw the diagonals of your rectangle. Write their lengths, both in mm and in cm.

8 Copy and complete these balance sheets.

(a)

Details	+/−	£	p
From last page Pocket money	 +	8 1	61 50
1st balance Sweets	 −		 49
2nd balance Present for dad	 −	 1	 85
3rd balance Gift from Uncle Fred	 +		 75
4th balance			

(b)

Details	+/−	£	p
From last page Magazine	 −	8	52
Balance Pocket money	 +	8	17
Balance Sale of doll's clothes	 +	9	67
Balance Lipstick	 −	10	42
Balance		9	64

9 Construct a three-sided shape that will roll between two parallel lines spaced 4 cm apart, and at all times touch both lines.

10 One day in 1980, Jim said, 'The day before yesterday I was twelve. Next year I will be fifteen.' What was the date when he said this and what is his date of birth?

Paper Eight

1 **Examples** 4 cm = 0.04 metre;   3 cm 5 mm = 3.5 cm = 0.035 metre

Write:
(a) 5 cm in metres   (b) 0.07 metres in cm   (c) 2.6 cm in metres
(d) 3 cm 8 mm in cm   (e) 3 cm 8 mm in metres   (f) 0.065 metres in cm
(g) 7 cm in mm   (h) 80 mm in cm   (i) 4 km in metres
(j) 1 km in centimetres   (k) 1 kilometre in mm.

*2 How many:
(a) millimetres in a centimetre   (b) centimetres in a metre   (c) metres in a kilometre?

*3 Copy Figure P12, which shows a sectional view of a bowl. Use compasses to construct the 60° angles as shown.

Fig. P12

30 mm

6 cm

30 mm
Fig. P13

4 Using compasses for the two 60° angles, construct Figure P13 to the size marked on it. Do not erase your construction lines.

5 **Example** 0.466 m = 46.6 cm = 466 mm

Write as in the example:
(a) 0.555 m   (b) 0.66 m   (c) 0.7 m   (d) 8.8 m.

6 I have 0.6 metres of wire. How many centimetres is each side if I use the wire to make:
(a) an equilateral triangle   (b) a regular hexagon   (c) a regular octagon
(d) a rectangle with the length twice the width?

7 All but six of my shirts are white; all but six are blue; all but six are grey. I have no shirts of any other colour. How many blue shirts have I?

1 Multiply 97 by:
   (a) 8   (b) 10   (c) 18   (d) 78.

*2 Ebenezer Scrooge never spent his pocket money.

On January 7th he had £59.68 saved up. On January 8th he was given £1.16 pocket money. His new savings, the Balance, came to £60.84. On January 15th he was given £2.06.

Copy and complete Ebenezer's account book if he was given:
£1.23 on January 22nd;   £1.09 on January 29th;   £2.92 on February 5th;
£3.89 on February 12th.

		My Savings, by E. Scrooge	
	Date		
	7.1.83	Balance	£59.68
	8.1.83	Pocket money	£ 1.16 +
		Balance	£60.84
	15.1.83	Pocket money	£ 2.06 +
		Balance	£

*3 Jane has been collecting for a charity. How much is there in the following envelopes?

   (a) Anna's: seven 10p's, four 5p's.

   (b) Sylvia's: five 10p's, six 2p's.

   (c) Bridget's: two 50p's, five 20p's; eight 5p's.

   (d) Janet's: one 50p, five 5p's, eight 2p's, 7 pennies.

4 Copy these company accounts and fill in the missing amounts.

DETAILS	+/−	1983	1982	1981
Home Sales		£36505	£34341	£32016
Overseas Sales	+	£21886	£20346	£
TOTAL SALES		£	£	£50231
Tax	−	£15345	£10777	£
PROFIT after tax		£	£	£30604
Bank Interest	−	£12588	£ 9780	£
NETT PROFIT		£	£	£21878
Dividends paid	−	£12554	£ 9028	£
PROFIT retained		£	£	£13085

5 Change 60 km/h to: (a) km/min   (b) m/min   (c) m/s.

6 Find and describe a method to find the centre of a circle drawn on a piece of paper (e.g. using an inverted cup) if you may only use a pencil (no ruler, etc.).

Paper Ten

1 (a) 1.7×5 (b) 6.3×4 (c) 1.2×2.4 (d) 3.5×14

2 (a) 5×10 (b) 5.6×10 (c) 8.2×10 (d) 8.36×10 (e) 7×100 (f) 7.1×100
(g) 7.12×100 (h) 71.2×10 (i) 783×10 (j) 84.2×100 (k) 0.976×10

3 **Example** $26 \times 13 = 338$
So: $2.6 \times 13 = 33.8$; $2.6 \times 1.3 = 3.38$
$0.26 \times 1.3 = 0.338$; $0.26 \times 0.13 = 0.0338$

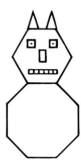

In Octaland, $47 \times 14 = 724$.
What would the answer be in Octaland for:
(a) 4.7×14 (b) 4.7×1.4 (c) 0.47×0.14
(d) 47×0.14 (e) 0.47×1.4 (f) 4.7×0.14?

*4 Name the shape used in Figure P14 for:
(a) the ears   (b) the eyes   (c) the nose
(d) the head   (e) the body.

Fig. P14 An octapussy

5 Follow the instructions given in Figures P15 and P16. Write on the polygon you cut its name, then stick it in your book.

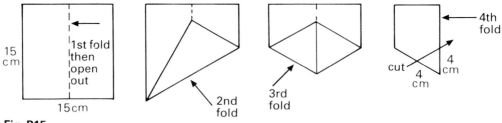

Fig. P15

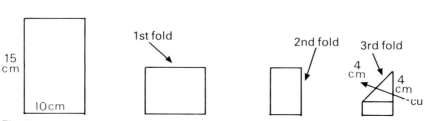

Fig. P16

6 A large piece of paper, 0.1 mm 'thick', is cut in half, then each piece is cut in half, then each piece is cut in half again (making 8 pieces) and so on, 20 times altogether. How high would the pieces be in metres if they were piled on top of each other?

You might now try to find the answer for 30 times!

Paper Eleven

1 (a) How many eights make fifty-six?

(b) How much each if £1000 is shared equally between eight people?

*2 The **sum** of 18 and 3 is 21: sum is the answer to an addition.

The **difference** between 18 and 3 is 15: difference is the answer to a subtraction.

The **product** of 18 and 3 is 54: product is the answer to a multiplication.

The **quotient** of 18 and 3 is 6: quotient is the answer to a division.

Find the sum, the difference, the product, and the quotient, saying which is which, for:
(a) 15 and 3   (b) 28 and 4   (c) 567 and 7   (d) 100 and 20.

*3 John has a bag of 40 sweets. He shares them equally between himself and his friends. Any left over he gives to his sister. A likely story!

How many sweets are left for John's sister if he has:
(a) 2 friends   (b) 3 friends   (c) 4 friends   (d) 5 friends   (e) 6 friends
(f) 7 friends?

4 Divide by 7:
(a) 84   (b) 175   (c) 770   (d) 3710   (e) 1463.

5 Divide the numbers in question 4 by eight, giving the answers as a mixed number, like $3\frac{3}{8}$.

6 Copy Figure P17, making it twice as large. The rectangle framework should be drawn faintly first. Centres are marked with dots. You could colour your finished picture.

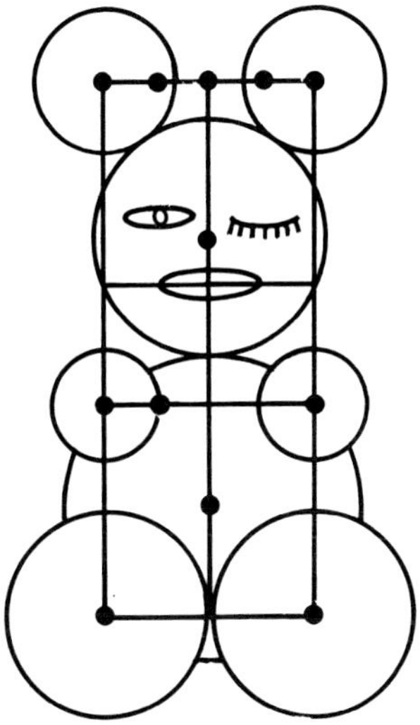

7 Which number between 1 and 50 will divide exactly by more integers than any other?

Fig. P17

8 A clock takes 12 seconds to strike 4 o'clock (four equally spaced dongs). How long will it take to strike 8 o'clock?

Paper Twelve

1 (a) List set $A = \{$multiples of 23 below 231$\}$.　　(b) Is $170 \in A$?　　(c) What is $n(A)$?

*2 Using your answer to question 1(a) to help you, find:
(a) $805 \div 23$　　(b) $1311 \div 23$　　(c) $1725 \div 23$　　(d) $690 \div 23$　　(e) $2323 \div 23$.

*3 The answer to $17 \div 3$ can be written as $5\,r\,2$ or as $5\frac{2}{3}$.

Write in both ways: (a) $13 \div 3$　　(b) $15 \div 7$　　(c) $61 \div 8$　　(d) $80 \div 9$　　(e) $60 \div 7$.

*4 Copy and complete this route matrix for the network in Figure P18.

	To			
	A	B	C	D
A	0	1	1	0
B		0		
C			0	
D				0

(F r o m)

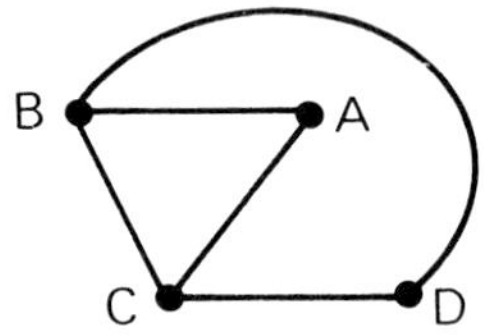

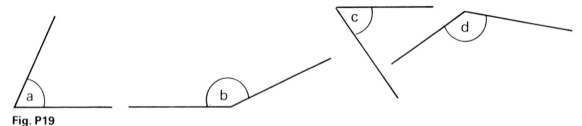

Fig. P18

*5 What is the correct name for:

(a) a point like B in Figure P18　　(b) a line like BC in Figure P18?

*6 Measure each angle in Figure P19.

Fig. P19

7 (a) Copy the nodes in Figure P20, then draw the one-way network for this matrix:

● A 　 ● B 　 ● C 　 ● D

Fig. P20

	To			
	A	B	C	D
A	2	2	0	0
B	0	0	1	0
C	0	0	0	2
D	0	0	0	1

(F r o m)

(b) How many nodes, arcs and regions in your network? (Count a loop as *one* arc.)

(c) Is your network traversable (ignoring arrows)? If yes, where do you start and finish?

8 A man notes his car's distance meter, which registers in miles, at the start and finish of three journeys. How many miles has he gone on each journey?
(a) 17 604; 18 039   (b) 18 039; 18 109   (c) 18 109; 18 754

9 Find each journey in question 8 in kilometres, taking 5 miles = 8 kilometres.

10 How many litres of petrol will the car in question 8 use altogether during its three journeys if it averages 8 km to a litre?

11 A train takes 1 hour between stations A and B. Trains leave A bound for B, and B bound for A, on the hour every hour.

How many trains does a passenger see on the journey?

Paper Thirteen

1 Find the sum, difference, product and quotient (see Paper Eleven) of 646 and 19.

Fig. P21

Questions 2 to 5 refer to Figure P21.

*2 The ratio of AB to CD is 1 : 2.

What is the ratio of:
(a) AB to EF   (b) EF to AB   (c) CD to EF   (d) EF to CD?

*3 If AB is really 3 cm long, how long is:
(a) CD   (b) EF?

*4 If CD is really 8 cm long, how long is:
(a) AB   (b) EF?

*5 If EF is really 15 cm long, how long is:
(a) AB   (b) CD?

*6 For every twelve pupils on an outing, there has to be one teacher. How many pupils could four teachers take?

*7 Draw a circle of radius 3.5 cm. In your circle draw a chord of length 5 cm.

205

*8 Roy has a distance meter on his bicycle, registering miles. Before a ride it read 3128 and after the ride it read 3146. How far was the ride?

9 AB : CD = 1 : 3   AB : EF = 1 : 4   AB : GH = 2 : 5

(a) If AB = 6 cm, find CD, EF and GH.

(b) If CD = 9 cm, find AB, EF and GH.

10 Divide by 19:   (a) 494   (b) 1919   (c) 17 233   (d) 13 319.

11 In March 1980, Concorde flew from New York to London in 24 s under 3 h. She averaged 1175 m.p.h.

(a) How long did she take in hours, minutes and seconds?

(b) How far did Concorde fly on that record-breaking journey?

12 To find what day of the week you were born (from 1900 to 1999).

Month	J	F	M	A	M	J	J	A	S	O	N	D
Number (Leap year in brackets)	1(0)	4(3)	4	0	2	5	0	3	6	1	4	6

A = last two figures of year.
$B = A \div 4$ (ignoring remainders). If no remainder it is a leap year.
C = month number (see table).
D = date in month.
$E = A + B + C + D$.
Divide E by 7, take remainder.
Remainder gives day of week, where $1 \Rightarrow$ Sunday, $6 \Rightarrow$ Friday, $0 \Rightarrow$ Saturday.

Example 2nd July 1941
$A = 41$; $B = 10$; $C = 0$; $D = 2$; $E = 53$.
$53 \div 7$ gives remainder 4, so the day was a Wednesday.

How does it work?
You sort that out! (*Hint:* 1st Jan. 1900 was a Sunday.)

Paper Fourteen

1 Use your protractor to draw an angle of 75° and an angle of 135°.

*2 How many centimetres is:
(a) 20 mm   (b) 1 m   (c) 5 m?

*3 How many metres is:
(a) 1 km   (b) $\frac{1}{2}$ km   (c) 200 cm?

*4 **Example** 35 mm can be written as 3.5 cm.

Write: (a) 47 mm in cm   (b) 8.7 cm in mm.

*5 If, on average, 1 km of motorway costs £800000 to build, how much on average would 1.5 km of motorway cost to build?

*6 Construct, using compasses and a ruler, an angle of 60°. Check your accuracy with a protractor.

*7 Use your protractor to help you copy Figure P22. Colour the flag if you like.

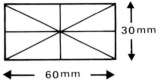

Fig. P22

8 $a = 6.35$ metres $b = 8.01$ metres $c = 6.5$ kilometres $d = 4.25$ kilometres

(a) How many centimetres is $a + b$?

(b) How many metres is c?

(c) How many metres is d?

(d) How many centimetres is $c + d$?

(e) Rewrite a, b, c and d if each is made ten times further.

(f) Write one hundredth of a, b, c and d in centimetres.

9 Construct, using compasses and a ruler, an angle of:
(a) 60°   (b) 120°   (c) 300°.

10 A boy lying down 30 metres from the base of a tower on the same level as him finds that if he turns his head up 45° he can see the top of the tower. By a scale diagram find the height of the tower. Find the height of a tall object near you in the same way.

11 Construct Figure P23. Make the two circles 5 cm and 4 cm in radius.

Fig. P23

207

Paper Fifteen

1 In Figure P24 name:
(a) line OA (b) line OB (c) point O.

2 In Figure P24, state the co-ordinates of:
(a) P (b) Q (c) R (d) O.

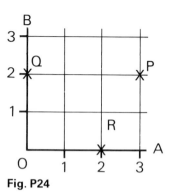

Fig. P24

*3 A teacher reckons that for every word she says, Pat says ten. If the teacher says, 'Pat, do try to control your tongue!', how many words does Pat say?

*4 Pat and Jane agree to share the lines the teacher gives to Pat in the ratio 3 : 1. That is, Jane does one for every three that Pat does. If the teacher sets 100 lines, how many does Pat have to do?

*5 Find what number the letter must be if:
(a) $x + 9 = 16$ (b) $20 - e = 12$ (c) $6a = 60$ (d) $y - 17 = 21$ (e) $7z = 56$
(f) $p + p = 12$

*6 **Example** $3a + 2a$ can be simplified to $5a$.

Simplify:
(a) $2x + 5x$ (b) $5x - 2x$ (c) $3x + x + 7x$.

*7 Draw very accurately a square of side 5 centimetres.

8 Ann and Lee agree to share the 100 lines that Ann was given in the ratio 7 : 3. How many lines does Ann have to do?

9 Seven tins of soup cost £2.66. What is the cost of one tin?

10 Find p if:
(a) $p + p + 4 = 14$ (b) $p \div 7 = 8$ (c) $3p + 1 = 13$ (d) $8 \div p = 2$.

11 State the next two numbers in the sequence:
(a) 1, 4, 16, 25 (b) 3, 7, 15, 31 (c) 0.25, 2.5, 25 (d) 1, 8, 27
(e) 1, 4, 5, 9, 14 (f) 1, 4, 10, 28, 76

12 Draw a square made up of 16 squares each of side 1 cm. How many squares in your drawing?

Paper Sixteen

1   Copy the following sets and ring the unlike terms.

   Example   {2x, ③, 5x}

   (a) {4a, 7, 2a}   (b) {2, 5, 3a}   (c) {a, 3a, c}

*2   Only like terms can be added or subtracted.

   Examples $3x + 7x \rightarrow 10x$ **but** $4a + b$ and $5 + 2a$ cannot be simplified.

   Simplify if possible:
   (a) $2a + 5$ (b) $3x + 2x$ (c) $x + x$ (d) $7 + a$ (e) $2a + a$.

*3   Draw x- and y-axes from 0 to 4 each. Write on them 'x-axis' and 'y-axis'. Mark each of the points (4,2), (0,3) and (2,0) with a cross, writing the co-ordinates next to the cross.

*4   Copy Figure P25, then work out:

   (a) its perimeter in centimetres

   (b) its area in cm^2 (divide it into two rectangles).

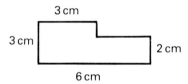

Fig. P25

*5   (a) $7.16 + 3.8$ (b) $4.29 - 1.8$ (c) $5.8 - 1.66$ (d) 4.2×5 (e) 2.6×1.1

*6   Find the area (in cm^2) and the perimeter (in mm) of a rectangle 6.7 cm long and 2.1 cm wide.

*7   What fraction of an hour is:
   (a) 15 min   (b) 20 min   (c) 5 min   (d) 90 min?

*8   Calculate the angle between the hands of a clock at:
   (a) 3 o'clock   (b) 4 o'clock.

9   Simplify:
   (a) $3a + 4a$ (b) $5b - 2b$ (c) $3c + 2c + 1$ (d) $4d + 4 + d$ (e) $3e + 3 - 2e$.

10   If $h = 4$, state the value of:
   (a) 2h   (b) h^2 (c) $2 + h$ (d) $h - 2$.

11 $a = 4.73$ $b = 36$ $c = 3.5$ $d = 0.38$

   Find the value of:
   (a) each figure 3   (b) $a + b + c + d$ (c) $b - a$ (d) $c - d$ (e) $a \times b$
   (f) $c \times d$ (g) $a \times d$.

209

12 Calculate the perimeter in cm and the area in cm² of the shapes in Figure P26.

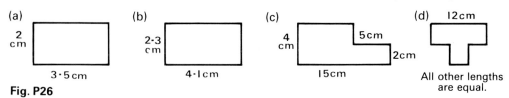

(a)
2 cm
3·5 cm

(b)
2·3 cm
4·1 cm

(c)
4 cm
5 cm
2 cm
15 cm

(d) 12 cm
All other lengths are equal.

Fig. P26

13 Calculate the angle between the hands of a clock at: (a) 4:00   (b) 4:20   (c) 4:40

14 Find three answers to '1 added to 16 four times'.

Paper Seventeen

1 Cancel the following fractions to make them as simple as possible.
(a) $\frac{10}{20}$ (b) $\frac{12}{15}$ (c) $\frac{24}{30}$ (d) $\frac{36}{40}$ (e) $\frac{25}{35}$ (f) $\frac{16}{48}$ (g) $\frac{28}{49}$

*2 $A = \{\frac{5}{10}, \frac{6}{18}, \frac{3}{6}, \frac{4}{12}, \frac{5}{20}, \frac{7}{28}, \frac{15}{30}, \frac{10}{30}\}$

List sets B, C and D where:

B is a set made up from the elements of set A that are equal to a half;

C is a set made up from the elements of set A that are equal to a third;

D is a set made up from the elements of set A that are equal to a quarter.

*3 (a) £8.08 − £3.25   (b) £4.26 × 5   (c) 2006 − 197   (d) 4.6 × 7.2
(e) 0.46 × 7.2 (Use the answer to (d).)

*4 Draw lines AB, CD and EF, making AB = 30 mm, CD = 4.5 cm and EF = 2.3 cm.

*5 If each line in question 4 was lengthened in the ratio 2 : 1, how many millimetres long would each become?

*6 Taking 5 miles as being 8 kilometres, how many kilometres is 30 miles?

7 (a) Copy and complete: $\frac{2}{\ \ } = \frac{4}{6} = \frac{\ \ }{9} = \frac{22}{\ \ }$

(b) Arrange in descending order of magnitude (i.e. biggest first):
$\frac{2}{3}$; $2\frac{1}{4}$; 0.6; 0.25; $\frac{16}{48}$; $\frac{7}{2}$; 0.7

(c) Which of the following fractions is nearest to a whole one?
$\frac{17}{20}$; $\frac{14}{17}$; $\frac{16}{19}$; $\frac{8}{11}$; $\frac{13}{16}$

8 A 6.3 cm nail is driven 14 mm deep into a plank. What fraction of the nail is still showing?

9 Simplify the ratio:
(a) $4:8$ (b) $6:30$ (c) $8:56$ (d) $25:200$ (e) $32:60$.

10 If the first part of each ratio in question 9 is £16, how much is the second part?

11 Take a piece of paper about 30 cm by 2 cm. Tie a single knot in it and flatten out the knot. Name the shape made by the knot when it is held up to the light.

12 My car's fuel consumption averages 45 miles to the gallon. Convert this to litres per 100 km. (Take 5 miles = 8 km and 1 gallon = 4.5 litres.)

13 Once every hour a train leaves Chufftown for Bigtown, and once every hour a train leaves Chufftown for Smalltown. Both trains stop at Midway Junction. I arrive at the station at Chufftown at different times each day and travel to Midway. I nearly always catch the Bigtown train. Why do you think this is?

Paper Eighteen

1 (a) 316×25 (b) 100×7.65 (c) 10×0.8 (d) 200×300 (e) 4.1×6
(f) 4.1×6.2 (g) $1505 \div 5$ (h) $3006 - 899$

2 **Example** $0.85 = \frac{85}{100} = \frac{17}{20}$ (dividing both 85 and 100 by 5)

Write as a simplified common fraction, as simply as possible:
(a) 0.25 (b) 0.5 (c) 0.7 (d) 0.8 (e) 0.95 (f) 0.08

*3 Change to a decimal fraction, by dividing the top number by the bottom number, or otherwise:
(a) $\frac{3}{4}$ (b) $\frac{3}{8}$ (c) $\frac{4}{5}$

*4 Copy and complete the arrow diagram for the relation 'is a third of'.

is a third of

$9 \longrightarrow$ ____

$2 \longrightarrow$ ____

$3 \longrightarrow$ ____

$4 \longrightarrow$ ____

$\longrightarrow$ ____ 21

$\longrightarrow$ ____ 36

*5 Using your protractor to help you, draw a clock face on a circle of radius 4 cm. Make the clock show 'half past nine'.

6 What decimal fraction is the same as:
(a) $\frac{3}{100}$ (b) $\frac{17}{20}$?

7 Look at the tables in exercise 17B. Then, for values of x from 0 to 4, draw a table for the mapping:
(a) $x \rightarrow x + 3$ (b) $x \rightarrow 3x$ (c) $x \rightarrow x^3$.

8 Plot co-ordinates from question 7 (a) and (b), but not (c), on a graph, with the x-axis from 0 to 4 and the y-axis from 0 to 12. Join the set of points for each mapping with a straight line, using a ruler.

9 List: (a) $\{x : 1 < x < 5,\ x \text{ integral}\}$ (b) {factors of 84}.

10 (a) Change 75 m.p.h. to km/h, taking 5 miles = 8 km.

(b) How many metres per second is 75 m.p.h.?

11 Draw a clock face numbered from 1 to 12. Show how to divide it into three parts with two straight lines so that the sum of the numbers in each part is equal.

Paper Nineteen

1 For Figure P27:

(a) Draw up the route matrix for the network.

(b) State the order of nodes A, B, C and D.

(c) How many regions are there in the network?

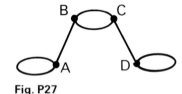
Fig. P27

*2 Write the word PAPER as it would appear when reflected in a mirror.

*3 Calculate the perimeter and the area of a rectangle 2 cm long and 1.5 cm wide.

*4 Write in shorthand:
(a) $c \times c$ (b) $c + c$.

*5 If $y = 4$, find the value of:
(a) $2y$ (b) y^2 (c) $y + 6$.

*6 **Example** $3x + 2 + 4x \rightarrow 7x + 2$

Simplify:
(a) $2x + 2 + 5x$ (b) $3a - 2 - a$.

*7 Frank and Peter decide to share their pools win of £500 in the ratio 2 : 3. That is, for every £2 that Frank receives Peter will receive £3. To do this they first divide the money into five equal piles. How much money does each receive?

8 Which of the shapes in Figure P28 have the same area?

Fig. P28

9 If $y = 7$ state the value of:
(a) $2y$ (b) y^2 (c) $y - 7$ (d) $2y + 1$.

10 Simplify:
(a) $5x + 1 + 7x$ (b) $5x - 1 + 7x$ (c) $3 + 2a + a$ (d) $4x + y - 2x - y$.

11 If a set $A = \emptyset$:

(a) What is n(A)?

(b) Describe a set that A could be.

12 Divide £180 in the ratio 4 : 5.

13 A clock ticks once a second. How many days, hours, minutes and seconds will it take for a million ticks?

14 A donkey's right legs walk 12 km a day but his left legs walk 11 km a day. Suggest what the donkey's job might be.

Paper Twenty

1 Copy the grid in Figure P29. Label the x-axis and the y-axis. Plot the points whose ordered pairs are (2,1), (0,1) and (1,3). Join them to make a triangle. Draw the triangle's line of symmetry. Reflect the triangle in the mirror line, m.

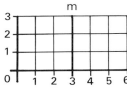

Fig. P29

2 (a) Name the point where the axes of a graph cross.

(b) What other name have you met for 'ordered pair'?

(c) Write the ordered pairs for the three corners of your image triangle in question 1.

*3   Add £3.68, £5, £4.06 and 25p.

*4   Find the change from £10 if you spend: (a) £1.96   (b) £3.85   (c) £2.18

*5   Taking 5 miles as about 8 kilometres, suggest a sensible speed limit in km/h to replace:
(a) 30 m.p.h.   (b) 50 m.p.h.   (c) 70 m.p.h.

*6   Find the sum, difference and product (see Paper Eleven) of 17.6 and 0.97

*7 $A = \{$multiples of 13$\}$. Is $143 \in A$?

*8   If $d = 5$, what is the value of: (a) d^2 (b) $2d$?

*9   Calculate the perimeter and area of Figure P30.

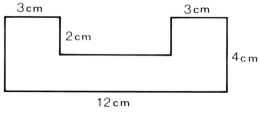

Fig. P30

10   I buy six pens @ 35p each, four writing-pads @ 84p each, two books @ £3.92 each and three tubes of glue @ £0.56 each. What is the total cost and the change from a £20 note?

11   The circumference of a circle can be found fairly accurately by multiplying the diameter by 3.14. The hands of a clock, measured from the centre of the clock face to their tips, are 6 cm and 8 cm long. How much further does the tip of the minute hand travel in one hour than the tip of the hour hand?

12   A man walks 6 km at 6 km/h, then 6 km at 3 km/h.

(a) How long does the journey take?

(b) What is his average speed over the whole journey?

Paper Twenty-one

1   How many:
(a) days in December   (b) degrees in a complete turn   (c) eggs in a dozen
(d) grams in a kilogram   (e) metres in a kilometre   (f) volts in a kilovolt
(g) mm in 4.2 cm   (h) cm in 3.01 metres   (i) cm in 3.1 m
(j) quarters in a half   (k) eighths in a whole   (l) seconds in an hour?

214

*2 Copy the shapes in Figure P31, together with their names.

Mark on each shape all its lines of symmetry.

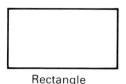 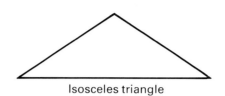 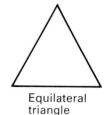

      Rectangle   Square   Isosceles triangle   Equilateral
                                                                                       triangle
Fig. P31

*3 A right-angled triangle has one angle of 40°. How many degrees are the other two angles?

*4 (a) $1.05 + 21 + 3.6 + 8.023$ (b) $3 - 1.5$ (c) $4 - 1.32$ (d) 0.82×3.3
     (e) $\frac{1}{4}$ of £100   (f) $\frac{1}{2}$ of 3.2   (g) $3621 \div 17$ (h) 200×200

*5 How much each if four friends share £5 equally?

6 Can a triangle have angles of 108°, 62.5° and 10.5°? Explain your answer.

7 Construct a triangle with the longest side 50 mm and two of its angles 105° and 45°. Measure the shortest side in millimetres.

8 $j = 3000$ $k = 200$ $l = 17.6$ $m = 0.25$

Find:
(a) $j + k + l + m$ (b) $j \times k$ (c) $l \times m$ (d) $k - l$ (e) $j \times l$ (f) $k \times l$
(g) $k \times m$ (h) $j \div k$.

9 Construct an equilateral triangle of side 4 cm using the compass method (not a protractor) for the 60° angles.

Join each vertex (corner) to the mid-point of the opposite side.

Draw a circle which:
(a) just fits in the triangle (called the incircle)
(b) the triangle just fits in (called the circumcircle).

Measure the radii of the two circles in millimetres.

10 (a) Write $<$ or $>$ between each pair (see exercise 16A, question 19):
     (i) $\frac{5}{8}$ $\frac{9}{13}$ (ii) $\frac{5}{18}$ $\frac{9}{34}$ (iii) $\frac{7}{8}$ $\frac{11}{13}$

(b) Arrange the six fractions in order of size, smallest first.

11 'You have half as long left as you have had' said the maths teacher during a one-hour maths exam. How long is there left?

Paper Twenty-two

1 Give answers to all the following in kilograms.
  (a) 5 kg 214 g + 3 kg 126 g   (b) 7 kg + 4 kg 846 g + 324 g
  (c) 3.648 kg + 1.632 kg   (d) 4.623 kg − 1.728 kg   (e) 7 kg − 1.247 kg
  (f) 7.324 kg × 6   (g) 2.416 kg × 7   (h) 6.524 kg ÷ 4   (i) 7.304 kg ÷ 8

*2 (a) Copy Figure P32 onto squared paper.

  (b) Plot on the grid the points (3,2), (3,3), (4,3), (4,5), (5,5), (5,3), (8,3), (8,2), (9,2), (8,0), (2,0).

  (c) Use your ruler to join these points in order.

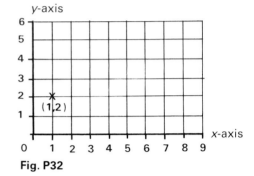

Fig. P32

*3 **A number can be divided by 3 if its digit-add is 3, 6 or 9.**

  Example The digit-add of 4295 is 4 + 2 + 9 + 5 = 20 → 2 + 0 = 2.
    4295 will *not* divide exactly by 3, as its digit-add is 2.

  For each of the following numbers, write 'Yes' if it divides exactly by 3, and give the answer to the division.

  Write 'No' if it will not divide exactly by 3.

  (a) 4218   (b) 5142   (c) 7129   (d) 1004   (e) 4215

4 Copy each shape in Figure P33, writing under it its correct name chosen from:
Concave hexagon; Quadrilateral; Triangle; Concave octagon; Convex hexagon; Convex octagon; Concave pentagon.

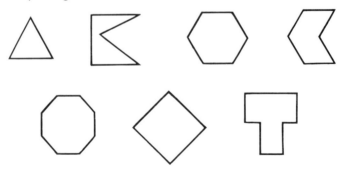

Fig. P33

5 Use 'digit-add' (see exercise 10C, question 6) to list x if x∈ {2, 3, 6, 9} and x is a factor of:
  (a) 2247   (b) 4266   (c) 824 197   (d) 841 275.

6 Distown lies on the same road as Ayetown and Beetown. A signpost at Ayetown says Distown is 3 miles away and a signpost at Beetown says Distown is 5 miles away. What is the distance along the road from Ayetown to Beetown? (You should be able to give more than one answer.)

7 What fraction of 3p is one third of 2p?

Paper Twenty-three

1 What is: (a) 20% of £1   (b) 40% of £10?

2 Write in words: (a) 72   (b) 116   (c) 8000   (d) 24 000   (e) 1 000 000.

3 (a) $16 \times \frac{1}{2}$ (b) $\frac{1}{4} \times 12$ (c) $\frac{3}{4} \times 3$ (as a mixed number)   (d) $12 \times \frac{5}{6}$
 (e) $9 \times \frac{5}{12}$ (f) $\frac{24}{14} \times 7$

4 **Examples** $5a + 6a + 3a \rightarrow 14a$ $9a - 2a \rightarrow 7a$

Simplify:
(a) $7a + 2a + 5a$ (b) $9a + 7a + a$ (c) $7a - 3a$ (d) $11a - 7a$.

*5 Cancel to make the bottom number as small as possible:
(a) $\frac{3}{6}$ (b) $\frac{5}{10}$ (c) $\frac{12}{16}$ (d) $\frac{25}{100}$ (e) $\frac{32}{40}$

*6 Copy the diagrams in Figure P34 onto squared paper, then draw the reflection of each in the mirror line m.

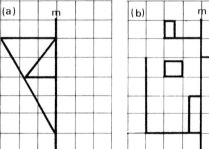

Fig. P34

*7 Write in figures:
(a) six hundred and three
(b) seven thousand and eight
(c) fifty thousand, one hundred and nine
(d) five million, twenty thousand.

8 In a survey to find which sweet some pupils liked best, 15% said Minto, 35% said Minchew, 25% said Peppo, and 10% said Spearmint.

(a) What percentage of those asked did not choose any of the sweets named?

(b) Write the given four percentages as fractions, with the denominators as small as possible.

9 Simplify:
(a) $3a + 7a - 4$ (b) $4a - 3a + 5$ (c) $3 - 2a + 6a$ (d) $a + a$ (e) $a \times a$.

217

10 Find the values of the expressions in question 9 if $a = 2$.

11 Copy and complete:

(a) $\frac{1}{5} = \frac{2}{10} = \frac{}{15} = \frac{}{20} = \frac{}{55} = \frac{6}{} = \frac{9}{} = \frac{15}{}$

(b) $\frac{1}{8} = \frac{2}{} = \frac{}{24} = \frac{}{32} = \frac{}{64} = \frac{10}{} = \frac{12}{}$

12 If 660 pupils took part in the survey in question 8, how many chose each sweet?

Paper Twenty-four

1 Write as a percentage:
(a) $\frac{4}{5}$ (b) $\frac{11}{20}$ (c) $\frac{17}{20}$ (d) $\frac{1}{8}$.

2 Figure P35 shows a unicursal curve, that is, a diagram made from one continuous line which returns to its starting point. Draw your own unicursal curve. Find how many colours are needed if regions with a common arc are to be different colours.

Fig. P35

*3 If $a = 2$, $b = 3$, $c = 0$ and $d = 4$, find the value of:
(a) $3a$ (b) $a + b$ (c) $3c$ (d) $2d + 4$ (e) $18 - 4b$ (f) $3ab$
(g) $2acd$ (h) $4d - 3a$.

*4 Add, giving your answer in metres:
126 cm;   48 cm;   212 cm;   7 cm;   106 cm.

*5 How many centimetres make:
(a) 1 m   (b) 1 m 28 cm   (c) 3 m 8 cm   (d) 2 m 6 cm   (e) 2.46 m
(f) 10.04 m?

6 In the fifth year of a school there are 180 pupils. Thirty of them are prefects.

(a) What fraction of the year are prefects?

(b) What percentage of the year are prefects?

7 If $a = 3$, $b = 5$, $c = 0$ and $d = 1$, find the value of:
(a) $2a - b$ (b) $14 + 2b$ (c) $5c + 5d$ (d) $3ab$ (e) $4ac$ (f) $3d - 2c + 7$
(g) abc (h) $a + bd$ (i) $4c + 3d$ (j) $72abcd$.

8 Five children have heights of 1 m 64 cm, 148 cm, 1.5 m, 1 m 49 cm, and 157 cm.

What is their total height in: (a) cm   (b) metres?

9 A roll of tape is 50 m long. How much is left after nine 1 m 48 cm pieces have been cut from it?

10 Write in km:
(a) 3649 m   (b) 4204 m   (c) 461 m   (d) 27 m.

11 Write *x* grams in kilograms.

12 What is the number which is half as big as *k*?

13 Add VAT at 15% to the following prices.

Trousers, £20;   Coat, £46;   Socks, £1.20.

Paper Twenty-five

1 (a) Copy and complete the mapping diagram.

(b) Write the pairs of values as co-ordinates: (0,3), (1,4), etc.

(c) Plot the co-ordinates on a grid labelled 0 to 4 along the bottom and 0 to 7 up the side.

Join the points together.

$$x \rightarrow x + 3$$
$$0 \rightarrow 3$$
$$1 \rightarrow 4$$
$$2 \rightarrow 5$$
$$3 \rightarrow$$
$$4 \rightarrow$$

2 Draw a diagram like the one in question 1 for the mapping $x \rightarrow 3x$. Use the same values of *x*. Plot and join the points, using 0 to 4 along the bottom and 0 to 12 up the side.

3 Round to the nearest 10:
(a) 463   (b) 5326   (c) 741   (d) 1026.

4 Round the numbers in question 3 to the nearest 100.

5 Write in both words and figures the times shown on the clock faces in Figure P36.

Fig. P36

6 Write your answers to question 5 in 24-hour-clock time, if all the times are past noon.

219

7 Copy Figure P37, then draw the images of the shapes in the sloping mirror line. You can check your answer by using a real mirror.

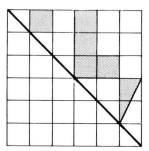

Fig. P37

*8 Amy sells 63 raffle tickets, numbered in order. If the first ticket she sells is number 24, what is the number of the last one?

9 A pond-lily leaf doubles its size each day. It completely covers the pond in twenty days. How long would two leaves take to cover the same pond if they both start at the same size as the first and grow at the same rate?

Paper Twenty-six

1 Copy each diagram in Figure P38 onto squared paper, then draw all the lines of symmetry.

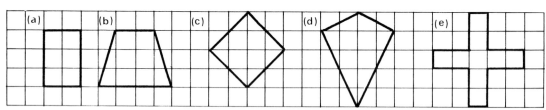

Fig. P38

2 Find the value of the letter if:
(a) $3x = 9$ (b) $a + 7 = 10$ (c) $a - 7 = 4$ (d) $7 - a = 6$ (e) $2c + 6 = 24$
(f) $3d - 5 = 7$.

3 Find the sizes of angles a, b and c in Figure P39.

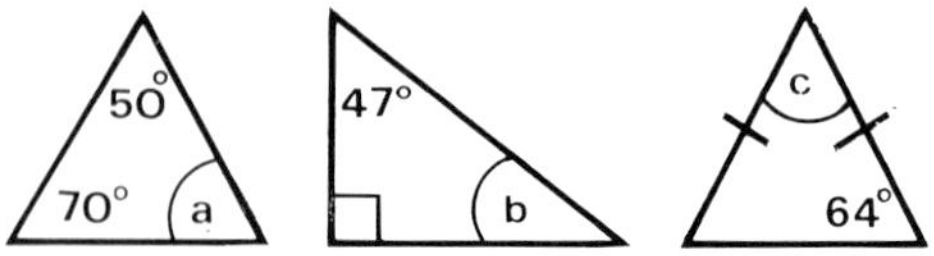

Fig. P39

4 Write as a decimal fraction:
(a) $\frac{1}{2}$ (b) $\frac{1}{4}$ (c) $\frac{2}{5}$ (d) $\frac{3}{4}$ (e) $\frac{4}{5}$ (f) $\frac{5}{8}$

5 **Example** $0.26 = \frac{26}{100} = \frac{13}{50}$

Write as a common fraction, simplified if possible:
(a) 0.4 (b) 0.65 (c) 0.17 (d) 0.05

*6 How many squares can be made by joining any four dots in Figure P40?

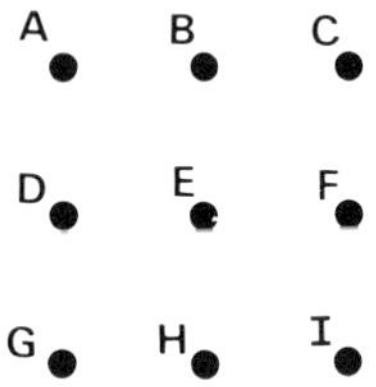

Fig. P40

220

7 Find the value of *n* if:
(a) $1.3n = 11.7$ (b) $4.7 + n = 6.2$ (c) $3.1 - n = 2.4$

8 The twelve people at a meeting each shake the hand of everyone in the room. How many handshakes will there be? Can you find a rule to give the answer for any number of people?

Paper Twenty-seven

1 Raj pays £967.20 rent per year. How much does he pay per week?

*2 $A = \{174.8, 3000, 416.25, 2187.2, 96.8\}$

Rewrite set *A* with each element divided by:
(a) 10   (b) 100.

*3 (a) $17.24 \div 4$ (b) $30.065 \div 5$ (c) $160.24 \div 8$

*4 Find the value of the letter if:
(a) $a - 4 = 0$ (b) $3c = 21$ (c) $3c - 4 = 8$.

*5 Write 12 mm in:
(a) cm and mm   (b) cm.

*6 The passenger train in Figure P41 is the same length as six goods trucks. It has four coaches. Another train has six coaches. How many goods trucks long is it?

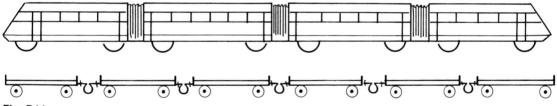

Fig. P41

*7 Calculate the perimeter and the area of each shape in Figure P42.

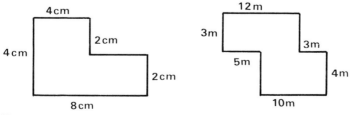

Fig. P42

8 (a) 46.5 km ÷ 3 (b) 57.764 kg ÷ 7 (c) 387 litres ÷ 12 (d) 12441 kg ÷ 6

9 Express in grams:
(a) 4 kg (b) 3 kg 246 g (c) 7 kg 48 g (d) 4.605 kg (e) 3.6 kg.

10 Express in ml:
(a) 3 litres (b) 2 litres 460 ml (c) 5.79 litres (d) 6.403 litres.

11 Find the cost of 5 kg of grass seed if 200 g costs 75p.

12 State the values of (a) to (h) in this table.

Example Scale measure 3 cm; Scale 1 : 10000;
Real measure = 3 cm × 10000 = 30000 cm = 300 m = 0.3 km

Scale measure	5 m	1.7 m	10 cm	2.8 cm
Scale	1 : 7	1 : 50	1 : 5	1 : 100
Real measure	(a) m	(b) m	(c) m	(d) m

Scale measure	7.6 mm	1.46 mm	4 cm	4.8 cm
Scale	1 : 3	1 : 1000	1 : 10000	1 : 50000
Real measure	(e) cm	(f) km	(g) km	(h) km

Paper Twenty-eight

1 The midday temperatures at noon each day for a week were 16°C, 21°C, 20°C, 19°C, 14°C, 16°C, 20°C. What was the mean temperature for the week?

2 (a) h min
         1   24
       +3   36

(b) h min
     6   27
   +8   39

(c) h min
     6   37
   +4   52

(d) h min
     8   00
   −5   40

(e) h min
     6   20
   −4   30

(f) h min
     8   36
   −5   46

***3** Draw an example of:
(a) an acute angle (b) an obtuse angle.

4 Copy the shapes in Figure P43 onto squared paper. Then draw the reflection of each shape in the mirror line, m.

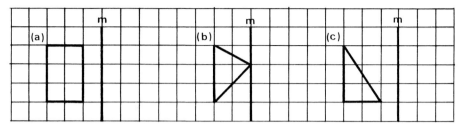

Fig. P43

*5 Noah's Ark was 300 cubits long, 50 cubits wide and 30 cubits high. One cubit is about 52 cm (the length of a man's arm from elbow to middle-finger tip). Find the dimensions of Noah's Ark in metres.

6 At what hours o'clock is the reflex angle between the hands 300°?

7 Sketch the diagrams in Figure P44, then draw their reflections in the mirror lines marked m.

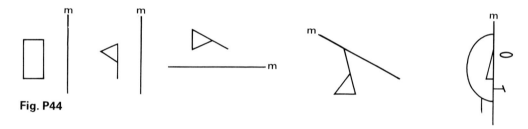

Fig. P44

8 Arrange in order, largest first:
$\frac{2}{5}, \frac{4}{6}, \frac{3}{8}, \frac{5}{9}, \frac{6}{10}, \frac{7}{11}$.

9 Figure P45 represents a negative lying on the print made from it. Trace the diagram. Can you find a point on the negative which is directly above the same point on the print?

10 Referring to Figure P45, investigate the coincidence of points for other positions of the negative.

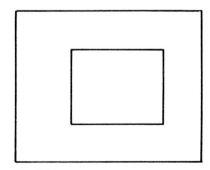

Fig. P45

223

Paper Twenty-nine

1 $N = \{3, 5, 7, 8, 9, 11, 12, 13, 16, 18, 19, 21, 22, 24, 27, 29, 30, 93, 100\}$

List the following sets of elements from set N.
(a) $P = \{$prime numbers$\}$ (b) $S = \{$square numbers$\}$
(c) $T = \{$triangular numbers$\}$ (d) $F = \{$Fibonacci numbers$\}$

2 Figure P46 shows three bar-codes. What six figures should be printed under the third one?

  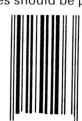

Fig. P46 302395 001861

3 (a) 9109×1 (b) 9109×2 (c) 9109×3

(d) Write the next six terms in this sequence.

(e) Explain the connection between your answers and the multiples of nine.

*4 A ticket machine only accepts 5p and 10p coins. Using o for a 5p and O for a 10p, copy and complete the table to show all the ways and orders of putting 5p, 10p, 15p, 20p and 25p into the machine. 20p is done for you as an example.

		Total ways
5p		
10p		
15p		
20p	o o o o | o o O | o O o | O o o | O O	5
25p		

5 Draw a circle, centre O, of radius 35 mm. Draw a chord AB of length 0.06 m, then draw the radii joining A and B to the centre.

Measure:
(a) ∠ AOB obtuse (b) ∠ AOB reflex (c) ∠ OBA acute (d) ∠ OAB acute.

6 (a) Find the pattern in each column of this table, then write the next two rows.

(b) Take each row in turn. Square each number and find a connection between the three answers.

3	4	5
5	12	13
7	24	25
9	40	41

224

Paper Thirty

1 A circle has a diameter of 9 cm. What is its radius in mm?

2 What will five copies of a book cost if one costs £3.94?

3 An isosceles triangle has one angle of 100°. Calculate the other two angles.

*4 State the missing number:
(a) 1, 3, 6, ..., 15   (b) 1, 4, 9, ..., 25   (c) 1, 1, 2, 3, 5, ..., 13

*5 A man walks 20 km in 4 hours. Assuming his speed is the same all the time:

(a) What is his walking speed in km/h?

(b) How many minutes does he take to walk 1 km?

(c) How many metres does he travel in 1 min, correct to the nearest metre?

*6 Write the numbers from 1 to 100 in rows of ten as in the diagram.

1	2	3	4	5	6	7	8	9	10
11	12	13	14	15	16	17	18	19	20
			etc.			etc.			

Put a ring round all the multiples of 3. Put a cross over all the multiples of 7. Which numbers have both a ring and a cross? What can you say about these numbers?

7 In one minute a car passes three posts set 500 metres from each other. Find its speed in km/h.

8 (a) $7 \times 11 \times 13$

(b) Write any three-figure number twice (like 104 104).

Which of the following are factors of your six-figure number:
(i) 7   (ii) 11   (iii) 13   (iv) 1001?

9 Draw, colour, and cut out four L-shapes, each made up of four 1 cm squares, as in Figure P47.

Arrange the shapes so that only the eight coloured squares can be seen (you need to overlap them of course). When you have succeeded, try getting just the white squares to show.

Fig. P47

Glossary

If you cannot remember what a word means, or cannot find a particular topic in the book, this glossary should help you.

Notes   When you are told to 'see ...', this refers you to the heading in the Book One Summary, which comes after this glossary, and to the chapter in the book where you can find more information.

Words in italics, like *power*, can themselves be looked up in the glossary if you do not know what they mean.

A
Acute An angle between 0° and 90°.
Arc Part of a circle: see CIRCLES (5).
Part of a network: see NETWORKS (11).

B
Bar-chart A diagram to show information by a series of columns or bars. See chapter 33.

C
Chord See CIRCLES (5).
Construct Draw accurately, usually using only a ruler and a pair of compasses.
Co-ordinates The method of fixing the position of a point on a grid; also called an Ordered Pair. See GRAPHS (13).
Cube Shape: a solid with six square faces; dice are cubes.
Algebra: A number or letter multiplied by itself, then multiplied by itself again, e.g. k^3 (k cubed) $= k \times k \times k$.
Cubic As in cubic centimetre (cm^3). $1\,cm^3$ is the volume of a cube of side $1\,cm$. It is also the volume of anything with the same volume as this cube.

D
Denominator The correct name for the bottom number in a fraction. It 'denominates' (names) the kind of fraction that it is, e.g. the 4 in $\frac{3}{4}$ tells you that the fraction is quarters.
Diameter See CIRCLES (5).
Difference The result of a subtraction.
Digit One of the figures 0, 1, 2, 3, 4, 5, 6, 7, 8 and 9.
Digit-add Used in this book for the result of continually adding the digits of a number until a single digit results, e.g. the digit-add of 156 is 3. See DIVISIBILITY (10).
Domain The set of numbers, or the *region*, from which you start. See MAPPINGS (17).

E
Element A member of a set. $3 \in F$ says '3 is an element of set F'.
Equilateral Equal-sided. See TRIANGLES (20).

F

Face	A flat side of a solid.
Factor	See KINDS OF NUMBERS (30).
Figure	A diagram, or a *digit*.

I

Image	The result of transforming an *object*, e.g. by reflecting it. See REFLECTION (18). Also the result of a *mapping*, e.g. Under the mapping $y \rightarrow 2y$, the image of 6 is 12.
Improper fraction	A top-heavy fraction, like $\frac{13}{2}$.
Index/Indices	The raised figure (figures) that gives the *power*, e.g. the 2 in x^2.
Infinite	Without ending.
Integer	A *whole number*, like 4 or 18.
Isosceles	With two equal sides. See TRIANGLES (20).

L

Litre	The metric unit for liquids. See METRIC SYSTEM (21).
Locus	The path made by a moving point.

M

Mapping	The change of one number to another by a given rule, or the rule itself, e.g. $y \rightarrow y^2$ is a mapping which changes a number into its square, so that 4 maps onto 16 and 5 maps onto 25. See MAPPINGS (17).
Mixed number	Consisting partly of an *integer* and partly a common fraction, like $3\frac{3}{4}$.
Multiple	See KINDS OF NUMBERS (30).

N

Natural number	A number used to count objects, like 1 and 14.
Network	A diagram of connected lines. See NETWORKS (11).
Node	A junction of *arcs*. See NETWORKS (11).
Null set	A set with no elements.
Numerator	The correct name for the top number in a fraction. It tells you how many of that kind of fraction there are, e.g. the 3 in $\frac{3}{4}$ tells you there are 3 quarters.

O

Object	The point or shape that is being transformed, e.g. by a reflection. See REFLECTION (18). Also the number that is going to be mapped by a *mapping*.
Obtuse	An angle between 90° and 180°.
Ordered pair	Another name for the *co-ordinates* of a point.
Origin	The point (0,0) on a graph. See GRAPHS (13).

P

Pentagon	A five-sided shape. Not to be confused with *polygon*.
Perimeter	The distance or line round a shape.

Pictogram	A chart showing information by means of picture symbols that represent a certain amount. See chapter 33.
Pie-chart	A chart showing information by dividing up a circle. See chapter 33.
Polygon	A many-sided shape. See POLYGONS (9).
Power	The result of multiplying a number by itself a number of times, e.g. '5 raised to the power 3' is $5 \times 5 \times 5 = 125$. It can also be shown by an *index*, e.g. 5^3.
Prime	A number with only two *factors*, 1 and itself. See KINDS OF NUMBERS (30).
Product	The result of a multiplication.

Q

Quotient	The result of a division.

R

Radius	See CIRCLES (5).
Range	See MAPPINGS (17).
Ratio	A comparison between two amounts, usually written with 'to' or a colon (:), e.g. the ratio of boys to girls at a party was $3:4$. See RATIO/SCALES (12 & 32).
Rectangular	Number: see KINDS OF NUMBERS (30).
Recur	To repeat, as in recurring decimals, e.g. 0.333 333 3... The recurrence is shown with a dot (or two dots), as in 0.3̇ for 0.3333... and 0.1̇45̇3 for 0.145 345 345 3...
Reflex	An angle more than $180°$.
Region	A special area of a diagram, especially of a graph or a *network*. See NETWORKS (11).

S

Square	Algebra: a letter with *index* 2, like x^2.
	Number: a *whole number* that is made by multiplying another whole number by itself. See KINDS OF NUMBERS (30).
Standard form	The method of writing a number as a number between 1 and 10 multiplied by a *power* of ten, e.g. 2.5×10^6 is the standard form way of writing 2 500 000.
Sum	The result of an addition.

T

Tonne	A metric unit of weight, equal to 1000 kg.
Topologically equivalent	See TOPOLOGY (11).
Triangular number	See KINDS OF NUMBERS (30).

V

Vertex	The mathematical name for a corner.

W

Whole number	A number with no fractional part. 4 is a whole number, $5\frac{1}{2}$ is not. Also called *integers*.

228

Note Only 'key facts' are given in this summary. The numbers in brackets refer you to the book chapters, where fuller details will be found.

Basic Arithmetic (2, 4, 8, 10, 28)

You should be able to apply the following operations to all integers and decimal fractions, except division by a decimal fraction.

Addition, giving a **sum.**
Subtraction, giving a **difference.**
Multiplication, giving a **product.**
Division, giving a **quotient.**

Sets

'List a set' means write all its **elements,** e.g. $A = \{1, 3, 5\}$
'Describe a set' means write what the elements are in words, e.g. A is the set of odd integers from 1 to 5.
$1 \in A$ means '1 is an element of set A'.
$n(A) = 3$ means 'the number of elements in set A is 3'.
$\emptyset$ or $\{\}$ is a null set. It has no elements.

Angles (3)

Acute: less than 90°.
Obtuse: between 90° and 180°.
Reflex: more than 180°.

Circles (5)

The **circumference** is the special name for the perimeter of a circle (all the way round it).
An **arc** is part of the circumference.
The **diameter** is twice the **radius** ($d = 2r$).

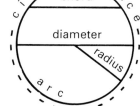

Metric System (6, 21)

Prefixes: milli $\Rightarrow \frac{1}{1000}$ **centi** $\Rightarrow \frac{1}{100}$ **kilo** $\Rightarrow 1000$
      Note: $\Rightarrow$ is the symbol for 'implies'.

Length: 1000 millimetres (1000 mm)   = 1 metre (1 m)
      100 centimetres (100 cm)   = 1 metre
      1000 metres (1000 m)   = 1 kilometre (1 km)
Conversion: 5 miles $\backsimeq$ 8 kilometres
      Note: $\backsimeq$ is the symbol for 'is approximately'.

Examples   28.5 mm = 2.85 cm   3.5 km = 3 km 500 m   3.05 km = 3 km 50 m

Weight: The basic unit is the **gram.** 1 g is a very small weight; about the weight of two drawing pins.
      There is an extra unit of weight, the **tonne,** equal to 1000 kg.

229

Conversion: 1 kg is about $2\frac{1}{4}$ lbs (pounds weight).

Capacity: Usually used for liquids. The basic unit is the **litre**, but the 'kilolitre' is not used, e.g. 30000 litres, not 30 kl.

Conversion: 1 litre is about $1\frac{3}{4}$ pints; 1 gallon is about 4.5 litres.

Constructions (7)

You should be able to construct a 60° angle.

Polygons (9)

A **polygon** is a shape with any number of straight sides. Special polygon names (number of sides in brackets) include: triangle (3); quadrilateral (4); pentagon (5); hexagon (6); octagon (8); decagon (10).

 Convex

 Concave

Divisibility (10)

Note: In all the following, divide ⇒ (implies) divides exactly a whole number of times.
Last figure: even ⇒ divides by 2; 0 ⇒ divides by 2, 5 and 10; 5 ⇒ divides by 5.
Digit-add: 3, 6 or 9 ⇒ divides by 3 (and by 6 if an even number); 9 ⇒ divides by 9.
A number divides by 4 if the last two digits divide exactly by 4.
A number divides by 8 if the last three digits divide exactly by 8.

Networks (11)

This is a **network**. The **nodes** are marked •. The numbers give the orders of the nodes (the number of **arcs** that leave them).

This network has 4 **regions** (remember the outside). A corner with two arcs does not have to be a node. We have shown one that is and one that is not.

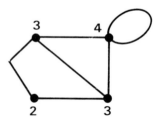

Topology (11)

Topology is the study of shapes that are distorted (stretched or shrunk) without changing: (a) the nodes or their orders, (b) the number of regions or their position relative to each other, (c) the number of arcs.

 is topologically equivalent to (the same as)

 is topologically equivalent to and to

Route Matrix (11)

A route matrix describes a network.

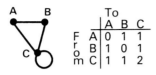

		To		
		A	B	C
F	A	0	1	1
r	B	1	0	1
o	C	1	1	2
m				

Note: The loop at C counts as one arc but two ways of going from C to C, clockwise and anticlockwise.

Sometimes the arcs are one-way, shown with arrows.

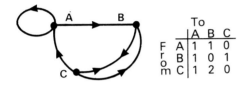

		To		
		A	B	C
F	A	1	1	0
r	B	1	0	1
o	C	1	2	0
m				

Ratio and Scales (12, 32)

8 parts   4 parts

3 parts   2 parts

AB is divided at X in the **ratio** of 8 parts to 4 parts.
AX : XB = 8 : 4 = 2 : 1 (dividing both by 4); if AX : XB = 2 : 1 then AX = 2XB.

CY : YD = 3 : 2, so CD is divided into 5 parts (3 + 2).
If CD is 15 cm then each part is $15 \div 3 = 3$ cm, so CY = 9 cm and YD = 6 cm.

A drawing to a **scale** of 1 : 30 has 1 unit of the drawing representing 30 units of the real object, so that a book 30 cm by 15 cm would be drawn 1 cm by $\frac{1}{2}$ cm.

Graphs (13)

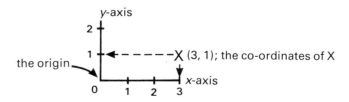

Algebra (14, 24)
Like terms have the same letters; they can be added or subtracted.
Examples $3x + 4x \rightarrow 7x$
$\qquad\qquad$ $2 + 2x + 3 \rightarrow 5 + 2x$ (but you cannot add 5 to $2x$)
$\qquad\qquad$ $5a - a + c \rightarrow 4a + c$ (but you cannot add $4a$ to c)
$a \times a$ is written a^2 and is called 'a squared'. The raised 2 is called an **index**.
$3 \times a \times b + 2 \times a$ would be written as $3ab + 2a$.

Rectangles (15)
Area = length times width (or base times height).

Fractions (16)
You should be able to change common fractions to decimal fractions and vice versa.

Examples $\frac{3}{5} \rightarrow 5\overline{)3.0}^{\,0.6}$ $\quad \therefore \frac{3}{5} = 0.6$

$\qquad\qquad$ Note: $\rightarrow$ is used in this book to mean 'becomes'.
$\qquad\qquad\qquad$ $\therefore$ is the symbol for the word 'therefore'.
$\qquad\qquad$ $0.6 = \frac{6}{10} = \frac{3}{5};$ $0.65 = \frac{65}{100} = \frac{13}{20};$ $0.654 = \frac{654}{1000} = \frac{327}{500}$
$\qquad\qquad$ Note: 10 at the bottom when the last figure is in the tenths column; 100 at
$\qquad\qquad\qquad$ the bottom when the last figure is in the hundredths column.

Cancelling: Fractions are cancelled to make the numbers smaller. Each number must be
$\qquad\qquad$ divided by the same amount. We usually cross out the figures when doing this.

Example $\dfrac{65}{100} \rightarrow \dfrac{\cancel{65}^{13}}{\cancel{100}_{20}} = \dfrac{13}{20}$

Mappings (17)
A **mapping** changes one number to another by a given rule.
Example $x \rightarrow x - 3$ changes 12 into 9, 10 into 7, 8 into 5, etc.
In the example, {12, 10, 8} is called the **domain**; {9, 7, 5} is called the **range**.

Reflection (18)
The line joining O (the **object**) to I (the **image**) crosses
the **mirror line** (m) at right-angles. The image is the
same distance behind the mirror as the object is in
front.

Line Symmetry (19)
It is easiest to think of the line (or axis) of symmetry as a fold line or a mirror line.

No line of symmetry.

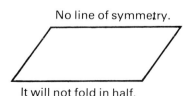

It will not fold in half.

Triangles (20)

The three angles of a triangle add up to 180°.

Angles: Acute   Obtuse   Right

Sides: Scalene   Isosceles   Equilateral

Fraction multiplied by Integer (22)

Examples $\dfrac{8^2}{\cancel{12}_{3\ 1}} \times 9^3 = 6;$ $7\frac{3}{8} \times 12 \rightarrow \dfrac{59}{\cancel{8}_2} \times \cancel{12}^3 = \dfrac{177}{2} = 88\frac{1}{2}.$

Percentages (23)

Percentage (%) means 'out of 100', so $35\% = \frac{35}{100} = \frac{7}{20}$.

To change a fraction to a percentage, multiply it by 100%.

Examples $\dfrac{3}{5} \rightarrow \dfrac{3}{5} \times 100\% \rightarrow \dfrac{3}{\cancel{5}_1} \times \cancel{100}^{20}\% = 60\%.$

$0.8 \rightarrow 0.8 \times 100\% = 80\%.$

Approximations (26)

Approximate means 'roughly the same as'.

Examples 1365 → 1370 to the nearest 10 (the tens figure is the 6, the key figure is 5, so round the 6 up to 7).

Note: 1360 is equally correct, but usually we 'round up'.

1365 → 1400 to the nearest 100 (the hundreds figure is the 3, the key figure is 6, so round 3 up to 4).

1365 → 1000 to the nearest 1000 (the thousands figure is the 1, the key figure is 3, so leave the 1 unaltered).

Remember: Key figure 5 or more ⇒ round up.

Mean (Average) (29, 31)

The **Mean** (one of the three statistical averages, but commonly just called 'the average') is found by dividing the total sum by the number of items.

Average Speed is Total Distance divided by Total Time.

Remember: Speed equals Distance over Time.

233

Kinds of Numbers (30)

Multiples are made by multiplying a number by an integer.
Example   Some multiples of 8 are 8, 16, 48 and 64.

Factors divide exactly into a number.
Example   The factors of 12 are 1, 2, 3, 4, 6 and 12.

Prime numbers have only two factors, 1 and the number.
Example   Some primes are 2, 3, 5, 7 and 11.

Rectangular numbers are all those not prime, except 1. They can be shown as a rectangle of dots or a square of dots.

Square numbers can be drawn as a square of dots. All square numbers except 1 are also rectangular numbers.
Example   Some square numbers are 1, 4, 9, 16, 25, 36, 100, 121, 144.

Triangular numbers can be drawn as a triangle of dots.

The number 1 is a square number and a triangular number. It is not a rectangular number nor a prime number.

•   ••   •••   ••••

1,   3,   6,   10   etc.

Two Number Patterns (30)

Pascal's Triangle

```
        1
      1   1
    1   2   1
  1   3   3   1
1   4   6   4   1
      etc.
```

Fibonacci's Sequence
1, 1, 2, 3, 5, 8, 13, etc.